William & Regina
I love what
you are to
for me. John Mark

MW00563253

Yet Will I Trust Him

John Mark Hicks

Yet Will I Trust Him

Understanding God in a Suffering World

John Mark Hicks

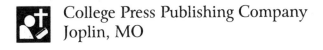
College Press Publishing Company
Joplin, MO

Copyright © 1999
College Press Publishing Company

Printed and Bound in the
United States of America
All Rights Reserved

Cover Design by Brett Lyerla

All Scripture quotations, unless indicated, are taken from
THE HOLY BIBLE: NEW INTERNATIONAL VERSION®.
Copyright © 1973, 1978, 1984 by International Bible Society.
Used by permission of Zondervan Publishing House.
All rights reserved.

Quotations marked NRSV are taken from the New Revised
Standard Version, © 1989, Division of Christian Education
of the National Council of Churches of Christ in the USA,
and used by permission.

Library of Congress Cataloging-in-Publication Data

Hicks, John Mark.
   Yet will I trust him: understanding God in a suffering
world/John Mark Hicks.
     p. cm.
   Includes bibliographical references.
   ISBN 0-89900-861-5 (pbk.)
   1. Providence and government of God. 2. Suffering—
Religious aspects—Christianity. 3. Theodicy. I. Title.
BT135.H53 1999
231'.8—dc21   99-18728
                                   CIP

Dedication

To

Sheila Pettit Hicks (wife, died in 1980),

Mark N. Hicks (father, died in 1994), and

Joshua Mark Hicks (son, terminally ill),

all of whom I have loved more than my own life,

but through whose illnesses and deaths

God transformed my vision of his glory.

Acknowledgments

Thanks to John Hunter and the editorial staff at College Press for their work and the opportunity to share this material.

Thanks to my students at Harding University Graduate School of Religion who have encouraged me and helped me think through God's story. They have raised appropriate questions, probed me and enlightened me.

Thanks to the numerous churches who listened to me tell this story. In particular, I thank the members of the Ross Road Church of Christ in Memphis, Tennessee among whom I ministered for over seven years as much of this material was developed, tested, and written.

Thanks to Allen Black, David Fletcher, and Bob Lewis who engaged me in conversation and read the manuscript in various forms. Thanks to Keith Stanglin, my graduate assistant, who checked many details for me. Their help has been invaluable, though the finished product, of course, is my responsibility alone.

Thanks to my mother, Lois Hicks, for her constant encouragement to complete this project. Her life of faith has inspired my own, and her demeanor has always provided a Christian model for my life.

Most of all, thanks to my wife, Barbara, and my children — Ashley, Joshua, and Rachel — for their patience and generous allotment of time that enabled me to complete this work. They are my joy and my life, and I could not have completed this task without their support and encouragement. They are God's most precious gifts to my life.

TABLE OF CONTENTS

Preface

This has been a difficult book to write. My understanding of God's providence and the meaning of suffering has changed many times over the past twenty years. I fear that once this is printed it may already inaccurately reflect my changing perspectives. Nevertheless, I am convinced that the basic story line is biblical, and I hope the form in which I offer it is helpful.

I have aimed this book at upper level undergraduate students in a way that would stretch them. It is intended to provide church leaders and health care workers with a theological framework for thinking about suffering and helping sufferers. It provides the theological values which are important for enduring suffering and comforting sufferers. The book, then, is a theological story. It is the story of God's history with his people and how suffering functions in it — what God is doing *with* suffering and what he will do *to* it.

This is not a philosophical theodicy. My purpose is to tell the biblical story in a wholistic manner so that we can see the beginning from the end. Once we know God's story, then we will have the appropriate lens through which to interpret our own personal stories. My task, then, is an exercise in biblical theology, not philosophical theology.

While some of the chapters call for greater theological acumen than others, the first and last chapters are the "bottom line" of the book. Chapter one tells my own personal story and chapter ten provides the basic theological values that sufferers and would-be comforters need.

My prayer is that this book will help you interpret your own personal story of suffering and that it will provide a "lens" through which you may see how God's story intersects with your own. I am confident that God's story — his goals, purposes, and intents — intersects with every person. I hope this book helps you see how, even in the experience of suffering.

ADDITIONAL MATERIAL AVAILABLE ON THE INTERNET

Due to length I could not include all the material I would have liked. Consequently, through the labor of Bob Lewis, additional material relevant to this book is available on the College Press website. These two additional chapters are more technical in character as they interact with current scholarly thought, though they have important practical dimensions.

"What Should I Believe about Providence? Options in Contemporary Theology." This chapter offers a typology for understanding current views of providence. It explains the widely divergent understandings of providence under the headings of "premodern (interventionist), modern (deist), and postmodern (personalist)." It is found at *www. collegepress.com/jmhicks/providence.htm.*

"A Reasonable Theodicy? The Traditional Problem of Evil." This chapter interacts with the traditional formulation of the problem of evil. It provides a theodicy that arises out of the material in the book but puts it into a form that follows more traditional discussions of evil in philosophical literature. It is found at *www.collegepress.com/jmhicks/theodicy.htm.*

You may also offer comments, suggestions or ask questions on the website at *www.collegepress.com/jmhicks/default.htm*. I would appreciate any help the reader may offer as I plan to continually revise my understanding of this topic.

My vita is also available at *www.collegepress.com/jmhicks/cv.htm*.

Chapter One

Where Is God?
A Personal Story

Men cry out under a load of oppression;
*   they plead for relief from the arm of the powerful.*
But no one says, "Where is God my Maker,
*   who gives songs in the night?"*
*   Elihu to Job, Job 35:9-10*

I do not remember a time during my youth when I did not believe in the goodness of God. I grew up under the godly training of faithful parents. My father, Mark N. Hicks, began preaching in 1950 and he remained in ministry until his death in 1994. My mother, Edith Lois Hicks, is a retired public school teacher. Both formed my infant faith by their example and guidance. They raised me within the life of the church and in a family that understood Christianity as a way of life. In many respects I was sheltered, and I am grateful. Consequently, throughout my first twenty-one years I never seriously questioned the goodness of God, his world, and the church. My vision of God had been shaped by a wonderful family and church life.

On May 22, 1977 I married. I was young, only nineteen, and even though I had already earned a B.A. degree in Religion at a private Christian college, I was incredibly naïve about the world's evil and pain. I had not experienced the pain of personal suffering, nor had my understanding of God been radically challenged. Suffering, I thought, does not come from God — only good. Those who live before him faithfully can expect only good things from a good God. While I value my undergraduate training and would not trade it for any other, my education had, with some notable exceptions, reinforced my belief system rather than challenged it. I was still sheltered even though I was introduced to intellectual rigor. I had grown up in faith and had never doubted who my God was nor what he could do. I had him in a box that I could inspect. I knew what he could and could not do. I was comfortable with my God. My life's plan was fairly set, and I knew exactly where God fit into it.

However, in 1980 this vision was shaken. My innocence was shattered and my naïve, simplistic belief in God's providential goodness was tested. On April 30, 1980, Sheila, my wife of less than three years, died suddenly and unexpectedly at home while recovering from surgery when a blood clot stopped her heart.

We had hoped for children in the near future. In fact, Sheila underwent back surgery so she could carry a child full term. We had already experienced one miscarriage, and we wanted to avoid another. We had planned to pursue a missionary career in Germany where we hoped to minister in the eastern block. We had planned, prayed, and pursued so much, but on April 30, 1980 all those dreams were dashed. The pillars of my faith were shaken by her death and cracks began to emerge. Had we not dedicated ourselves to God's service? Had we not prayed for health and protection? Now my prayers asked, "why?" Why had God not heard our prayers? Why had God not empowered us for ministry in Germany? Why had God not preserved the life of my spouse? Where was God when that blood clot entered my wife's heart? Could he not have stopped that clot? Had I not prayed faithfully? How could it be his will that my wife die? Does not my God give good things to his servants? Where are his blessings now? Why would he not spare her life?

In the midst of personal suffering, the suffering of all others seems inferior to our own. Suffering is an intensely personal experience. Others cannot experience what the sufferer at that moment experiences. They cannot understand. Sufferers discover that no one is truly empathetic in that tragic moment. The sufferer sits alone, like Job, on the trash heap. Only in the aftermath of suffering does one come to realize that suffering is not *sui generis* (one of a kind) but that suffering is something shared by all. Yet, even then, we still believe that there is something terribly unique about our own suffering. Nevertheless, the questions, doubts, and despair of the single sufferer are the same as those of a million sufferers. We all ask: "Why me?" "Why this?" "Why now?" and "Why doesn't God do something?" We all ask: "Where is God?"

The circumstances of my tragedy brought me face to face with doubt and despair. It reminded me of the Rabbi in Eli Wiesel's *Night* who in the midst of Auschwitz lamented, "It's the end. God is no longer with us. . . . Where is the divine Mercy? Where is God? How can I believe, how could anyone believe, in this merciful God?"[1] The words of this Rabbi resonated with me then, and even now, after twenty years, I sense their power. It was exactly how I felt. Like C.S. Lewis, after the death of his wife of three years, I was not "in much danger of ceasing to believe in God" as much as "coming to believe such dreadful things about Him."[2] To hear the taunting question, "Where is God?" from unbelievers is expected, as several examples in Scripture demonstrate (Joel 2:17; Micah 7:10; Psalms 42:3,10; 79:10; 115:2), but to hear it from the lips of believers reflects the distress and despair of the believing sufferer. The Rabbi's question expresses the despair of believers who suffer.

But I could not accept the full implications of that despair, though it was tempting. Instead, I renewed my study of Scripture. Could Scripture speak to the aching heart? Could it provide a place for lament? In particular I

studied Psalms, Job, and Ecclesiastes. I reread the narratives
of God's story. It was as if I had never read that literature
before — and, in a very real sense, I had not. Before my suffering I could never empathize with Job. Before my suffering I could never understand the intense emotions of the
psalmists. Now, I too, had suffered, and it opened up the
possibilities of an empathetic reading of Scripture. This
renewed reading opened up a world I never knew existed. I
discovered that one can read accounts of suffering empathetically only if one has already suffered. No amount of
textbook exposure can generate that genuine empathy.

At one point I can remember believing that such a
world of suffering could not exist in the believer's life. I
remember thinking that the world is God's good creation,
God is good, and therefore I should expect good, especially
in the light of the resurrection of Jesus. There is no room
for despair in a world where God has dispelled it through
Jesus Christ. We should always rejoice and never lament.
My motto was Philippians 4:4 — a triumphalism that others around me shared. Christians should always wear a
smile. They should always be happy because of Jesus Christ.
However, through an empathetic reading of Psalms, Job,
and other parts of Scripture, I entered a new world, the
world of *faithful lament*.[3]

Faithful lament was a new category for me. How can
lament, with its accusations, bewilderment, doubt, tears, and
frustrations, express faith? Prior to my own personal suffering, lament was unknown to me. I had not recognized it in
Scripture. I had not noticed it in my church. Christianity was
a faith of joy, celebration, and hopeful anticipation. Life
taught me to rejoice, look forward to the future, and celebrate God's victory through ministry.

My worldview was dominated by that triumphalism.
God's army will conquer. We will set the world aright. We
will establish the perfect church. My outlook had no room
for lament (and little room for failure) since such would
accuse God or fault him for suffering. Suffering was the

responsibility of someone other than God, and the proper response to suffering was to punish its cause. But my own suffering forced me to lament because the believer, who continues to believe, can only lament in the midst of suffering. Lament, with all its confusion, desperation, and doubt, expresses the sufferer's faith. Lament does not disown God; it appeals to him. It calls upon God to do something, to help, to rescue the one who has been faithful to him. It cries, "my God!"

I learned to lament through my own experiences and by meditating on Psalms and Job. The dimensions of Scripture which give expression to lament became my prayers as I personally appropriated them and gave voice to them. Biblical lament became my lament.

By God's grace, however, those early years of lament turned to praise because God refreshed my spirit and renewed my joy through Barbara, whom I married in November of 1983. Our union included a fifteen-month-old ball of fire named Ashley. She has always filled our home with love, excitement, and unpredictability. In 1985 God blessed us with a son whom we named Joshua Mark. We hoped his name would give him a vision for how he might one day serve God and lead his people, like Joshua of old (his name also honors my father, Mark Hicks, another of God's leaders). In 1987 God blessed us with another beautiful girl, Rachel Nicole. The biblical name reflected her own beauty and our prayer that God would use her in his service as well. These times of divine refreshing enabled me to identify with the ending of Job. God had richly blessed me in the aftermath of my suffering. He fulfilled my dreams, hopes, and expectations. My family and my ministry were my joys, and Jobian suffering seemed a thing of the past. Though some past questions remained fundamentally unanswered, God had blessed me with a new family. Yet, even as I gave credit to God for the joys of my new family, I still wondered about the meaning of the suffering I had endured. Should God get credit for that as well?

As I now look back upon the suffering of my youth, I must admit that a genuine sense of gratitude arises within me. It may sound harsh — and if it does, then this book will serve a useful purpose — but I confess with the psalmist that "it was good for me to be afflicted" (Psalm 119:71). Of course, affliction is never good in an absolute sense (death is something that God never intended; it is his enemy), but sometimes it is good in a relative sense. The relative good of his suffering, according to this psalmist, is related to the waywardness of his life prior to his affliction. He wrote: "Before I was afflicted I went astray, but now I obey your word" (Psalm 119:67). While all suffering cannot be so categorized (as, for example, in the case of Job), I identify with the psalmist's perspective.

Sheila and I were planning to spend several years on the mission field, but in my heart I was also planning to study there (under some "famous" theologian) and return to the States triumphantly. I would have a Ph.D. in one hand and the glory of missionary experience in the other. I would have been trained at a European university and have returned home as an eastern block missionary hero. I thought no Christian college would deny me the opportunity to teach. I was arrogant in my theology — I knew what was right, preached maliciously against error, and chastened everyone who left the "old paths" of my tradition. I had sided with the right wing of my heritage, and was closely associated with an editor, lecturer, and publisher who epitomized that "right wing." He published me, and I invited him for speaking engagements. My spirit was contentious, my attitude was arrogant, my theology was perfect and my goal was selfish. Of course, at the time, I would have never admitted these things. Indeed, I did not understand them about myself, and probably very few if any recognized them in me. I did not see myself for what I really was. Youth has its many blind spots. I know my 21-year-old self better now than I did then. Twenty years later I am able to analyze my own heart better than I could then. Hindsight is better than foresight or even present insight. I can now see where I would have ended up had something not happened to change my direction.

Sheila's death changed me. Scripture changed me. My encounter with the God of Scripture changed me. God changed me as I experienced his comforting presence and transforming power through suffering. The effect of that change was such that whereas I once had God so pegged that I knew what to expect from him and could plan out the course of my life without interruption, I now realized that my attitude must be one of submission. Humility must replace arrogance, submission must replace pride, and gentleness must replace contentiousness. In other words, God's glory must replace my selfishness. Without that experience — at that moment — my heart may have hardened, and my path may have been set.

God used Sheila's death to change me. But was that fair? Why should Sheila suffer for my good? Why her instead of me? I was the problem, not her! I was filled with pride, but she was not. I wanted to move up the "hierarchical" ladder of my church, but she just wanted to serve God. I wanted to be noticed, but that did not consume her. Why her instead of me? These questions have often plagued me. They are difficult questions, but in lament faith asks. But no matter how they are answered, I must thank God for the change he worked in my life. Through my suffering — whatever the origin and reason for that suffering — God worked powerfully to effect good in my life. He opened my heart to his transforming presence.

Despite the questions, I confess with the psalmist that it was good for me to have been afflicted. My sense is that if I had not been tried by suffering, my heart would have continued down its selfish, prideful, and arrogant path. My life would have been very different. Now I praise God for that affliction and I thank him for the change he worked in me. I did not change myself; God changed me as I sought him. But that change came in the context of prayerful lament over Sheila's death. I fear that I would have never changed had Sheila not died. But how can I thank God for the death of one I loved so dearly? The questions continue.

Nevertheless, since 1983 I have constantly thanked God for the renewal he has given me through Barbara, Ashley, Joshua, and Rachel. However, late in 1990 lament again entered my life. Joshua had always been a strong, strapping, and energetic boy. He was hyperactive and always getting into trouble. He enjoyed breaking things, was constantly disruptive, and was quickly expelled from the 4K program of a local Baptist church. Even though his behavior was never malicious, for a time we thought we would spend our twilight years visiting him at San Quentin. We knew we had a problem. Joshua was developing slowly and he was extremely aggressive. He never said more than one sentence at a time, and his sentences were never more than four or five words. He could never color between the lines, never learned the alphabet, and could rarely do anything that other four- and five-year-olds could do. He was developmentally delayed and socially dysfunctional.

We began to seek remedies. We doubted our parenting skills and sought help. We took Joshua to a child psychologist. We tried drugs for hyperactivity. Nothing seemed to work. Instead of progressing, Joshua began to regress. He began to lose what communication skills he had. He returned to wearing diapers, and his aggressiveness increased. Eventually, at the prodding of a Christian nurse to whom we are extremely grateful (she was surely the Lord's blessing), we took him to a pediatric neurologist. He immediately recognized a genetic condition. That day we discovered that our son would never get better, and in the first few months of 1991 we learned that his genetic condition was terminal. Joshua has Mucopolysaccharidosis IIIA (Sanfilippo Syndrome A) which is a genetic storage disorder. He is missing an enzyme which breaks down storage. The condition destroys the brain and debilitates the body due to waste buildup. According to case histories, Joshua will probably leave us sometime before his sixteenth birthday after a slow mental and physical degeneration.

Joshua is now fourteen. He can no longer communicate verbally. He cannot walk or stand by his own strength. His mental age is about six months. He wears diapers. He will eventually be bedridden. He will die a lingering death unless his heart or liver or pneumonia takes him first.

Suffering has again entered my life and the life of my family. It has attacked one of my children. And once again, I identify with Job. His children were his joy, his spiritual concern, and his investment in the future, but he lost them in his suffering. Now my joy, my investment in the future, is gone; my only son will soon die. He will not be the leader among God's people as we had hoped his name would reflect. He will not even play little league baseball, or ever again say the words "I love you."

But this time my perspective is different. Suffering is not a new experience for me, even though each experience of suffering is new. The hopes we invested in our son when we named him have been dashed. Our dreams for him as a leader of God's people are gone. Now our greatest joy is hearing him laugh and listening to him coo as we tell him that we love him. Yet we long to hear him say, "I love you," in response. We have accepted his eventual death, but we lament our plight. We have learned how to lament as a family, and we have experienced the anger and depression that comes with grief.

Nevertheless, God's renewal in my life through Barbara, Ashley, Joshua, and Rachel remains joyful though it is tinged with lament. Joy still abounds in our family, but it is a joy that lives alongside of lament, alongside of anger, sadness, and sometimes doubt. It is a joy mixed with tears and refined by suffering. It is a joy that has seen God in the midst of suffering and finds comfort in his presence. This joy is a song God has given us in the night of our suffering — it is given through lament so that the joy is greater, deeper, and fuller than a joy without lament.

I have experienced both kinds of joy: joy without previous lament (life with Sheila) and joy with lament (life with Barbara). Joy without lament can be superficial and fleeting, but through lament joy is better appreciated and, I believe, more deeply experienced. Joy with lament has a substance that remains. It is rooted in the experience of "seeing" God as we sit on the trash heap (see Job 42:5). It is a confidence that comes through experiencing God's presence in the sanctuary (see Psalm 73:17). The Psalms and Job point us to this kind of lament through which God gives songs to the heart. Elihu, as quoted at the beginning of this chapter, pointed Job toward the God "who gives songs in the night" (Job 35:10). God can give joy in the midst of lament. He can give a song of praise in the middle of suffering's darkness. Lament gives way to joy as it gives way to praise. Elihu pointed Job in the right direction. When Job finally "saw" God, he found a song of praise, even during his night of suffering (Job 42:2-6).

Nevertheless, it is still lament. We still question, wonder, despair, cry, and doubt. Lament often turns to praise, but sometimes lament needs to continue to complain, question, and plead. Had we not prayed for Joshua's health? Did we not ask God to raise him up as a leader among his people? Why has God denied us this joy? Why has God denied himself a servant? How can Joshua serve God in the grave? The questions remain. The laments continue. But there are also "songs in the night." How can both exist together? Scripture and experience have taught me that God gives songs of praise to his people who experience the night, but he does it in unexpected and surprising ways.

My renewed study of Scripture in the wake of suffering and my continued attempts to understand providence and suffering have shattered my previous vision of God. I no longer have "God in the dock" (or, God on trial) and I no longer have him in a box though I am often sorely tempted to do both. Let God be God; let God speak, and let us submit in humility. This is the ending of Job. God spoke, and

Job bowed in humility before God's transcendent sovereignty. When the psalmist entered God's presence, the thoughts that once oppressed him dissipated (Psalm 73:17). Let God be God.

"Where is their God?" the unbelievers taunt. "Our God is in heaven," the believing community replies, "he does whatever pleases him" (Psalm 115:3). "Where is God?" He is present. God comes to Job and answers him in the whirlwind. God comes to the psalmist in the temple sanctuary and gives him peace. God comes through the incarnation, through Jesus, where he speaks to us and empathizes with us. God comes through the transforming and comforting presence of his Holy Spirit. God is coming again and he will renew the world. The old things will pass away and everything will become new. God will again be "all in all" (1 Corinthians 15:28). "Where is God?" He is present within his creation. He sustains and comforts his people. God is working. He is actively bringing about a glorious goal where he will dwell with his people in a new heaven and new earth.

This book is about the story of God in his world. He created it, and because it is now filled with pain and death, he seeks to redeem it — both in our present experience and in the new heaven and new earth. What God created has fallen from its original peace and harmony, and what has fallen God seeks to restore to its original peace and harmony. The story of God involves the suffering of a fallen world, and it also involves the suffering of God. God enters our suffering in order to redeem it.

This is the story I hope to tell in this book. When we understand God's story, then it enables our stories — those of joy and those of suffering — to find meaning. We must see our story in the grand scheme of his. Only then will we find comfort, peace, and joy as we live within this fallen world. God's story answers our vexations with evil and suffering, and it offers us peace and hope. This story enables me to lament with hope. It enables me to end my laments with praise. I hope you will read my retelling of God's story, reflect on it, and, as far as you see my retelling as true, allow it to give meaning to your own story of suffering.

---

[1]Elie Wiesel, *Night*, trans. Stella Rodway (New York: Avon Books, 1960), p. 87.

[2]C.S. Lewis, *A Grief Observed*, with afterword by Chad Walsh (New York: Bantam Books, 1976), p. 5.

[3]See Claus Westermann, *Praise and Lament in the Psalms*, 2nd ed., trans. by K.R. Crim and R.N. Soulen (Atlanta: John Knox Press, 1981); "The Role of Lament in the Theology of the Old Testament," *Interpretation* 28 (1974): 20-38; Walter Brueggemann, *Finally Comes the Poet: Daring Speech for Proclamation* (Minneapolis: Fortress Press, 1989) and *The Message of the Psalms: A Theological Commentary* (Minneapolis: Augsburg, 1984); and André Resner, Jr., "Lament: Faith's Response to Loss," *Restoration Quarterly* 32 (1990): 129-142.

Chapter Two

How Involved Is God in His World?
The Modern versus the Biblical Story

Although I am blameless,
I have no concern for myself;
I despise my own life.
It is all the same; that is why I say,
"He destroys both the blameless and the wicked."
When a scourge brings sudden death,
he mocks the despair of the innocent.
When a land falls into the hands of the wicked,
he blindfolds its judges.
If it is not he, then who is it?
Job to Bildad, Job 9:21-24

A Dialogue

"That was an awful storm we had last night!" Mary commented as she met Jill in the hall.

"Yeah," her coworker, replied. "I was scared to death. I don't think I've ever seen it hail so hard. All I heard on the radio and TV last night were tornado warnings and tornado watches."

"But hearing a tornado warning on the radio, and hearing the tornado itself are two different things," Mary responded. "One of those tornadoes went right over our townhouse about one o'clock this morning."

"You're kidding! Did it really? Were you scared?"

"Scared out of my wits, but I just thank God that it didn't hit my house. Unfortunately, it destroyed the Anderson's home, and killed Jim and his two-year-old son Joshua. The whole neighborhood is shocked and devastated. He was a good man, and Joshua was such a sweet boy."

"How sad. Tornadoes are horrible things. But, Mary, you must feel very lucky. That tornado could have hit your house and killed you!"

"Oh, it wasn't luck," Mary said. "God was looking out for us. He protected us. We are so grateful to him. He answered our prayers, and let me tell you, we prayed hard last night."

"Uh . . . ," Jill muttered in a state of shock. "You really mean that, don't you?"

"Of course!" Mary continued. "I believe God has a special care for those who love him and pray to him. We knew these storms were coming from the late news, and we prayed for protection. Our prayers were answered when that tornado lifted over our house. . . ."

"But," Jill interrupted, "it hit the Anderson's house and killed a two-year-old child. Why didn't God protect them? Weren't they good people too? Was it just because they didn't pray? Or maybe they prayed but God didn't answer them like he did you. Did God prefer you over Joshua? Mary, this kind of talk bothers me. I don't think God had anything to do with it. Tornadoes are simply things that happen, and whatever they do is the result of natural forces and luck — good or bad."

Confused by Jill's rebuke, Mary asserted her faith. "I believe my prayers were answered. How else can I explain the fact that the tornado jumped over my house when it could have leveled it? How else can I give God glory if I do not acknowledge his hand? How can I thank him for saving my family if he did not have anything to do with it? Shouldn't I thank him for his protection?"

"Mary, I can sympathize with the way you feel," Jill responded. "But this is the twentieth century, not the Middle Ages. There is no need to bring God into this thing. We live in a scientific age where these random natural events are explained in terms of winds, rains, and whatever else science has discovered."

"It could never explain how that tornado missed my house and saved the life of my family without God's direction," Mary retorted with a finality that dared any challenge.

Jill, frustrated with Mary's naïveté and her seeming unreasonableness, responded in kind: "And no faith can explain why God would permit a tornado to kill an innocent two-year-old child! How can you believe in a God who protects you and kills a two-year-old boy? God had nothing to do with saving your life or taking his! God just doesn't do things like that."

Mary, insulted by the threat to her faith, did not respond, and the conversation ended abruptly. Mary was left with the mystery of her faith, and Jill was left with the randomness of luck.

The above dialogue is not a fictional one (though the names have been changed), and, I dare say, it is not a rare one, even among Christians. In fact, a similar exchange recently took place in the Arkansas State Legislature. Gov. Mike Huckabee, a Baptist minister, refused to sign a bill that "appeared to blame God for the tornadoes and floods that hit Arkansas on March 1." But Rep. Jimmie Wilson responded that "to say God didn't create tornadoes is like saying that He doesn't bring the spring rains."[1] Gov. Huckabee appears to see the world like Jill, and Rep. Wilson more like Mary.

Though the names and particulars may change, the story line remains the same — a narrow escape from death in a car accident, or a taxi delay prevents someone from boarding a plane that later crashes, or a cancer remission, or something as common as sweating through a fever. While the topics change, the conversations remain the same. Those conversations are focused on a single question: How involved is God in his world?

The differences between Mary and Jill are not small ones. The way they look at reality (their "worldviews") are totally different. Mary is willing to see natural events as God's acts. Jill simply thinks of them as random natural occurrences. One sees a role for divine action, and the other sees nature as a closed system that operates independently of God (whether he exists or not) or at least where nature functions chaotically without rhyme or reason. Mary's faith in God includes a belief in God's personal activity on her behalf. Jill does not believe that God works in the way that Mary thinks he does.

The difference between Mary and Jill is a large chasm. Jill looks at Mary and thinks, "She's living in the Middle Ages." Mary looks at Jill and thinks, "She's an unbeliever." According to Jill, Mary is naïve about science. According to Mary, Jill has lost touch with the reality of God in her life. Behind every act of nature Mary sees the hand of God. Behind every act of nature Jill sees the luck of the cards.

The difference between Mary and Jill is the difference between the premodern world in which the Bible was written and the modern, scientific world of recent centuries. Job's world, for example, would have immediately seen an act of God in the tornado Mary experienced. It may have been viewed in strikingly different, even contradictory, ways, but everyone would have agreed that God had something to do with it. The modern world strips away the "mythology" of divine action, and gives nature its own independence. Nature has become a closed system in which science will ultimately explain all events in terms of natural causes.

Since science provides a sufficient and reasonable explanation for tornadoes, why invoke the hand of God? God is no longer necessary to explain natural events, nor is he needed to produce them. Indeed, if we invoke God as the explanation for a natural disaster, we create the problem of how to relate "innocent suffering" to the goodness of God. How do we explain the death of a child in a tornado if God is the root cause or if God is in any sense responsible for the direction of that tornado? If God is responsible for the tornado, then he is responsible for the death of an innocent child. How do we reconcile the death of a child with the goodness of God? Our modern world removes God from all participation in nature, and thus absolves him of all responsibility in the suffering of the innocent through natural disasters. God is saved by his disengagement from the world. He cannot be blamed because he is not involved.

How did we move from a sense of God's pervasive involvement in the world through nature to the absence of God from nature? What has the modern world learned or lost which makes the biblical world seem so naïve? How can modern people learn anything from the Bible when they can no longer realistically enter that world to listen? How can Mary still cling to the primitive and unsophisticated notions of "acts of God" in nature?

The Context: Secularization

There is a fundamental sense in which a secular perspective undermines the biblical God. Broadly, secularization represents the decline of religious beliefs, authority, and perspectives in society at large. It is the displacement of religious institutions and practices with nonreligious ones. Secularization is the desacralization of institutions, the transposition of religious functions into the secular domain and the differentiation of sacred and secular so that the sacred loses its overarching claim.[2] Paul Pruyser sees secularization in all facets of society. Governmental agencies have replaced churches in social services. State universities have replaced Christian institutions in education. Science has toppled mythological and religious explanations for natural events. Psychiatry has displaced pastoral care.[3] These examples are but symptoms of the real problem. The basic problem is a philosophical one. It is a matter of vantage-point as well as starting-point. Secularization in its basic philosophical or intellectual sense refers to the "norms of intelligibility, standards of sense and nonsense, which prevail in our society and which are logically alien to religious belief."[4]

This is exactly the problem between Jill and Mary in the above dialogue. Neither one could understand the "norms of intelligibility" the other was using. For Mary it is perfectly intelligible to believe that God could and often does act through nature. For Jill that is nonsense. Mary's "norms of intelligibility" include a sovereign God who works providentially through nature in order to protect and preserve the lives of his people. It is perfectly understandable that Mary would read the tornado incident as an answer to prayer, especially since she had just prayed about it. Her view of nature is "sacred." Jill's worldview, however, excludes God as any reasonable explanation for natural events. Her "norms of intelligibility" rendered Mary's assessment of the tornado incomprehensible. God, if there is one, does not do things like that, especially when it entails the suffering of an innocent child. Jill's view of nature, therefore, is "secularized."

Mary's views do not dominate the modern scene. Her views are no longer normative in the church, much less in society at large. Modernity has secularized the world so that there is no need to seek divine meaning in natural events, coincidental circumstances, or personal tragedy. Luck has displaced God; scientific causes have displaced divine ones. What has happened to permit this widespread displacement of religious belief? What are the root causes of this secularization that levels everything to "natural" or "secular" explanations?

Reason

The causes of secularization are many and varied. But two causes are particularly significant. First, modernity has supreme confidence in Reason. (I have intentionally capitalized "Reason.") Reason has become, for all practical purposes, its own god. Modernity has supreme confidence in its ability to discern truth, solve problems, and understand reality. Indeed, Reason has become the standard of all judgment, and it stands in judgment over Scripture. The appeal to mystery, or what is hidden, is regarded as a retreat into irrationality. This exaltation of Reason, which became dominant during the Enlightenment of the seventeenth century (though its autonomous character has been present throughout history), has made humanity the measure of all things, and God's judge.[5] Reason is set over against Revelation. Humanity's ability to discern truth is set over against God's unveiling of hidden truth. Moderns have the marked tendency to dispel mystery and to accept only what their Rationality can judge. The cultural movement known as postmodernism is, in part, a reaction against this tendency.

The believer, of course, does not reject reason. Biblical religion is rational, that is, it is reasonable and coherent. Believers cannot avoid the use of reason and they should not try. But this is quite different from exalting Reason to a prominence which denies the possibility of mystery or where faith must submit to the lofty demands of Reason. It is also different from exalting Reason to a prominence which denies the possibility of anything which is beyond reason itself. The believer does not view human reason as the ultimate reality. Rather, believers understand that human reason is a finite attempt to understand and comprehend the infinite God. Believers use reason to understand Revelation, but they also accept that Revelation often unveils truths that are beyond reason and reveals a reality beyond our finitude. That is the essential difference between Reason and reason.

One, *Reason*, is arrogant and proceeds with unrelenting vigor to accomplish its goal of deconstructing and reconstructing knowledge in the optimistic expectation that it can fully accomplish its task. The other, *reason*, accepts its limitations and stands in awe of the mysteries of the universe, and in particular the mystery of God himself. The former is driven by arrogance to exhaust the universe and stand with pride on top of a mountain of accumulated knowledge. The latter is driven by a sense of God's transcendence which submits to the mysteries of God even while it seeks to understand what God has given us. One asserts itself in arrogance while the other submits itself in humility. One seeks understanding without faith while the other is faith seeking understanding. As Luther put it, the former asserts a *magisterial* control over faith, but the latter serves a *ministerial* function in relation to faith.[6]

Science

Modernity also has supreme confidence in Science (intentionally capitalized). Our age is an age of Science. There are more scientists alive today than the total number of scientists in previous generations. Science has a mystique for modern people. It can explain anything and create anything if it is given enough time. Indeed, reality is judged by what we can demonstrate, observe or prove by scientific inquiry. For some the only genuine knowledge is scientific knowledge. We are overwhelmed by mass media and educational materials which praise Science. A scientific authority or study legitimates any conclusion. This exaltation of Science is reinforced by the technological development of society (inventions, cures, and discoveries, etc.) which has certainly benefited humanity.

Nature, therefore, is the arena of Science, not God. Science can discover, explain and understand the vast workings of nature. There is no need to invoke God as the cause or agent of a natural event. Science has, for the modern person, stripped God from nature. God is no longer needed. He may still fill some gaps but those gaps are growing fewer in number. Indeed, the goal of Science is to eliminate them. This is particularly true in the context of Darwin's evolutionary theory and its subsequent revisions and variations. After the publication of the *Origin of Species* in 1859, and the *Descent of Man* in 1871, Science became increasingly dominated by antitheistic perspectives, or at least nontheistic perspectives. Nature has become an independent body of data from which God is excluded and to which Science alone has genuine access.

Believers, of course, do not object to science. We value it as a resource for exploring, developing, and caring for God's earth. We applaud its positive uses as it benefits humanity and dispels myth and superstition. Believers do, however, reject an omniscient and omnipotent Science. Science, like reason, must recognize its limitations. Certainly, it can search out the natural forces which produce a tornado, but it can make no judgment about whether God is active in the event. Such a judgment cannot be made because God is inaccessible to the scientist, as are other data concerning God. In fact, quantum physics has taught scientists that their scientific realism can only go so far. Nature, at bottom, is unpredictable and its root causes are unseen and unknown. Some scientists now talk about the universe in terms of chaos.[7] Order is only apparent and superficial. Scientists can no more eliminate God from a role in natural acts than they can determine the predictability of an electron (e.g., physicists cannot predict whether a particular electron will move to the right or to the left). The scientist cannot tell us whether a given event was an answer to prayer because ultimately in quantum theory the scientist is uncertain about the basic functioning of the universe. The scientist as scientist cannot discover whether God is at the root of the universe beyond the theories of quantum physics or whether it is the will of God that moves electrons. They cannot know whether a particular cancer remission was the result of some random event in nature or God's answer to prayer.[8] That kind of judgment cannot be made by science.

While believers rejoice in the progress of science, they also recognize that science cannot answer every question. Science can only study what is immediately and directly available to its methods. Therefore, it cannot prove or disprove God. It cannot speak about God at all. It can only study what God has created. The study of God himself is the subject of revelation, not science.

The combination of an optimistic view of Reason and Science, however, dealt a deathblow to the old "mythological" worldview of the Bible. Reason and Science have both significantly reduced the need for theistic perspectives and explanations of world events. However, the rise of postmodernity, whatever that turns out to be, has created the potential for dialogue between faith and science. It has deconstructed the arrogance of Reason and Science and created an opportunity for reintroducing a theistic worldview commensurate with reason and science.[9]

Prayer and the Subtle Influence of Secular Culture

The rise of scientific observation in the seventeenth century challenged the theistic understanding of a providential and involved God. Empirical science recognized a regularity in nature that could predict natural events with increasing accuracy. But if what was going to happen could be predicted, how could it be God's intervention? Comets are no longer seen as divine warnings. God no longer stands behind every natural event. Scientists no longer give any credence to the idea that God is actively behind events in the natural world.

As a result, a new understanding of God appeared. It was the deistic God, the watchmaker, who creates and sustains, and may occasionally tinker through some *super*natural act. This became the dominant image of God for the modern world. The world was no longer a place where God acted, but where we acted alone. God began the world and he would end it, but he would not intervene within it. The natural world was just that — natural, not *super*natural. Nature was secularized.

While the modern view of God emphasizes his transcendence (God stands aloof from the world in Deism), the postmodern understanding of God emphasizes his immanence (God is present within the world). For postmoderns the immanence of God is primarily if not exclusively within the subjectivity of the human soul. Faith is a human commitment to the hidden and unseen God. The world is an ambiguous place, but God is active in human subjectivity though he is not active in the empirical world. The presence of God is subjective and ambiguous, but real.

Modern and postmodern understandings of God reject the traditional view of a providential, involved God who rules his universe as the Sovereign Lord. For the modern, God is withdrawn and absent, and for the postmodern, God is the hamstrung encourager of godly values in the human story. In this context, it is important to understand how moderns and postmoderns understand prayer.[10]

Modern and Postmodern Views of Prayer

For *modern* theology God is the "God of the gaps." God fills in what science cannot explain, but as science increasingly explains things, the gaps disappear and the need for God in the natural world dissipates. Everything is explicable in terms of natural causation. Moderns believe God has so regulated the natural world that it functions autonomously and without partiality. God created his watch, and now he need only watch it tick.

Moderns view petitionary prayer as superstitious magic which misperceives God as a cosmic Santa Claus to whom we appeal for our personal benefit. They reject any notion that God intervenes to fill the gaps of our experience. As they see it, God is revealed through the order of nature which he created and sustains. Everything is under God's control, but rather than constantly adjusting, God controls the perfect system. Prayer is part of the system, but it does not appeal to God to act in any manner. God does not intervene within the human drama.

The modern's prayer, then, thanks and praises God for the wisdom and goodness of his purposes, humbly admits sin, confesses dependence upon God's gracious maintenance of natural laws, and commits to functioning as an instrument of God's grace in the world. Within a modern understanding, the prayer "Thy will be done" is a confident assertion. God's system is perfect. It is only due to human ignorance and obstinacy that everything in the world is not perfect. The effectiveness of prayer is rated on the basis of how much it changed the one who prayed. Prayer does not change the world. It only changes the self. When the people

of God pray, they stimulate moral dispositions within themselves. It is a kind of deistic self-help therapy.

The *postmodern* understanding is that God is hidden and
ambiguous. While "laws of nature" are dependable for
superficial experience, they are not the basis for knowing
the certain outcome of every natural occurrence. Chance
(what is incapable of prediction) is always part of the natural world and human experience. The postmodern God is
hidden. He does not act in the natural world. God has
designed the game of life with a set of rules and has given
humanity freedom to play it. Reality is an interaction
between the rules, choices, and chance. God is the promot-
er of "fair play." God's relation to the world is one of influence, not cause; and his influence is limited to those who
listen to his voice. God acts in the subjectivity of the
human soul to promote good, but he does not cause or
force anything. Rather, he leads those who listen to him.

Postmoderns use prayer to express commitment to
God. They pray to express their deepest desires for the
world. They articulate how they want the world to be.
Their prayers express a longing for God's moral will to
become a reality in the world, and they commit to partici-
pating in its implementation. Their choices and commit-
ments make a difference in the world. Since the world is an
ambiguous place where God's kingdom can either be present or absent, their commitment is important for God's
agenda.

God does not act in the empirical world. Rather, he
motivates within the subjectivity of the human soul. God
depends upon the human agent to accomplish his will in
the world. The prayer "Thy will be done!" is a prayer of
commitment. It does not expect that God's desire will in
fact be accomplished by some divine intervention, but that
the believer will desire and long for God's intentions to be
accomplished through them. Prayer facilitates a deeper
commitment to God. Here God acts in the subjectivity of
the individual to comfort and reveal himself so as to influ-

ence the believer toward the good that God intends. But
the rule of God's kingdom in the world is dependent upon
our choices and involvement. If God's will is to be done in
the world, human beings must do it. Otherwise, it will not
happen.

Moderns and postmoderns struggle with the concept of
prayer. Many have adopted a secularist view of prayer. For
them prayer is simply a means of self-actualization. It is
self-induced therapy; a psychological couch which emboldens us to seek change in the world. Secularized prayer is
often simply a method for self-motivation. It does not, as
Coleman writes, "intend to move [God] to intervene or to
change [an] external circumstance. The [secularist] prays
for justice, healing, comfort, peace, thinking that these
things will be accomplished if he does them."[11] Secularized
prayer looks to the human achiever rather than the divine
giver; it redeems by works rather than grace.

The Problem: The Point of Prayer

The role and purpose of prayer provides the best illustration of the difference between the biblical world and
ours.[12] It illustrates the difference between the faith which
sees God active in his world and the faith which removes
God from his world. About what may we legitimately pray?
May we expect God to do something? What sort of thing
may we expect God to do? May we ask him to do anything
other than help us bear with our suffering?

Jill (modern), Carol (postmodern), and Mary (premodern) represent three different worldviews which result in
different ways of understanding prayer. Mary believes that
through the power of prayer God may decide to act on
behalf of the believer. Consequently, when Mary heard
reports about tornadoes in her area, she prayed for protection. As far as Mary is concerned, God answered her prayer
when the tornado jumped over her house. Prayer, then, is
among other things petitionary. It requests God to act con-

cretely to change situations, circumstances, and prospects. As Coleman writes, "It does not matter whether God acts indirectly or directly, immediately or later, naturally or miraculously; what matters is that God does act on behalf of the petitioner."[13] In response to God's answer, Mary offers praise and thanksgiving. God receives the credit for the survival of her family.

Jill and Carol also believe in God. However, their prayers would not ask God to divert a tornado. God does not do such things. Rather, their prayers would focus on the faith, patience, and anxiety of the family and ask God to help them through the situation. Carol would be more prone to ask for God's strength and commit herself to God's mercy by helping those who might be injured by the storm. But they do not believe that God acts to control natural forces. They do not expect God to redirect the tornado. Rather, they believe prayer changes the individual and pushes people to self-involvement in the world so that they effect change and endure suffering. Prayer is, more or less, a psychological couch upon which believers struggle through their deepest anxieties in the presence of God. But they do not expect God to do anything concrete. What Carol does expect is that God would provide the strength to endure the anxiety that a tornado creates. Jill, however, is often left with no other recourse than to pray as a means of encouraging her own faith.

The following chart illustrates the differences between Jill, Carol, and Mary. The only thing Jill can find in prayer is self-actualization. Through prayer she gathers her own strength to endure the anxiety of the tornado. Carol, however, calls upon God's strength which will empower her to endure those same anxieties. But Mary not only "gathers herself" and seeks God's strength, she also calls upon God to redirect the tornado so that it misses her home and spares her family.

The Point of Prayer	Jill	Carol	Mary
Prayer as a Means of Self-Actualization and Self-Motivation	Yes	Yes	Yes
Prayer as a Means of God's Activity within the Subjectivity of the Human Soul	No	Yes	Yes
Prayer as a Means for Changing Empirical Realities	No	No	Yes

Jill and Carol reflect a secularist attitude toward prayer, while Mary's world is entirely sacred. Jill and Carol do not expect God to change the empirical realities of the world, e.g., redirect a tornado or change the course of a hurricane. Their natural world is secularized. But Mary seeks God's protection, not just from spiritual realities, but also from the natural evils that afflict his people.

Kushner's *When Bad Things Happen to Good People*, particularly his chapter "God Can't Do Everything, But He Can Do Some Important Things," illustrates the secularist attitude toward prayer.[14] Kushner believes that we need to rid ourselves of "unrealistic expectations." For example, he characterizes petitioning God for "food, clothing, prosperity, a safe return" as a "long list of demands." People do not receive such things as a result of prayer any more than "children who pray for bicycles, good grades, or boyfriends get them as a result of praying." God, apparently, is not in such control of the universe that he can provide such things. There are some things God cannot do in his world. It is not that he will not do it. It is that "He can't do that." God does the best he can in this world. We must revise our expectations of what God can do.[15]

As a result, it makes no sense to pray that God will "cure malignancies and influence the outcome of surgery," Kushner writes. "Praying for a person's health, for a favorable outcome of an operation has implications that ought to disturb a thoughtful person." If the person is not healed, am I to conclude that God did not want her healed? Is God somehow malevolent and sadistic? Or, am I to conclude that I did not pray hard enough? Did God say: "I could have made your mother healthy again, but you didn't plead and grovel enough?" Kushner dismisses these thoughts. God is good. The prayer of faith is commendable. His answer is: there are some things that God cannot do even though God would like to do them.[16]

There is, however, something positive about prayer according to Kushner. It is the way we are "put in touch with" other people and God. We share with others the joys and sorrows of life in prayer. Put in "touch with God" we draw strength from "the knowledge that God is at the side of the afflicted and the downcast." Prayer, then, is where we "pray for courage, for strength to bear the unbearable." There we tap the "hidden reserves of faith and courage which were not available" to us previously. Thus, God has no responsibility for the suffering — he can neither prevent it nor relieve it, but he does give "strength to cope with the problem." But it is difficult to determine whether this means anything more than that prayer is the means by which people find strength in themselves. It is unclear what exactly God really does for his petitioners, but he does not do anything concrete or empirical.

It appears that Kushner's idea of prayer is simply a means for self-actualization or perhaps the openness that God requires to provide strength to a believer. It may be nothing more than self-induced therapy or a form of self-help, or it may be the ambiguous work of God in the subjectivity of the human soul.[17] But it is clearly not activistic, that is, God does not act in the empirical world to change the fallen realities that face God's people. God would like to heal the sick, but he cannot.

Summary

How one prays, then, is an important signal as to how a person interprets God's involvement in the world. Mary does not see prayer as simply therapeutic. It is more. She will pray for a successful operation. She will pray for the safe return of her husband. She will pray for small things as well as catastrophic things. She will pray for help in finding her keys as well as for the health of her child. She still lives in a world where God acts in concrete ways. God involves himself in the lives of his people, and he acts on their behalf.

For Jill and Carol, as well as for Kushner, prayer signals a very different view of the world. It is a world where God no longer acts, or perhaps could never act, on behalf of his people in a concrete way. It is a world where prayer for health is excluded, and only prayer for strength remains; a world where prayer for the relief of oppression is excluded, and only prayer for endurance remains.

But Jill's and Carol's world are not the biblical world. In Scripture, God acts in concrete ways as he responds to the cries of his people. It is a very different world from the one in which Jill, Carol, and Kushner live.

According to the biblical story, God is interactive and personally engaged with his world in both the empirical and subjective dimensions. Subsequent chapters will note the many ways in which God is involved in his world. We must immerse ourselves in the story of Scripture, and view our lives through its lens which provides the interpretative framework for the eye of faith. We must interpret our experience in the light of Scripture. The biblical story must interpret our story.

Contrary to the way many moderns and postmoderns describe it, the biblical story is not some manipulative game that God is playing. On the contrary, God is involved in our story in order to win us to himself — to draw out our love for him — and to enter into relationship with us. He moves within nature and history as well as within our souls to help us find him, so that we learn to love him for his own sake rather than for our sakes. God searches among humanity for those who will enter into loving fellowship with him.

This is the driving force behind God's actions in the world. It is the structural principle out of which his actions flow.

When the people of God "call upon" their God within the biblical story, it is with the confidence that God seeks out his people, draws them to himself, and will remain faithful to his covenant of love. Prayer makes certain assumptions about whether God cares, whether he is present, and how he relates to the world. Prayer is fundamentally the believer's personal engagement with God. Prayer is fellowship between the God who seeks out a people for himself and a people who seek their God. It is a moment when God engages his people and they engage him. Prayer, then, assumes God's care, presence, and power. Prayer assumes God's total involvement with his people.

The Cause: Innocent Suffering

In the aftermath of World War I, World War II, and the Holocaust, the problem of innocent suffering has destroyed the last vestiges of the biblical worldview in the minds of modern people. Even Science and Reason could not destroy humanity's sixth sense (the sense of divinity in our souls) that God is involved in his world. But what Science and Reason could not do, the radical evil of the Holocaust (and other similar events) did. A secularized world seems the best explanation for the radical evil of Hitler's concentration camps and gas chambers. As Wiesel's *Night* evidences, the horror of the Holocaust murdered the Judeo-Christian God.[18] One of his most potent statements recalls the first night he saw the flames of Auschwitz:

> Never shall I forget that night, the first night
>   in the camp, which has turned my life into one
>   long night,
>   seven times cursed and seven times sealed.
> Never shall I forget that smoke.
> Never shall I forget the little faces of the children,

whose bodies I saw turned into wreaths of smoke
    beneath a silent blue sky.
Never shall I forget those flames which consumed my
  faith forever.
Never shall I forget that nocturnal silence which
  deprived me,
    for all eternity, of the desire to live.
Never shall I forget those moments which murdered
  my God
    and my soul and turned my dreams to dust.
Never shall I forget these things,
    even if I am condemned to live as long as God
      Himself.
Never.

No longer was it possible to believe naïvely in the God who routinely delivers the innocent from the oppressor. No longer was it possible to believe in the goodness of an omnipotent God. No longer was it possible to believe in a God who acts in history to prevent radical evil. The destruction of this naïveté — whether it comes from the Holocaust or out of the experience of the impoverished in the third world or out of racial discrimination in mid-20th century America — has accelerated secularization in both society and theology. Indeed, it has led many to deny the existence of God, or at least to revise the biblical picture of God.

Innocent suffering is undeserved suffering that is not directly related to the actions of the individual sufferer. It bears the consequences of an evil uncommitted. We expect the punishment of criminals. Rapists and murderers deserve incarceration. But innocent suffering is not construed as punishment for some wrongdoing. Modern people understand the difference between innocent and deserved suffering. Hitler deserved suffering, but the children he murdered did not.

Tragically, our world is well acquainted with the suffering of innocents. Whether it is gassing a million children in the Holocaust, a baby born with AIDS, children killed by a bomber in Oklahoma City, a child born with a terminal condition, or the death of thousands in an earthquake, the enduring question of such horror is: "Why do children die?" "They did not deserve this," it is lamented. "Why are babies born with AIDS?" Surely, no newborn infant deserves to die. We all share the same vision of the *prima facie* innocence of children, and we are all aware that innocence does not preclude suffering. When the drunk driver collides with another vehicle and kills all the family members, no one thinks that the family somehow deserved to die or that the family bears any immediate responsibility for their own deaths. Most would agree that the responsibility for the tragedy rests upon the drunk driver. But when a tornado kills a child, who bears the responsibility — no one or God?

Innocent suffering poses a problem for the theist who lives in the biblical world. Jill raised it succinctly to Mary. Can we honestly believe in a God who permits (or worse, directs) a tornado to hit the Anderson's house and kill his toddler? If God is ultimately responsible for such events like tornadoes, if God is active in the natural order, why does he not prevent such undeserved suffering? For Mary the problem is acute because her faith involves God in this world. For Jill God is not part of the equation. For Carol, God is only present to comfort and embolden the soul to endure. For both Jill and Carol, no one is responsible for the tornado. It is simply part of nature's chaos. They quickly move on to another question.

In a secular world, their position is comfortable. It does not charge God with any ultimate responsibility for the tornado that killed Joshua. The secularist sees the world as a morally neutral realm in which good or evil may take place. Whatever does happen, happens "naturally," that is, it is explicable in terms of observable phenomena. It is the result of natural forces or luck, whether good or bad. Thus, the death of thousands in an earthquake or the death of a child in a tornado has no moral meaning. No one is responsible — that's just the way things are. It is bad luck, not divine acts, which the sufferer must endure. It is chaos, not design. No one can charge God with any ultimate responsibility.

Conclusion

How did the quintessential biblical sufferer (other than Jesus himself) view God's relation to his world? Job believed that God was ultimately responsible for his suffering. While we will discuss this point later, here it is important to emphasize the disjunction between Job's world and ours. Job makes statements which no modern or postmodern could accept as true. Indeed, they would find them blasphemous or unimaginable. Even Mary might have a problem with the boldness and audacity with which Job assigns *all* his suffering to God's hand.

Job believes that God alone is in control of the world and its events. Consequently, only God is ultimately responsible for them. Job asks, "If it is not he, then who is it?" (Job 9:24c). Ask the animals who is responsible for his situation. "Which of all these does not know," Job protests, "that the hand of the LORD has done this?" (Job 12:9). Job cannot divorce God from his world. Whether the wicked prosper, or the righteous suffer, God controls his world. Just as he causes the wicked to prosper and the righteous to suffer, God is responsible for Job's suffering.

Yet this creates a problem for Job, as it does for all believers. Job knows his suffering is not deserved. He certainly knows that he is not like the wicked who reject God and believe it is futile to serve him (cf. Job 21:14-15). But he also knows that God has brought this suffering upon him. The problem is this: since God controls the world, why does not the world reflect his justice and his compassion? The righteous sufferer, whose questions become bold accusations, addresses this problem when he asks, "Does it please you to oppress me, to spurn the work of your hands, while you smile on the schemes of the wicked?" (Job 10:3).

Job does not deny God's existence, but he does wonder about his justice. Job felt unfairly treated by God. How could God be just and yet permit bad people to enjoy good things? How could God be just and yet permit good people to suffer bad things? According to Job, the universe had lost its moral bearings and God is responsible.

God is responsible for his world. Job understands this. But the modern believer shrinks back from the thought. The modern world understands the question. Indeed, the seeming horror of the possible answer has driven Jill to a Deism (where God allows the world to run much like we watch a clock tick), and has driven others (e.g., Kushner, Carol) to revise the traditional Judeo-Christian doctrine of God. Can God really be responsible for this world where radical evil is so pervasive? The modern believer seeks to absolve or justify God by removing him from involvement in the world or, as in the case of some postmodern believers, by understanding ("forgiving") God's limitations.[19] The modern/postmodern believer wants to isolate God from the problem; push him back into a corner where he can be justified or, at least, understood. The believer must defend God; or, at least, he must make excuses for him. There is only so much God can do. He has his limitations. God does the best he can do with the world he has made; he does the most he can do.[20] We must understand God's predicament. We must forgive God. Job, however, will have none of this divine coddling. God is responsible or he is not God.

If the answer has seemed so elusive to modern thinkers, how did the ancient authors of the Bible think through it? Where will God's story take us to enable us to endure undeserved suffering? The biblical story will lead us through the maze — through despair, anger, and questions — and bring us into the reverent awe of divine transcendence as God comes near to us in our suffering. The biblical story will tell us about creation, the fall, God's initiatives in history to redeem, the empathetic incarnation of God, the experience of God's power through the presence of his Holy

Spirit and the triumphant hope of the resurrection. The biblical story tells us how God has suffered with us and for us so that we might know his communion even in the midst of suffering.

---

[1]Joan I. Duffy, "Legislature Keeps 'Acts of God' in Bill," *Commercial Appeal*, March 21, 1997.

[2]See Karel Dobbelaere, "Secularization: A Multi-Dimensional Concept," *Current Sociology* 29 (Summer 1981): 1-213.

[3]Paul W. Pruyser, *Between Belief and Unbelief* (New York: Harper & Row, 1974), p. 15.

[4]W. Donald Hudson, *A Philosophical Approach to Religion* (New York: Macmillan Press, 1974), p. 110.

[5]See Nicholas Wolterstorff, *John Locke and the Ethics of Belief* (Cambridge: Cambridge University Press, 1996).

[6]See William Lane Craig, *Reasonable Faith: Christian Truth and Apologetics* (Wheaton: Crossway Books, 1994), pp. 36-48.

[7]J. Gleick, *Chaos: Making a New Science* (New York: Penguin, 1987) and David Ruelle, *Chance and Chaos* (New York: Penguin, 1993). For some theological reflections on chaos theory, see John Jefferson Davis, "Theological Reflections on Chaos Theory," *Perspectives on Science and Christian Faith* 49 (June 1997): 75-84 and J.T. Houghton, "New Ideas of Chaos in Physics," *Science & Christian Belief* 1 (1989): 41-51.

[8]Arthur A. Vogel, *God, Prayer & Healing: Living with God in a World Like Ours* (Grand Rapids: Eerdmans, 1995), pp. 93-106.

[9]See Diogenes Allen, *Christian Belief in a Postmodern World* (Louisville, KY: Westminster/John Knox Press, 1989), pp. 1-19; Timothy R. Philipps and Dennis L. Okholm, eds., *Christian Apologetics in the Postmodern World* (Downers Grove, IL: InterVarsity, 1995); David S. Dockery, ed., *The Challenge of Postmodernism: An Evangelical Engagement* (Wheaton, IL: Victor Books, 1995); and J. Richard Middleton and Brian Walsh, *Truth Is Stranger Than It Used to Be: Biblical Faith in a Postmodern Age* (Downers Grove, IL: InterVarsity, 1995).

[10]These categories and some of this material is dependent upon Philip Dale Krumrei, "The Relevance of Secularization for Interpreting and Nurturing Spirituality in Dutch Churches of Christ; An Analysis of the Relation of Pre-Modern, Modern and Post-Modern Paradigms of Faith and the Practice of Prayer" (D. Min. dissertation, Harding University Graduate School of Religion, 1992), pp. 240-246. For a fuller discussion of premodern, modern, and postmodern understandings of providence, see my web article at *www.collegepress.com/jmhicks/providence.htm*.

[11]Richard J. Coleman, *Issues of Theological Conflict: Evangelicals and Liberals* (Grand Rapids: Eerdmans, 1972), p. 195.

[12]My discussion is partly based upon Coleman, *Issues,* pp. 183-204.

[13]Ibid., p. 196.

[14]Harold S. Kushner, *When Bad Things Happen to Good People* (New York: Avon Books, 1981), pp. 113-131.

[15]Ibid., pp. 122, 124, 125.

[16]Ibid., pp. 113-114.

[17]Ibid., pp. 119, 122, 125, 127.

[18]Wiesel, *Night,* p. 44.

[19]Kushner, *Bad Things,* p 148.

[20]E. Frank Tupper, *A Scandalous Providence: The Jesus Story of the Compassion of God* (Macon, GA: Mercer University Press, 1995), p. 75; cf. pp. 78-81, 116-119.

Chapter Three

Why Did God Create This World?
Creation and Fall in the Biblical Story

In the beginning God created the heavens and the earth. . . .
So God created man in his own image,
in the image of God he created him;
male and female he created them. . . .
God saw all that he had made, and it was very good.
Genesis 1:1,27,31a

To the serpent,
"Because you have done this,
Cursed are you above all the livestock
and all the wild animals! . . .

To the woman,
"I will greatly increase your pains in childbearing;
with pain you will give birth to children.
Your desire will be for your husband,
and he will rule over you."

To the man,
"Because you listened to your wife. . . .
Cursed is the ground because of you;
through painful toil you will eat of it
all the days of your life.
Genesis 3:14a,16,17

Did God create this world? Well, yes and no. What God created was "very good," but what now exists is "cursed." God created life, harmony, and joy, but death, hostility, and pain now fill the earth. What happened? The answer to that question is the story of creation and fall.

It is important to understand this part of the story because here we see God's loving intent through divine creation and we see the introduction of evil, suffering, and death through human sin. Yet, despite the curse, God still seeks what is good for his creation. God's intent remains the same, and he will use whatever means are appropriate to achieve that end. The story of providence, then, begins with God's intent in creation.

Creation: What Did God Intend?

God's first gracious act toward humanity was not the Exodus nor the Cross, it was Creation. When God created, he acted freely and without compulsion. Humanity did not deserve to be created. It had no inherent right to exist. Neither was God compelled by some inner necessity. Creation was an act of unmerited love which arose freely out of his will (Revelation 4:11).

The model for understanding God's gracious act of creation is God's two great redemptive acts (one of which prefigures the other): the creation of Israel and the creation of the church. Both of these moments in redemptive history reflect God's original intent. Indeed, the creation of Israel and the church are the extension of God's original act of creation. God now seeks to redeem what is fallen. God's re-creation is driven by the same motive and interest that moved God to create in the first place. God decided to create, just as he decided to redeem, out of his love.

Israel did not create herself nor did she have some inherent, irresistible value as a nation. God was not compelled to call Abraham, nor was he obligated to choose

Jacob over Esau (cf. Romans 9:10-13). God did not choose Israel because they were so numerous (as if God must choose the largest nation), nor did he choose Israel because they were so faithful (as if any nation's righteousness could put God in their debt). God chose Israel despite the fact that they were the "fewest of all peoples" (Deuteronomy 7:7) and a "stiff-necked people" (Deuteronomy 9:6). God chose them because he loved them (Deuteronomy 7:8-9). God chose Israel for the same reason he created the cosmos.

The church did not create herself nor did she have some inherent, irresistible value as a people. God was not compelled to send his Son, nor was he obligated to redeem sinful people. God did not elect us in Christ because we were so holy (as if we could pretend to be such), nor did he elect us in Christ because we are so inherently valuable (as if we could arrogantly claim that something in us is so wonderful that God had to redeem us). Rather, God chose us out of his loving grace (Ephesians 1:4-6). Christ died for us despite the fact that we were sinners and God's enemies (Romans 5:6-10). God demonstrated his love for us through the gracious gift of his Son. "This is how God showed his love among us" (1 John 4:9). This is God's redeeming love, and it is the same love that moved God to create the cosmos.

But this still seems to leave us questioning. If God created out of his love, what does this mean? How are we to understand this divine act? Was his love some kind of compulsion that forced him to create? Was it deficient until he created us?

God Seeks a People for Himself

Why did God create the cosmos, or more specifically, why did he create us? This question has often perplexed theologians as well as children who begin to wonder about it in their first Bible classes. It is tempting to answer that there was something lacking in God, that God had some need to fulfill or some inner desire to satisfy. But then

God's act of creation would not be gracious, but self-interested. God created, according to this scenario, because God was selfish or ego-centered, or somehow deficient in his own being. An inner necessity compelled God to supply something lacking in his own life. That would be tantamount to saying that God created us because he was incomplete. God, then, would have created out of necessity rather than grace. We would exist because God needs us. This puts God in our debt instead of we in his.

If we are to grasp why God created, we must understand what he created, and how this is reflected in God's other gracious acts in history (such as the creation of Israel and the church). What did God create? He created a community — a male and a female who would fill the earth with their descendants, and consequently fill the earth with God's glory (Genesis 1:28; 9:1). When God created Israel, he chose Abraham and Sarah whose descendants would be a people which would glorify God among the nations. When God created the church, he chose Christ who would be the author of salvation for the brothers and sisters he would bring to glory (Hebrews 2:10). God has always intended a people for himself. Whether in the original act of creation or in the redemptive act of re-creation, God gathers a people for himself. God intends to share his love with a community.

This is a pervasive theme in Scripture. When God entered into covenant with Abraham, he promised him that he would not only be Abraham's God, but also the God of his descendants after him. Abraham's descendants would be God's people, and he would be their God (Genesis 17:7-8). When God came to Israel in Egypt through Moses, he promised redemption and assured them that "I will take you as my own people, and I will be your God" (Exodus 6:7). When Israel set up the tabernacle in the wilderness, God's glory descended on it with the promise that there God would dwell among his people and be their God (Exodus 29:45; 40:34-35; Leviticus 26:11-12). The glory was repeated with the completion of the temple under Solomon (1 Kings 8:11; 2 Chronicles 5:14; 7:1-3). The prophets constantly reminded Israel of God's promise to be present among them (Ezekiel 34:30). Israel would be God's people, and he would be their God (Jeremiah 7:23; 11:4; 24:7; Ezekiel 11:20; 14:11; 36:28; 37:27; Zechariah 2:11; 8:8; 13:9).

Further, this promise was at the heart of the "new covenant." Through Jeremiah, God declared his intent to forgive Israel's sin so that he could fulfill his promise, that is, "I will be their God, and they will be my people" (Jeremiah 31:33). Paul, in the context of thinking about the ministry of this new covenant (2 Corinthians 3:6), reminds us that this promise has found expression in God's church where "we are the temple of the living God" (2 Corinthians 6:16). Leviticus 26:11-12 is fulfilled in the church, as God has said: "I will live with them and walk among them, and I will be their God, and they will be my people" (2 Corinthians 6:16 quoting Leviticus 26:12). In the church God has a people for himself. But the ultimate goal of this promise is the eschatological dwelling of God with his people in a community which he will establish when the new age is consummated. When the new Jerusalem descends out of heaven, then a loud voice will announce: "Now the dwelling of God is with men, and he will live with them. They will be his people, and God himself will be with them and be their God" (Revelation 21:3).

This redemptive-historical motif, that God seeks a people for himself, demonstrates that God's intent in redemption/re-creation is to dwell with his people in a communion of love. God seeks fellowship with his people. Since re-creation is modeled after creation, God's original act of creation had the same intent. He created a community, a people, for himself. He created a people with whom he could share a communion of love.

But why does God seek a communion of love with a people of his own creation? Is God a solitary figure whose loneliness drives him to create in order to have fellowship with others? Does God need company?

While the doctrine of "Trinity" (however that word may be defined) seems remote, speculative, and cumbersome to some, it is helpful in understanding God's purpose in creating the cosmos.[1] It does not take an astute theologian to recognize the impact that Trinitarian theology can have on one's understanding of God's creative act. Indeed, Scripture reveals that creation itself was a triune act. God the Father is the fountainhead of creation; he is the source and origin of everything that exists. Everything in the universe originated with him; it was "out of" or "from" him (Romans 11:36; 1 Corinthians 8:6). Yet the Son is the instrument of creation. He is the means by which the Father created (John 1:1-3; 1 Corinthians 8:6). The Father created nothing without the agency of the Son. The Spirit, as the breath of life, is God's dynamic presence which gives and energizes life in the world (Job 26:13; 33:4; Psalm 33:6; 104:30). The Spirit was present at creation, and was the power by which life invaded what was lifeless (Genesis 1:2; 2:7). Creation, therefore, is from God the Father through the agency of the Son by the power of the Spirit.[2] The one God, then, performed the mighty work of creation as a community just as that same God performs the mighty work of redemption as a triune community (cf. Ephesians 2:18; 1 Peter 1:2). Both creation and redemption are the work of the triune God.

The doctrine of the Trinity teaches that the divine reality is a community of loving fellowship between the Father, Son, and Spirit. It is a community of holy love which existed before the cosmos did. Jesus prayed that his disciples might see the glory that the Father had given him, and the Father gave him this glory because he loved him "before the creation of the world" (literally, before the foundation of the cosmos; John 17:24). This text provides a glimpse into the common life of the Father and Son before the act of creation. Before the cosmos existed, there existed a community of love (*agape*) which the Father and the Son shared.

The prayer also points us to the redemptive love of God which flows from the love the Father and Son shared. Jesus promised his Father that he would continue to make the Father known to his disciples "in order that the love you have for me may be in them" (literally, the love [*agape*] with which you have loved me; John 17:26). The intent of redemption is to bring the fallen world into the orbit of God's *agape* fellowship where, just as the Father dwells in the Son and the Son in the Father, God's people may dwell in them and they in God (John 17:21). God intends for us to share the fellowship of the Father and the Son (1 John 1:3). If the intent of redemption is modeled after creation, then the intent of creation is clear as well. God intended to create a people to share his loving community.

God did not create this fellowship out of loneliness. As Bloesch comments, "God is not a solitary being, detached and remote from the world of human discourse and activity, but a Trinitarian fellowship of love."[3] God did not create because he needed fellowship since he already enjoyed fellowship through the triune communion of the Father, Son, and Spirit. This fellowship was not created by God as though at some point in time God became a fellowship. Rather, it is who God is. God is a community of love because God is love. God is *agape* (1 John 4:8). Consequently, God did not need to turn to anything outside of himself in order to experience loving community. This was present through the mutual indwelling of God's triune fellowship.

I think the best analogy for understanding this divine act — as limited as the analogy is — is the decision of a couple to have children. Why do couples decide to have children? Certainly, in a fallen world, there are less than pure motives. But in the purest sense, couples decide to have children in order to share their love with another. The decision to have a child is, in the best of circumstances, a selfless decision. They share something that they could have kept to themselves. The love which exists between a husband and wife is a communion unsurpassed in human relations. When children are born into that loving communion, the children share something they did not create. The parents give something they were not compelled to share. Children — and we wish it were true in every instance — are born out of the loving communion between parents. The couple shares their love with another.

Following this analogy, when the triune community decided to create, they decided to share with another something they already enjoyed. We humans did not create that fellowship, but it is offered to us in love. God did not create in order to receive (as if he needed anything outside of himself). He created to give of himself. Thus, the act of creation is an act of gracious, selfless love.

Nevertheless, just as parents are enriched through sharing the experience of love with their children, so God is enriched. God created for himself, or as Scripture puts it, for his own glory. Just as God created Israel for his own glory and marked off the church as his own possession to his own glory (Ephesians 1:14), so God created the cosmos for his own glory (Isaiah 43:7; 48:11). Creation was an act of God for God. Everything exists for him (Hebrews 2:10; Romans 11:36), that is, it is for his glory, to his honor, and for his benefit. But this is not the act of an egotist. Rather, it is the joyous sharing of his own fellowship. This joy is his fellowship with his people. God glorifies himself in that loving fellowship. It is an other-centered love that gives and shares.

The purpose of creation, therefore, is to magnify the glory of the God who shares his love and fellowship with those whom he has created. God is glorified in the joy of communion. Thus God acts, whether in creation or redemption, to the praise of his glory which is expressed in the communion he has with his people (cf. Ephesians 1:6,12, 14). So also human beings exist to magnify and reflect the glory of God by enjoying fellowship with him.[4]

Creation expressed the grace of God. The gracious act of creation, an act of *agape* love, is God's decision to share what he already possessed. It was not to gain something he lacked. Rather, God decided to share his own loving fellowship within the triune community with others. This is an astounding but wondrous thought. God, without compulsion, decided to share his holy communion with those whom he created. Just as God so loved the world that he gave his Son, he also so loved that he created a world with which to share his love. God's love, by his free decision, is self-giving and other-centered so that it seeks to share the joy of divine communion with others.

Human Freedom and Communion with God

When God had finished creating, he looked at everything he had created and declared that it was "very good" (Gen. 1:31). The climax of this creation was humanity whom he created as male and female in his own image. The divine community created a human community with whom it could share its own fellowship. On the seventh day, God rested in the fellowship of his creation. God provided a place for this fellowship to grow and develop, which Genesis calls "Eden" (Genesis 2:10-14). It was a place where God freely walked among his people and they did not hide from him. The Garden of Eden was a place of joy and fellowship between God and his people.

Genesis does not describe the relationship between God and his people in abstract theological terms. Instead, it offers a relational narrative. God provides for his creatures. He provides life, as he breathed into Adam the breath of life (Genesis 2:7). He provides a garden furnished with all that is necessary for life. He provides a tree of life which offers everlasting communion in the presence of God (Genesis 2:9). He provides a task (Genesis 2:15) and gives humanity dominion over his creation as benevolent caretakers (Genesis 1:28-30). He provides companionship and community for his creatures by creating male and female. God is the Great Provider (thus, providence).

Aloneness, solitude, and individualism are not absolute values.[5] Rather, God created a community where a mutual relationship might enrich the life of the other. "It is not good for the man to be alone" (Genesis 2:18). Consequently, the communion between Adam and Eve, between husband and wife, is part of the reality that God created for the happiness of his people. That communion reflects the communion of God's own triune life. That they were both naked but neither was ashamed, underscores the intimacy, freedom, and openness of that relationship (Genesis 2:25), especially in light of the shame they would later feel (Genesis 3:7).

The divine community created a human community, and the human community bears the image of the divine. Just as God had created out of his love to share his triune communion, so God called for the human community to fill the earth with their descendants which would image God's act of creation (Genesis 1:28). By procreation, they would fill the earth with God's glory. Adam and Eve, as male and female, were to share their fellowship with God, with each other and with still others to whom they would give birth in love.

Adam and Eve were born into a divine community of love, just as children are (at least ideally) born into the loving communion of their family. Yet, in this communion, God offers his children a choice. All the provisions of the Garden are open to their use and cultivation except one. God placed the "tree of the knowledge of good and evil" (Genesis 2:9) in the middle of the Garden, and he forbade them to eat from it (Genesis 2:17). God set a choice before his children. As long as they lived in Eden, they would choose whether to obey God or disobey him; whether to eat or not eat of the forbidden fruit. Consequently, God created a place where humanity would have to choose communion with God over a "knowledge of good and evil."

This poses a serious question. Why does God offer his creatures a choice? Why could not God simply position the tree of life in the Garden without also planting another tree which symbolized their potential rebellion against God? Why did God put the "tree of the knowledge of good and evil" in that Garden where their communion with God was so pristine, innocent, and pure? Perhaps God sees some value in choice itself. Perhaps choice provides the opportunity for the genuine and authentic expression of love. Perhaps the reality of love is only known and experienced when there is choice.

Several years ago I attended the Broadway musical "Starlight Express" with my wife. It was a wonderful play where actors on roller skates simulated trains. Each actor/actress represented either an engine or a caboose. The plot revolved around the rivalry between an old steam engine and a modern electric engine. This rivalry created a crisis in the relationship between the old steam engine and his caboose (representing his lover). The caboose was tempted to attach herself to the newer, more modern engine. In an important scene, the old steam engine is trying to convince her to stay with him and he insists that she remain his caboose. She replies that authentic love means that he can make no such demand because if he forced her to stay then it would not be love. If she is truly free to stay, she must also be free to go. In other words, if the old steam engine desires genuine, authentic love, then he must permit her the freedom to stay or go. Without freedom, there can be no real love. Without freedom, there is only a coerced relationship of power and fear.

Why did God provide a choice in the Garden? The question raises the issue of God's intent. God intended to enter into a communion of love with his people as an extension of his own community of love. Yet the love of another must ultimately be a choice or it is not genuine love. God, therefore, provides a choice so that his people might experience genuine love. He provides them the opportunity to go or stay because what he desires is a genuine loving relationship born out of affection and loyalty. God's creatures must have the freedom to go if they are to have the freedom to stay. So, God offers them a choice: the tree of the knowledge of good and evil or the tree of life. Humanity may enjoy God's communion or seek its own way.

A common plot line illustrates my point. A wealthy prince has fallen in love with a peasant girl. The prince has a choice. On the one hand, he can send his royal guards into the village, kidnap the girl and force her to live in the palace. In response the young lady may resent the kidnapping and grow bitter about how she was forcibly separated from her family. Consequently, she would never authentically and genuinely love the prince even though she is forced to marry him. The prince, then, would never find what he seeks. He seeks a mutually fulfilling, reciprocal relationship of love. By forcing her into the relationship, he could never be sure about what kind of "love" he receives from his bride. On the other hand, the prince could woo the peasant girl by becoming a peasant himself.[6] He could live in the village and work alongside her as a peasant. Love would develop in freedom and this would ground its genuineness. She would not be forced into "love" nor motivated to love by the offer of wealth, power, and position. The prince, then, would know his bride loves him out of freedom rather than coercion.

God created Adam and Eve in a circumstance that permitted genuine choice. God offered his fellowship to them. He offered them a choice so that their love might be born out of freedom rather than coercion. It is certainly in God's power to coerce. Indeed, one day every knee will bow and every tongue will confess Jesus as Lord to the glory of the Father (Philippians 2:9-11). One day everyone will bow before the overwhelming manifestation of God's glory. One day God will coerce a confession from those who have not already done so willingly. But that is not what he seeks. He does not desire "forced confessions" or "coerced love."

Rather, just as within himself there is the freedom to love, so he seeks love that is born out of freedom among his creatures. God desires a reciprocal love that arises out of the freedom of relationship rather than a "coerced love" that arises out of God's decree.

God could drag us into the palace and force us to live with him, but he has decided to woo us with his love by identifying with us. In the Garden, God identified with his people by walking among them, and in redemption, God identified with his people by becoming one of them in the incarnation of the Son (John 1:1,14-18). God does not force us to live with him, but he leads us to desire him by the excellency of his love.

The analogy of parents and children again helps to illuminate this relationship. In healthy circumstances, children are born into a loving family where they are received and cared for by unselfish parents. Parents offer their love without condition, and they seek reciprocation. They want their children to love them as authentically as they are loved. Parents do not want a love that is coerced by household rules and regulations. We do not want forced hugs, and neither do we want a preprogrammed "I love you." Rather, we want our children to develop a relationship with us that is born out of freedom, gratitude, and genuine affection.

In the same way, God yearns for our love. Consequently, he provides a choice in order to ground the authenticity of that love. The provision of choice reveals God's intent to have a genuinely reciprocal fellowship.

The Fall: The Cursed Cosmos

God provided this newly created community with an environment where they could fill the earth with their offspring, care for their environment as benevolent royalty, and enjoy the presence of God. God created Paradise, the Garden of Eden. However, genuine, mutual love involved a choice. God explicitly set that choice before them. They had to decide. They could reciprocate God's love or they may seek their own "knowledge of good and evil."

The Risk of Human Freedom

When God provided humanity with a choice, he took a risk. He risked that some would not reciprocate his loving fellowship. Parents take the same risk when they have children. The potential in parenthood for mutual love and joy is immeasurable, but the potential for pain and hurt is equally immeasurable. When our children reciprocate our love, when they offer us hugs and kisses, when they express their care for us affectionately, the joy is almost unparalleled. God intended such relationships within families as a reflection of his own triune fellowship. However, when our children rebel, run away from home, or curse us, the pain is almost unimaginable. The potential for joy is balanced by an equal potential for hurt. God never intended the hurt when he created, but he risked it with the gift of human freedom.

God risked that some would choose their own interests over fellowship with him.[7] The gift of freedom means that humanity could either choose its own direction or share God's loving community. But if God were going to offer authentic mutual love, then he would have to risk the choice. Without the choice, the fellowship would have been superficial and inauthentic.

Some think it is strange to talk about God "taking risks." In fact, theologians line up on both sides of this question. Paul Helm, for example, argues that God's world is risk-free. God acts with certainty; he knows the future and he has determined what will happen. God does not take risks.[8] If God takes risks, it is argued, he cannot be the sovereign God of the Bible who knows all things, governs all things, and brings the world to a certain goal. Others, such as William Hasker, believe that the existence of free creatures involves God in risks so that "creating and governing a world is for God a risky business."[9] If God does not take risks, it is argued, then human persons do not have genuine freedom, for if they have genuine freedom, then they can act in ways that are contrary to God's intentions. Such a circumstance creates a risk for God.

There is a sense in which God takes risks and a sense in which God does not take risks. The scenario in Genesis 2, where God sets a choice before Adam and Eve, reflects a risky situation for God. If the choice is a real choice, that is, if God has not already predetermined what choice will be made, then the choice does present God with a risk. If it is a genuine choice, he risks rejection. He risks the hurt of rebellious children and broken fellowship. Where there is no choice, there is no risk. Where there is no risk, there can be no choice. It appears from the text that choice was genuine, and, therefore, God took a real risk. Adam and Eve were responsible for what they chose.

Nevertheless, there is a sense in which God does not take risks. There was no risk because God was not surprised by any of the choices that were made. God's knowledge is comprehensive, or as more classical theologians would say, God is omniscient (all-knowing). When God decided to create, he knew some would rebel against his intentions and reject his fellowship. God chose his Son as the world's redeemer even before the creation of the cosmos (1 Peter 1:20; cf. Titus 1:2). God knew the risks, and he knew the result of the risk. Before the creation he had already planned how he would respond to humanity's rebellion. God, therefore, was not surprised by the sin of Adam and Eve though he was hurt by it. God did not predetermine their choice, but he did know what they would choose and planned accordingly. God does not take a risk because God knows that his purposes will ultimately prevail and he will accomplish his intention for creation. God never loses control even though he offers his creation a genuine choice.

We must hold both of these biblical truths together even if there is some tension between them. On the one hand, Adam and Eve made a genuine choice for which they bore responsibility. On the other hand, God knew what choice they would make. Scripture seems to teach both points, and however we might harmonize them, it is important to believe both.[10] This tension teaches us that God does risk human rebellion by offering genuine choices but at the same time God is not surprised, circumvented or dethroned by those choices. God remains sovereign even while he offers genuine human freedom.

While we must constantly balance human responsibility and divine sovereignty (a theme to which we will return in later chapters), at this point in the story we must emphasize the genuine character of this human freedom. Adam and Eve were presented with an authentic choice. They had the power of "contrary choice," that is, they could choose to eat or not eat the forbidden fruit. The choice was not just between two alternatives, that is, to eat forbidden fruit A or forbidden fruit B. It was a choice between two contraries — between what was forbidden and what was not forbidden (any other fruit in the garden).

Further, it was not a choice that was determined by their nature, as if they had to choose according to predetermined dispositions. God created them, and they were "very good." They were not predisposed to rebel against God. It was not their nature to rebel. They were created to commune with God and they were living in communion with him. Consequently, their decision to eat the forbidden fruit was contrary to their nature. Nevertheless, they chose to eat it. We can only believe that their choice was self-caused. They decided for themselves to eat the forbidden fruit. They were not coerced by some evil impulse in their created nature.

Original humanity, then, was created with the potential to sin or not sin. There is no text that says God predetermined Adam and Eve's rebellious choice. God was in no sense the author of their evil. God knew they would sin, but he did not predetermine it. Neither was it predetermined by their nature since their created nature was pure and upright. Their choice was self-caused though influenced by the serpent. God gave them a genuine choice and they made the wrong one.

God, therefore, was responsible for the gift. The gift served God's intention because he desired authentic communion between himself and humanity. But the abuse of this freedom belongs at the feet of humanity.

Rebellion Brings Judgment

God centered the choice in two fruit trees: a "tree of life" and a "tree of the knowledge of good and evil." God's approach here has often been ridiculed or mocked by those who think it quite unfair to judge human destiny by a piece of fruit. What does fruit really matter anyway? Some think that God was just setting Adam and Eve up for a fall or that God was simply testing their obedience to see if they would obey in minor things, even in things that did not seem to matter. Both make God a sadistic manipulator of his people; a God who is only interested in seeing how he can make insignificant things into great tests of obedience, or a God who somehow enjoys watching us mull over whether a piece of fruit really matters. Such understandings, however, misread the significance of the trees in the Garden.

When God set the choice before Adam and Eve, it was not a frivolous test to see if Adam and Eve would cross a line which God had drawn in the sand. Rather, it was a choice about whether they would choose communion with God or a life independent of God. The trees are not about fruit. They are about fellowship. They are about life and death, a choice between life with God or life apart from God. The trees symbolize that choice, and the choice expresses what the heart truly desires.

What the "tree of knowledge of good and evil" represents has a long history of debate. Options range from sexual knowledge to omniscience to moral discernment to the experiential knowledge of sin.[11] But none of these are particularly appropriate. Adam and Eve already had sexual knowledge through their union as one flesh. God created them to fill the earth. They also had moral discernment since the choice they were offered involved a recognition that it was right to eat one fruit and wrong to eat another. They at least had the moral knowledge that it was wrong to eat the forbidden fruit. Omniscience was not an effect of having eaten the fruit. It cannot refer to the experience of sin because even God acknowledged that they had become like him in the knowledge of good and evil when he expelled them from the Garden (Genesis 3:22), and God has not experienced sin.

Hamilton suggests a better alternative. The phrase refers to the "moral autonomy" to formulate and pronounce a juridical decision. Hamilton concludes that what is forbidden to humanity "is the power to decide for [itself] what is in [its] best interest and what is not." That prerogative belongs to God alone, but humanity has become like God in that by "knowing good and evil" (Genesis 3:22) they have taken center stage by autonomously deciding what is moral and what is not. Adam and Eve became gods when they subverted God's moral authority. They came to know good and evil as autonomous agents who had rebelled against God's authority. As Hamilton comments, when humanity "attempts to act autonomously [it] is indeed attempting to be godlike."[12]

The choice that God offered Adam and Eve, then, was nothing frivolous or superficial. It is the basic choice we all face. Whom will we serve? It is a question of allegiance — whether we will submit to God in loving fellowship or whether we will seek independence from God on the basis of our own moral autonomy. The original sin of humanity is the basic sin of humanity — it is the arrogance of guiding our own path. Adam and Eve became like God when they took upon themselves the knowledge of good and evil (Genesis 3:5; cf. 3:22). The serpent enticed them. "You will be like God," the serpent promised; you will be autonomous and independent so as to make your own way in the cosmos. You will no longer depend upon or serve God. If you eat, humanity will come of age, and it can then seek its own path. This is the original Enlightenment mentality — the promise of maturity through autonomous rational decision.

The promises and threats attached to each choice indicate their significance. When humanity chooses to serve God, it chooses life, joy, and fellowship with the divine community. When humanity chooses to seek its own way, it may appear to be liberating, but it is actually the path of death. The choice between the two trees was a choice between life in the Garden with God and death in alienation from God outside the Garden. Because they chose autonomy and asserted their own authority, Adam and Eve were excluded from the Garden and God's communal presence (Genesis 3:22).

The death penalty is clearly stated in Genesis 2:17b, but there is disagreement about its primary meaning. The text literally reads, "in the day of your eating from it dying you shall die" (or, the NIV reads, "when you eat of it you will surely die"). Some have taken this to mean that God would immediately strike Adam and Eve dead as soon as they ate the forbidden fruit. Since God did not kill them the day they ate, some have concluded that God was only speaking in spiritual terms, that is, they would be separated from communion with God. However, this does not fit the meaning of "death" in Genesis. After chapter three, the consistent emphasis of Genesis, as if to remind us of the sentence passed upon Adam and Eve, is "and then he died . . . and then he died . . . and then he died . . . and then he died" (5:5,8,11,14,17,20,27,31; 9:29, etc.). In other words, the sentence had been carried out. Adam and Eve chose death by choosing their own autonomy, and death is what they passed on to their descendants (cf. Romans 5:12). Every other reference to death in Genesis, unless chapters 2 and 3 are the exceptions, is a reference to physical death.

There is no text in Genesis which portrays death in any other terms than physical, though spiritual death may be implied as well. Death reigns over humanity because Adam and Eve chose their own way.

It is best to interpret "you shall surely die" as the announcement of a penalty which carries not only the promise of death as a sentence, but also the formal declaration that the one so addressed deserves to die. This phrase is used in Genesis 20:7 and 26:11 with this dual connotation, and in both of those cases it is God himself who addresses the parties. God will exact this penalty. Other uses outside of Genesis also carry the idea that one has come under some kind of penalty that God or a royal figure has imposed (1 Samuel 14:44; 22:16; 1 Kings 2:37,42; 2 Kings 1:4,6,16; Jeremiah 26:8; Ezekiel 3:18; 33:8,14). There is nothing that demands immediate execution. Indeed, sometimes there is reprieve. As Hamilton notes, all that the phrase "clearly conveys is the announcement of a death sentence by divine or royal decree."[13] Further, the "day you eat" is more about certainty than about chronology or timing. For example, Shimei was threatened with death "on the day" he crossed the Kidron, but he was not executed the same day (1 Kings 2:37,42). The expression is a Hebrew idiom that emphasizes the certainty of death without necessarily defining the exact day. It is figurative, as Vos says, for "inevitable eventuation."[14] It declares that one deserves to die and the sentence will certainly be carried out though it may be delayed. "In the day . . . you shall die" refers to the time at which one comes under the condemnation of death, not the execution of the sentence.

The relationship between Adamic sin and death is a theme that Paul articulates in two New Testament texts. He explicitly correlates the sin of Adam with physical death, and not only Adam's own death, but the universal death that envelops all of creation. Adam's sin had a universal impact. It brought the sentence of death upon humanity. Whatever the particular meaning of Romans 5:12, it seems clear that Adam's sin brought death into the world and as a consequence death reigns. Death rules humanity because "in Adam all die" (1 Corinthians 15:22).

The death sentence had a universal impact because it involved the exclusion of the original couple from the tree of life. The "way to the tree of life" was blocked (Genesis 3:24), and consequently eternal life in communion with God was blocked. Humanity was not created immortal or else they would never have died. But death invaded this paradise as the penalty for their sinful choice. Excluded from the Garden humanity began to experience death (Genesis 5). Access to the tree of life means life in communion with God, but without access to the tree of life there is the loss of communion with God and inevitable death. Humanity was given a choice, and they chose death.

But why would they choose death when they could have chosen life? Would not everyone choose life? Perhaps, but if one were convinced that "to choose death" was deceptively labeled in order to prevent the choice of something better than "life," then one might choose "death." If "choosing death" really meant to receive a power and knowledge that would make one like God, then the choice for "death" would seem preferable. Is this not what happened to Eve? The serpent convinced Eve that eating the forbidden fruit would give her access to a knowledge that belonged only to God. And, in her pride, she wanted to become like God. She desired "wisdom" (Genesis 3:6), and so she ate what she knew was forbidden. But she thought it was forbidden because God was protecting his own turf and he did not want anyone else to know what he knew. Eve asserted her moral authority over God and acted autonomously to seize what she wanted. She ate because she thought God had deceived her and had prevented her from attaining equality with him. She chose what she thought was in her own best interest. But she was deceived.

The deceiver was the serpent. We do not know much about this serpent though he is often associated with Satan (an identification not made in the text itself), and we know that the text says that God created this serpent (Genesis 3:1). Most importantly, however, we know that, for whatever reason, he appears as a deceptive seducer. The serpent speaks to both (as the plural "you" in Genesis 3:2-5 indicates), but only Eve answers. Adam is "with her" (Genesis 3:6), but he does not speak. The serpent portrays God as a deceptive oppressor who manipulates the couple into doing his bidding. God does not want them to know what he knows. God does not really want them to become like him. God has a hidden agenda. But if you eat the fruit that God has forbidden, so the serpent promises, then you will become like him and you will see him for what he is. You will no longer need God, the serpent implicitly promises, because you will be wise like him.

Eve was deceived, so she ate. But Adam was not deceived (1 Timothy 2:14), but he ate anyway. Eve believed that she could possess God's wisdom and become like him. Adam chose Eve over God. Eve desired wisdom and took the initiative in sin. Adam desired Eve more than God and ate with her. Both sinned in their pride. Both chose the appeal of immediate gratification over communion with God. Both chose what God had created rather than choosing the creator himself. They chose the gifts over the giver.

The choice here was momentous. It was not frivolous or superficial. It went to the heart of God's intent for his creation. God intended to share his communion with his people, but his people chose their own version of communion. Instead of reciprocating God's offer of love, they asserted their own moral authority. Instead of enjoying the parental love of their God, they asserted their own independence. Their sin was not the theft of an apple from a neighbor's tree which might entail only a minor penalty. Rather, it was the assertion of their moral independence from God. It was an assertion of their own will. They chose their own path. The irony is that what they believed was in their best interest was actually the road to death. A Hebrew proverb summarizes the point: "There is a way that seems right to a man, but in the end it leads to death" (Proverbs 14:12).

The Meaning of the Curse

While God is often pictured as a sadistic judge, it is better to envision God in the narrative of Genesis 3 as a hurt parent. Certainly, death, as a legal penalty, is imposed, but God is not removed from the pain and shame of his original couple. God comes to them as parents go to their children in order to receive some explanation for their behavior. Parents usually seek such explanations because they are hurting and not because they are attempting to determine punishment. God asks a series of questions, not because he is ignorant, but because he seeks to engage his children. The questions are direct in their form, but subtle in meaning (Genesis 3:9-11). "Where are you?" God asks. "We are hiding because we are naked," Adam answered. "Who told you that you were naked?" God responded. These questions have the ring of a hurt parent rather than that of an angry judge, although the two are not mutually exclusive.

God is hurt, disappointed, and grieved by their sin. Adam and Eve violated God's command. But more than that, they chose to break communion with God. Every parent knows that it is not the rule but the relationship that is important. The rule is a symbol of that relationship. To break the rule, to go beyond the boundaries, is to destroy the communion that exists between a parent and child. Just as the rebellious assertion of independence by a child grieves its parents, so the sin of Adam and Eve grieved God. The tone of his voice was probably more like "how could you?" than "now I've got you."

Nevertheless, God does act as a judge here. The penalty is exacted. God is faithful to his promises and his threats. God is not a sadist. He is holy. The holiness of the community is at stake. God is light, and no darkness can exist within his community. The light must dispel the darkness because they cannot coexist at the same time in the same place. Humanity rejected God's offer of communion and asserted its moral independence. The holiness of God cannot commune with evil. The psalmist confessed, "You are not a God who takes pleasure in evil; with you the wicked cannot dwell" (5:4). Consequently, the penalty attached to humanity's disobedience must be exacted. God's condemnation, however, is not vindictive but rather the result of humanity's choice to embrace darkness which cannot abide in God's eternal light.

Death now reigns over humanity as a tyrant who cannot be satisfied. This is not what God intended. When he created humanity, he made them "a little lower than the heavenly beings and crowned [them] with glory and honor," and he gave them dominion over creation and put everything under their feet (Psalm 8:5-6). Humanity ruled creation. But now death rules humanity. Sin reversed their fortunes. They were created to inherit and care for the earth. But now they are dominated by an alien force which God never intended. The writer of Hebrews makes this very point when, after quoting Psalm 8, he notes: "Yet at present we do not see everything subject to" humanity. Rather, we see that humanity is subject to death (Hebrews 2:8-9,14-15).

Though God did not intend death, death is the penalty of sin. "The sting of death is sin" (1 Corinthians 15:56a). Sin brought humanity under the power of death. "The power of sin is the law" (1 Corinthians 15:56b). The law imposed the death penalty (a curse) for those who sinned. Sin is penalized by death. Whether that law is the Mosaic code (Deuteronomy 30:19-20), or the imperatives of Jesus (Matthew 7:21-23; cf. 1 Corinthians 16:22), or the law that existed between Adam and Moses (Romans 5:13-14), or the simple law given to the original couple in the Garden ("you must not eat of the tree of the knowledge of good and evil," Genesis 2:17), the law curses those who break it. It exacts a penalty. Death, therefore, reigns, because sin reigns

(Romans 5:12-14). When Adam and Eve sinned, they brought death into the world because death gains its power as a curse due to sin. Through sin God's good creation, therefore, fell under a curse.

Something changed when sin reared its ugly head in God's good creation. Death invaded and turned a good creation into a fallen one. It turned Paradise into a barren land. Where once God's intention of communion with his creatures was fulfilled in the joy of the Garden, now sin has broken that communion, and death has turned that joy to mourning. The world is different now. It is covered by death's shroud (Isaiah 25:7). It has been cursed and plunged into a spiral of deterioration, degeneration, and death. Because of sin, God has subjected his creation to "frustration" (Romans 8:20). The whole creation now groans under the burden of a curse.

The narrative of Genesis 3 summarizes this curse. It is a curse which God himself pronounces. God curses the serpent (Genesis 3:14) and he curses the ground (Genesis 3:17). In the context of these curses, God reveals the consequences that the sin of the original couple will have upon their life. Instead of the friendship which Eve and the serpent anticipated in their earlier dialogue, now there is hostility between them (Genesis 3:15a). Instead of the unmitigated joy of childbirth, now the woman will experience pain (Genesis 3:16a). Instead of the harmonious joy of marriage in a complementary relationship, now the woman will experience a desire to rule her husband and her husband will mistreat her with tyrannical power (Genesis 3:16b).[15] Instead of the joyous task of caring for the Garden of Eden, now men will work the land with pain and sweat (Genesis 3:17-19). Instead of enjoying communion with God through the tree of life, now humanity will return to the dust from which they came (Genesis 3:19).

The consequences of sin involve the destruction of relationships and harmony. The harmony between humanity and nature is destroyed since nature itself now rebels against its ruler. The serpent is hostile to the woman. Childbirth, as a natural event, has become a painful effort. The ground is hostile to man. The joy of work has become the pain of toil. The harmony between human beings has been destroyed. The woman will now seek to control her husband and the husband will now dominate and abuse his wife. And, as one can read in Genesis 4, brother will kill brother. Sin has disrupted the peace of creation. Sin is the "vandalism of Shalom."[16] It has introduced foreign elements like hostility, pain, and death into God's good creation. God did not create these and neither did he intend them, but they are the consequences of sin. This is what sin does. It has an inherent destructive quality. It corrupts what is good. It destroys what is virtuous. It brings death where there was once life. Sin is a dynamic power which works havoc in God's good creation. Like a strip-mining enterprise, sin strips creation of peace, joy, and harmony.

While God acts as a judge to curse his good creation in order to exact the penalty of sin, God is nevertheless the gracious parent. Even while he describes the just consequences and effects of sin, God offers grace to his children. Even though there is now hostility between the serpent and Eve, the offspring of Eve will ultimately crush the serpent (Genesis 3:15). The narrator envisions a time when good will triumph over evil. Ultimately, as we know in the light of fuller revelation, God through Jesus Christ will crush the evil that the serpent represents (cf. Romans 16:20). There is some sense in which this is the "first enunciation of the good news."[17]

Further, the human race will continue. Immediate death will not be imposed. Though Adam and Eve are expelled from the Garden where they will suffer eventual death, they will have a life outside of the Garden. Moreover, God continues the grace of childbearing though it is now tinged by pain. God still seeks a people for himself and by his grace he permits the human race to continue. By his grace, God continues the original vision of creation where humanity will fill the earth with their offspring and create a people for him. God's original intent guides his treatment of fallen humanity. He gives them the grace of life when they deserve death. The penalty will be imposed, but it is delayed as an expression of God's grace, just as the delay of the second coming of Christ is an expression of God's patient mercy (2 Peter 3:9).

The fundamental meaning of the curse is the expulsion of the original couple from the Garden which entailed two momentous events. First, it meant expulsion from a life in communion with God. No longer would they experience the presence of God as he walked in the Garden among them. Their expulsion meant separation from God's holy communion of love. Second, it meant eventual death. Since they no longer had access to the tree of life, they lived under the sentence of death. They deserved to die because outside of God's communion there is no life. Wenham emphasizes these points:

> Apparently then, man did not die on the day he ate of the tree. But in the closing verses of the chapter, sanctuary symbolism and language reappear (3:21-24). God clothes the human couple and then expels them through the east-facing entrance to the garden where cherubim are stationed to guard the tree of life. These features anticipate the design of the tabernacle and the regulations associated with it. Like the garden of Eden, the tabernacle was a place where God walked with his people. To be expelled from the camp of Israel or to be rejected by God was to experience a living death; in both situations gestures of mourning were appropriate. . . . The expulsion from the garden of delight where God himself lived would therefore have been regarded by the godly men of ancient Israel as yet more catastrophic than physical death. The latter was the ultimate sign and seal of spiritual death the human couple experienced on the day they ate from the forbidden tree.[18]

Physical death, then, was a penalty exacted in the light of spiritual death. The expulsion from the Garden symbolized both. It meant that humanity was excluded from the communion of God's life in the Garden and that the consequence of this exclusion was physical death itself. The tree of life is the biblical symbol for both kinds of life (spiritual and physical), and exclusion from it entails both kinds of death (spiritual and physical). Both deaths are part of the curse.

Summary

The story of creation reveals God's intent. He intended communion and life. God created life, provided sustenance, and offered the tree of life. God intended to create a community which would image and represent the harmony, joy, and fellowship of his community. He intended to share his dominion with those who bear his image so that they could care for the earth and serve as his representatives upon the earth. He intended his people to fill the earth with their children so that he might be glorified through communion with them.

This intent is highlighted throughout God's story as it is given to us in Scripture. From beginning to end, from creation to *eschaton*, God desires a people for himself with whom he can share a loving fellowship. God desires, to put it in New Testament language, *koinonia* (fellowship, communion). In redemption God has called us into the "fellowship of his Son" (1 Corinthians 1:9) to enjoy the "fellowship of the Holy Spirit" (2 Corinthians 13:14) as we also experience the "fellowship of the Father" (1 John 1:3). In redemption God offers us his triune fellowship just as he did in creation. Christians have all been baptized into the fellowship of the Father, Son, and Holy Spirit (Matthew 28:19). In both creation and redemption, this fellowship is God's goal, and it guides all his actions in the world. It is the fundamental structural principle of God's story. It shapes his providential work. God intends to have a people for himself — this was true in creation, and it is still true, even in a fallen world.

Genesis 2-3 explains what happened to God's good creation. What was "very good" has now fallen. The harmony of the original creation has been destroyed. The world, filled as it is with death, now looks very different from the world which God created. The original creation exhibited God's intention for harmony, peace, joy, life, and communion. But the present fallen world exhibits hostility, pain, brokenness, and death. The world is different because of sin. Humanity has chosen its own way rather than enjoying the communal life of God. Sin has destroyed God's original creation, and God has imposed a curse upon the fallen world. He has subjected it to frustration (Romans 8:20).

But the story is not simply about the original couple; it is also a paradigmatic account of each person's existential fall into sin. Every human being is Adam and Eve. We all have sinned (Romans 3:23). We have all fallen short of the glory God intended for us. We have each experienced our own fall into sin. We all look back to some kind of innocence from the vantage point of our fallenness. We were not aware of our innocence until we became aware of our sin. Now we lament the loss of innocence as we confess our sin. The story of Adam and Eve is our story. The writer intends for us to identify with Adam and Eve and recognize that their history is paradigmatic for ours. We, like they, have moved from innocence to rebellion. We have been expelled from the Garden. We too are subject to death. We too are under a curse. The story of Genesis 2-3 is the story of humanity's relationship with God. It is the story of creation, fall, and the promise of redemption. It is not just Adam's fall, it is *our* fall. It is not simply Adam's problem, it is *our* problem.

But God is gracious. He was gracious to Adam and Eve. He clothed them and gave them a life outside of the Garden. It is a circumstance other than that God intended. The world is a different place now that a curse has been imposed. But God's intention remains. He intends to have a people for himself with whom he can commune in holy love. God now has a redemptive intent for his fallen world. He has subjected the world to frustration, but he has also subjected it in hope (Romans 8:20-21). God intends to redeem the fallen world and release it from its curse. He intends to destroy death and renew his creation. One day, when the new heavens and the new earth appear, God will make everything new and "there will be no more death or mourning or crying or pain" (Revelation 21:4). There will be a day when "no longer will there be any curse" (Revelation 22:3a).

Given the fact that the world is now fallen, what is God doing? How does God relate to his fallen world in order to bring his original intent to fruition? What on earth is God doing? The story continues . . . .

---

[1]Ted Peters, *God as Trinity: Relationality and Temporality in Divine Life* (Louisville, KY: Westminster/John Knox Press, 1993), pp. 81-145, surveys contemporary thought. See Catherine Mowry LaCugna, *God for Us: The Trinity & Christian Life* (San Francisco: HarperSanFrancisco, 1991).

[2]Stanley Grenz, *Theology for the Community of God* (Nashville: Broadman & Holman, 1994), pp. 133-139.

[3]Donald Bloesch, *God the Almighty: Power, Wisdom, Holiness, Love*, Christian Foundations, 3 (Downers Grove, IL: InterVarsity, 1995), pp. 39-40.

[4]John Piper, *Desiring God: Meditations of a Christian Hedonist* (Portland, OR: Multnomah Press, 1986).

[5]God gifts some people with the grace of singlehood for the sake of his kingdom (1 Corinthians 7:7). But Christian singleness is not solitude because it exists within the context of the communal life of the church.

[6]Søren Kierkegaard, *Philosophical Fragments*, trans. David Swenson (Princeton: Princeton University Press, 1962), pp. 14-15, used this image as an analogy for the incarnation of Jesus.

[7]There were, of course, other choices. For example, whether Adam would love or hate Eve, whether he would abuse her, whether she would abuse him, etc. The trees, however, symbolically focused the choice between fellowship with God and human autonomy.

[8]Paul Helm, *The Providence of God*, Contours of Christian Theology (Downers Grove, IL: InterVarsity, 1994), pp. 39-68.

[9]William Hasker, *God, Time and Knowledge* (Ithaca, NY: Cornell University Press, 1989), p. 197.

[10]A good example of a theological harmonization would be Jack Cottrell, *What the Bible Says about God the Creator* (Joplin, MO: College Press, 1983), pp. 274-292. A good philosophical analysis would be Alvin Plantinga, *God, Freedom and Evil* (New York: Harper & Row, 1974), pp. 66-72. The classic discussion is Thomas Aquinas, *Summa Theologica,* Part I, Question 14.

[11]See the discussions by Gordon J. Wenham, *Genesis 1-15,* Word Biblical Commentary, 1 (Waco, TX: Word Books, 1987), pp. 62-64 and Victor P. Hamilton, *The Book of Genesis, Chapters 1-17,* The New International Commentary on the Old Testament (Grand Rapids: Eerdmans, 1990), pp. 163-166.

[12]Hamilton, *Genesis,* p. 166.

[13]Ibid., p. 174.

[14]Geerhardus Vos, *Biblical Theology: Old and New Testaments* (Grand Rapids: Eerdmans, 1948), p. 49.

[15]Cf. Susan T. Foh, "What Is the Woman's Desire?" *Westminster Theological Journal* 37 (1974/75): 376-383. On gender roles, see John Piper and Wayne Grudem, eds, *Recovering Biblical Manhood and Womanhood: A Response to Evangelical Feminism* (Wheaton, IL: Crossway Books, 1991); and Jack Cottrell, *Gender Roles and the Bible: Creation, the Fall, & Redemption* (Joplin, MO: College Press, 1994).

[16]Cornelius Plantinga, Jr., *Not the Way It's Supposed to Be: A Breviary of Sin* (Grand Rapids: Eerdmans, 1995), p. 7.

[17]See W.S. Lasor, "Prophecy, Inspiration, and *Sensus Plenior,*" *Tyndale Bulletin* 29 (1979): 57.

[18]Wenham, *Genesis,* p. 90.

Chapter Four

What Does God Permit in a Fallen World?
The Story of God, Satan, and Job

A Story

Near the region of Edom, in the land of Uz, there lived a man named Job. He was devoted to his God and he exhibited an immaculate lifestyle. His God blessed him with children and wealth; with health and prosperity. He was God's friend. Everything Job touched became a blessing to him. His God protected him.

Job was respected as a community leader who sat at the city gates with the elders. Young people would step aside when he entered a room. When they saw him coming, even the old men would rise to their feet. The chief men would listen rather than speak when Job was present.

Job was known as the defender of the oppressed. He rescued the poor from injustice. He took up the cause of the stranger. He assisted the orphan. The dying husband blessed Job because he knew that Job would care for his widow. Job brought joy into the lives of the oppressed and the handicapped. He pleaded their cause at the city gates. He pressed for righteousness and justice in the city. He snatched victims from the fangs of the wicked. Job epitomized just leadership, wise counsel, and a compassionate heart.

One day, however, God's blessings ceased. God's protection ended. Everything Job touched turned to ashes. In a single day, Job lost his wealth and his children. The Sabeans killed his servants and stole five hundred oxen and five hundred donkeys. The Chaldeans killed his servants and stole three thousand camels. The fire of God destroyed seven thousand sheep along with the servants tending them. A mighty wind collapsed the house where his children were feasting and killed them. In a single day, God's blessings had turned into God's calamity. In the space of hours, the God who blessed Job became the God who attacked him. That attack extended to Job's own body as he was covered with sores. He scraped the infectious puss with a broken potsherd while he sat on the town trash heap. God turned on Job with a ferocity and ruthlessness that only the wicked deserve.

Now the community avoids Job. Now children mock him. They spit in his face. His name has become a symbol of disgrace, a symbol of God's displeasure. His most intimate friends, whom he loved, have turned against him. His guests, whom he once entertained, now treat him as a stranger. The community that once sought Job's help and advice now keeps their distance. They ignore him. Job is now one of the oppressed, a social outcast. His community has stripped him of every honor.

Even Job's own family now avoids him. His wife is horrified by his condition. She prods Job to curse God and die, to end his suffering by provoking God to finish the job he started. Even she will not come close enough to smell his breath. His remaining servants will not go to him when he calls, even when he begs.

Job is alone. He has nothing but his own diseased skin and bones. He can do nothing but question, lament, and worship. He sits alone on the trash heap.

Why? What happened? The one who was once blessed was cursed in a single day. The one who had received so much good from God now has received trouble from the same God. How can one who images God so well — and there was no one else like him — be treated so badly by the one he images? Why? What happened?

— adapted from Job 1-2,19,29-30

The narrator of the above story tells it from an earthly, horizontal perspective. It is told as if the narrator were a contemporary observer. The community, Job's family, and Job himself only have this earthly perspective. They can only see the facts "from below" or "under the sun" (Ecclesiastes). They cannot see beyond the horizon. Job was a seemingly righteous man whom God at one time blessed but now curses. Now the community and family must respect God's curse — they must keep their distance from one who has so displeased God that such a catastrophic calamity has befallen him. Job is ostracized and separated from the community. God has cursed him. He is not as righteous as he appeared.

But as Job sits on the trash heap, his thoughts are rather different. He knows his own integrity. He knows he is not hiding some great sin. He knows his heart is dedicated to God. Yet he understands that his trouble has come from God. His questions do not have any obvious answers, but he certainly rejects the conclusion his community has drawn. Job has been attacked, but he does not believe it is a punishment for some hidden sin. Job has received trouble from God, but he still worships God. Job is ignorant about the reason for all this trouble, but it is clear that he will not reject his God. He will not curse God even though it appears God has cursed him.

The community and Job are both ignorant. Neither knows the reason for his troubles. The readers of the book, however, have a perspective that neither had. The prologue (Job 1-2) provides this perspective. It gives the readers a heavenly viewpoint. It is as if the readers are watching the whole event from an aerial vantage point. The readers are omniscient in relation to the text — they have a full view. The plot has been explained to them before they see the play. Even though the participants in the play are ignorant of the plot's drama and eventual outcome, the readers see it from beginning to end in the prologue (Job 1-2) and the epilogue (Job 42). The readers, then, have a distinct advantage over the participants in the story. They have a heavenly perspective that no participant in the story has. The prologue and epilogue provide a framework for understanding the book. They are the lens through which we read the ensuing dialogue and grasp the meaning of Job's suffering.

The Suffering of Job

The narrative that began this chapter only offers an account "from below" — an earthly perspective. The prologue, however, gives us an account "from above" — a heavenly perspective. The events that transpire in the heavenly arena are known only to the reader. Job is ignorant.

Yet Job's ignorance is our ignorance. While the reader understands that something more is happening than simply the random suffering of a good man named Job, when we readers suffer, our perspective is the same as Job's. We, like Job, are faced only with the fact of suffering. Like Job, we are ignorant of any heavenly transactions that may or may not have taken place. As a result, we can fully empathize with Job's predicament because it is ours. We are now as ignorant as Job was then concerning God's specific purposes.

However, as readers of Job's story, we see more than Job saw. We know exactly what is happening. We can see that the suffering, as undeserved as it may be, has meaning. What to Job seemed utterly senseless makes sense, at least in some provisional way, to the reader. Only meaning gained "from above" is definitive; all meaning gained "from below" is provisional, tentative, and fallible. That is why we need to see suffering through the eyes of God and in the context of the story God has provided. We need to see it from the perspective of the divine throne room, and the book of Job starts there.

God's Responsibility

The author places us in the presence of God. We see the "sons of God" (angels) present, but the Accuser, "Satan," is also present.[1] Both have come into God's presence to report their activities. No doubt what is pictured is an executive meeting of God's providential messengers. Angels are God's work force in providence (Psalm 104:4).

Satan is also at work. His power is subservient and secondary. Satan must apply for God's power to do his work. Satan has a role in God's providence, but he is not an independent, autonomous agent outside of God's sovereignty. He ultimately serves God's purposes.

God's question to Satan may seem difficult at first glance, "Where have you come from?" (1:7). Did not God know where Satan had been? Certainly, but God is seeking conversation. In effect, God gives Satan permission to speak in his royal court. He was not requesting information he did not already have. Much like God asks Moses, "What is that in your hand?" (Exodus 4:2), he asks, "What have you been doing lately?" Satan's generalized answer indicates his pervasive activity in the world. "From roaming through the earth and going back and forth in it," he replied (1:7). But God wants to get down to specific cases.

God initiates the whole drama by calling Satan's attention to Job. Satan is aware of Job. He does not deny Job's external righteousness, but he does attack his integrity. "Sure," Satan says, "Job is righteous. Why shouldn't he be? You have protected him from every disaster and given him every blessing. Who wouldn't serve you under those circumstances?" According to Satan, Job is righteous for a different reason than God will admit. Job serves God for profit. Satan accuses Job of selfishness. Job's worship is self-centered and self-interested. It is a "fair-weather" faith. God has bribed Job. Consequently, Satan asks, "Does Job fear God for nothing?" (1:9).

Satan's implied accusation is an accusation against all believers. It says that when we serve and love, we serve God for the rewards. Satan asserts that the basis of faith is profit or personal gain. As long as believers are prosperous, healthy, and happy, they will serve God. But let God permit some evil, permit the loss of a family member or the loss of a job, then believers will lose hope in him and reject him. Faith only exists when it is profitable. Believers are only faithful when they are happy. Job himself acknowledges that this is the attitude of the wicked. They ask, "Who is the Almighty, that we should serve him? What would we gain by praying to him?" (21:15). Will anyone love God even when there is nothing to be gained other than God's fellowship? Will anyone love God just to enjoy his fellowship? Will Job worship God despite the fact that he has lost everything? This is the trial of Job, and the test of all genuine faith. Job, however, will not give up his faith nor curse God despite his sufferings. Job rejects the counsel of the wicked. He knows "their prosperity is not in their own hands, so [he] stand[s] aloof from the counsel of the wicked" (21:16).

Satan recognizes that he cannot act against Job under the present circumstances. God had put a "hedge" or fence around him to protect him from disasters (1:10). God had limited Satan's access to Job. Satan understands that if Job is to be tested, if disaster is to come upon him, then God must act. God must remove his protection. Thus, he challenges God, "But stretch out your hand and strike everything he has, and he will surely curse you to your face" (1:11).

The hand of God, a metaphor for the power or activity of God, must move against Job if disaster is to strike his family. God must lift his hand — extend his power, act in some manner — if the heavenly council is to discover whether Job serves God for profit. Indeed, when Job passes the first test, God complains to Satan that "you incited me against him to ruin him without any reason" (2:3). God recognizes his responsibility for the test. God acted against Job. Again, in the second trial, Satan challenges God to "stretch out [his] hand and strike his flesh and bones" (2:4). An act of God is required if Job is to experience "evil" or calamity. The power went from God's hand to Satan's hand (1:11-12; 2:5-6). It was God's power, in the hands of Satan, that tested Job. Satan wielded God's power by God's own permission.

At the very least we must say that God permitted Satan to afflict Job when he could have prevented it. In fact, God had previously prevented Satan. But God lifted the hedge, and placed the power to act into Satan's hands with restrictions (1:12; 2:6). In the first test, Satan could not touch the person of Job, but he could destroy his property, servants, and family. In the second test, Satan could not kill Job, but he could inflict severe pain upon his body. Nevertheless, God was responsible even though Satan may have been the direct agent. He was at least responsible in the sense that he gave Satan *permission* and *power*. God could have refused Satan's challenge. He could have restricted Satan further than he did. He could have said, "Satan, you can destroy his property, but not his children." God determined the kind of power he would put into the hand of Satan, and he determined its limitations. God bears the ultimate responsibility for the evil that came upon Job because it did not have to come at all. God could have kept the "hedge" in place or he could have prevented what Satan sought to implement. God's hand acted against Job. God sovereignly decided to test Job in response to Satan's accusation.

Job saw this clearly. He did not know about the heavenly wager, but he did know that the world is God's. He did not know about the activity of Satan, but he knew that God is sovereign. He knew the hand of God was acting against him. Even God himself said that Satan had "incited" him "against" Job (2:3). The word "incite" is used to describe how God might stir up someone (1 Samuel 26:15), or influence someone toward an action (2 Chronicles 18:21). Both God and "Satan" incited David to take a census of his people (1 Chronicles 21:1; 2 Samuel 24:1). God himself recognized that he had acted against Job. "Satan" had incited him. God cannot be distanced from these disasters. God put the faith of Job at issue, removed the hedge, gave Satan the power and could have stopped the suffering at any time. God had moved "against" Job, and Job knew it.

To the first disasters, Job responded, "The LORD gave and the LORD has taken away; may the name of the LORD be praised" (1:21). Job recognized his children and his prosperity as gifts from God. But he also attributed to God the loss of those gifts. If we praise the Lord for the blessings he gives, we must also praise him for the blessings he takes away. Job, in the clearest of terms, asserted God's responsibility for his predicament. The Lord gave, and the Lord took away. God is as active in the taking as he is in the giving. Nevertheless, Job praised God.

Job responded similarly to the second disaster, "Shall we accept good from God, and not trouble?" (2:10). Literally, the Hebrew term translated "trouble" means "evil" as in 1:1,8; 2:3. God gives good things, but sometimes he also gives "evil" in the sense of calamity or disaster. According to Job, people of faith must be willing to accept both. The wise one of Ecclesiastes recognized this principle as well (7:13-14):

> Consider what God has done:
>> Who can straighten what he has made crooked?
>> When times are good, be happy;
>>> but when times are bad [evil], consider:
>> God has made the one as well as the other.

Although Job attributed these disasters to God, thus making God responsible for his troubles, the narrator makes it clear that in neither instance did Job sin with his lips nor did he charge God with any wrongdoing (1:22; 2:10). In other words, Job did not curse God even though he affirmed God's responsibility. God took his children and his prosperity — this is Job's charge against God. Nevertheless, Job did not charge God with wrongdoing. He did not sin in his words even when he attributed the death of his children to God's "taking away."

The perspective of the prologue is further emphasized in the dialogue. Again and again Job attributes his suffering to God. The disasters are "arrows of the Almighty" (6:4). God had made him "his target; his archers surround[ed]" him and "without pity, he pierce[d] my kidneys" (16:12b, 13). The "hand of the LORD" destroyed him (12:9). The "hand of God," Job says, "has struck me" (19:21). In prayer to God he says, "Surely, O God, you have worn me out; you have devastated my entire household" (16:7). Job believes that his continued suffering, not simply the past events, is due to the continued activity of God. He complains, "Even today my complaint is bitter; his hand is heavy in spite of my groaning" (23:2). God, in the words of Job, "has unstrung my bow and afflicted me" (30:11). Job saw that his continued suffering was the will of God or else God would have acted to put an end to it. Suffering continues because God's hand continues to oppress him (6:9; 10:7; 12:9; 19:21; 23:2; 30:1). God extended his hand to empower Satan, and God actively employs his power to continue Job's suffering. He continues to permit Satan to afflict Job and does not act to reverse Job's fortunes — at least not yet.

If the prologue, the friends, and Job agree upon anything, it is this: God is responsible for Job's suffering. If God would act, the suffering could end (as it does in the epilogue). If the suffering does not end, God has decided not to act. Either way, God is responsible. Either way, God has willed that Job suffer and continue to suffer.

The First Wave of Suffering

The first wave consisted of four events. First, the Sabeans raided Job's herds of oxen and donkeys and killed his servants (1:13-15). Second, "the fire of God" (lightning) started a fire which destroyed both his sheep and his servants (1:16). Third, the Chaldeans stole his camels and killed his servants (1:17). Fourth, a strong wind collapsed the house in which his children were feasting, killing all of them (1:18-19). These disasters involve two very different kinds of events: human and natural agency.

The Role of Human Freedom

Human agency involves the free, responsible acts of human beings — the Sabeans and the Chaldeans. They sinned when they stole Job's property and murdered his servants. They acted on their own volition. They did what they wanted to do. Yet Satan had empowered them to act against Job's property. By whatever means Satan may have incited the Sabeans and the Chaldeans — whether through circumstances and opportunities, or some other means — Satan stands behind these acts. Satan's act, it must be remembered, was also a free act. But he had received his power from God. Just as Satan, in some fashion, stood behind the acts of the Sabeans and the Chaldeans, so God, in some fashion, stood behind the acts of Satan. God was, at least, an indirect cause of the death of Job's servants. He empowered Satan who empowered the Sabeans and the Chaldeans.

While God and Satan both stand behind the suffering of Job, there is a qualitative difference between their intentions. They are motivated by different goals. Satan intends to destroy Job. His intent is malicious. He hopes to undermine Job's faith and entice Job to curse God. God, however, intends to test Job's faith as a means of strengthening it. God intends to refine Job's faith, develop his character, and achieve a cosmic victory through his endurance. Satan intended Job's troubles for evil, but God intended them for good (much like in the case of Joseph, Genesis 50:20). Satan acted with the maliciousness of a murderer and a thief, but God acted with the benevolence of parental refining. Satan tempted Job to curse God, but God tested Job's faith.

The same event is both a trial and a temptation. It is similar to Abraham's situation. God tried Abraham by commanding him to offer Isaac as a sacrifice (Gen. 22:1), but no doubt Satan also tempted Abraham to disobey God. Trials come from God, but temptations arise from our own lusts and selfish desires (James 1:13-15) as Satan incites them. Consequently, both God and Satan stand behind Job's troubles, but they intend them differently. Job's free response to his trouble will determine whether the trial will turn into a fruitful temptation or whether it will offer a cosmic testimony to the integrity of faith.

That God can stand behind "evil" human actions is nothing unusual for Old Testament theology. God used nations to punish other nations. For example, Assyria, the empire which wiped out the northern kingdom of Israel, was the rod of God's wrath (Isaiah 10:5). God asks, "Does the ax raise itself above him who swings it, or the saw boast against him who uses it? As if a rod were to wield him who lifts it up, or a club brandish him who is not wood!" (Isaiah 10:15). Indeed, God says that it was by his "hand" that Israel was destroyed (Isaiah 10:10). Assyria was the instrument by which God acted to destroy the northern kingdom of Israel. The God of Israel did not lose a battle with the Assyrian gods. On the contrary, God himself created these disasters for Israel. God was responsible for the Assyrian and Babylonian captivities, the wars that preceded them and the deaths they involved. The LORD himself declares, "I form the light and create darkness, I bring prosperity [peace] and create disaster [evil]; I, the LORD, do all these things" (Isaiah 45:7).

Another example is Babylon, God's "war club," his "weapon for battle" (Jeremiah 51:20). God declared his responsibility for the victories of Babylon over God's own people. God created the disaster, the evil, that befell Judah (Jeremiah 44:2, 11). God can speak in the first person as the agent who "shatter[s] nations" and "destroy[s] kingdoms" (Jeremiah 51:20). God declared, "with you I shatter horse and rider, with you I shatter chariot and driver, with you I shatter man and woman, with you I shatter old man and youth, with you I shatter young man and maiden" (Jeremiah 51:21-22). God takes responsibility for the destruction of his own people. Babylon was the instrument by which God shattered the nations. Babylon did not act autonomously. On the contrary, it acted under God's sovereignty.

God can also act through "Satan." Whereas 1 Chronicles 21:1 states that "Satan rose up against Israel and incited David to take a census," 2 Samuel attributes this to the

Lord himself as the means by which God would discipline Israel (2 Samuel 24:1). While "Satan" incited David to do evil, God stood behind that action as well. But they do not have the same purpose in mind. God's purpose in using "Satan" was to punish Israel — a just reason, but the adversary's purpose was to destroy the faith of Israel — an evil intent. "Satan" was malicious in his intent, but God was disciplinary in his. The same act is incited by both God and Satan, but for different reasons and with different goals. Nevertheless, it is God who sovereignly acts through Satan to accomplish his purposes. God seeks to draw them back into a relationship with himself.

Consequently, the fact that human actions are acts of responsible, self-determining, free agents (such as the Sabeans, Chaldeans, Assyrians, and David) does not necessarily imply that God has nothing to do with those actions. The free acts of human beings are subservient to the purposes of God, and God will use and direct them to accomplish his intentions. God is sovereign over human actions. He may permit, for example, the Sabeans to kill Job's servants and steal his property or he may not. God may use Assyria to punish Israel or he may not. God may incite David to take a census or he may not. God alone will decide. Job recognized the Lord's hand in the free acts of the Sabeans and Chaldeans. He credited God with taking away his blessings (1:21). He charged God with ultimate responsibility. In this, the narrator writes, Job did not sin.

This does not mean that the Sabeans and Chaldeans are not responsible for their actions. The text does not say that the Sabeans and Chaldeans were coerced against their will to steal and murder. They acted according to their own volition, and they sinned through their actions. Their sin arose from their own lusts and covetousness. Sin arises out of our own evil desires (James 1:14-15). We are responsible for our desires and our actions. No one can blame God for personal sinfulness. Sinners can only blame their own inward, evil desires.

Consequently, David sinned when he took the census. The Assyrians also sinned when they devastated Israel. Nevertheless, God was active in these events. God wielded the Assyrians like an ax; God incited David to take the census; and God, through Satan, empowered the Sabeans and the Chaldeans. Somehow, in some manner, divine sovereignty and human responsibility coexist. God is sovereign, but human beings are free. The Sabeans and the Chaldeans freely sinned and they bear the responsibility for their actions, but God was the one who "took away" Job's prosperity and his servants.

Mysteriously, God is responsible in such a way that he does not participate in the sinfulness of human or Satanic actions, that is, God is not guilty of moral evil.[2] This is why Carson believes it is valuable to retain the notion of "permission" when talking about God's actions "because it is part of the biblical pattern of insisting that God stands behind good and evil asymmetrically."[3] While Satan and God may have a "hand" in the same action, Satan intends it as temptation and God intends it as trial. God did not coerce Satan, the Chaldeans, or the Sabeans into evil, but he permitted, empowered, and limited the sinful actions which arose from their own evil desires. God did this for his own purposes and not for those which Satan intended.

The Role of Natural Causation

The second kind of disaster which came upon Job involved the use of nature. Nature's acts, just like human ones, are subservient to the purposes of God. The very name the author gives to lightning betrays his view of natural events. He calls it the "fire of God" (Job 1:16). God controls the lightning (Job 38:24). Satan acted, but God permitted. Satan acted, but God empowered. Nature acted as the direct cause, but God was the indirect cause. God is responsible for what nature does.

How different is a "mighty wind" off the desert from a raging tornado? The disaster that killed Job's children was a natural one, but it had a cause that science cannot discover. These events were not supernatural — they were not the miraculous interventionist activity of a supernatural energy. They were the result of natural forces. There was nothing miraculous about these natural disasters, but there was something divine about them. They were permitted and empowered by God. Satan created no miracle, and God broke no "natural laws." But God, through the power he had given Satan, brought suffering on Job by what appeared to be "natural events." The author of Job sees a divine hand in these events. Through these natural events, God "took away" Job's blessings.

This is nothing unusual for Old Testament theology. Natural events in Scripture are routinely described as "God's acts." Nature is at God's command and is moved by his will. We read of "lightning [literally, fire] and hail, snow and clouds, stormy winds that do his bidding" (Psalm 148:8). God is involved in his world — he causes the grass to grow (Psalm 104:14) and he feeds the lions (Psalm 104:21,27). The Lord is sovereign over his creation, and the psalmist declares this unequivocally (Psalm 135:6-7):

> The LORD does whatever pleases him,
>> in the heavens and on the earth,
>> in the seas and all their depths.
> He makes clouds rise from the ends of the earth;
>> he sends lightning with the rain
>> and brings out the wind from his storehouses.

When read in the light of the natural disasters that hit Job, this text is a chilling assertion of God's authority over his world (see also Jeremiah 10:13; 51:16). Lightning and wind are at God's command, and it was lightning and wind which destroyed Job's prosperity and his children. No wind nor lightning could have destroyed Job's prosperity and children unless God himself had, at the very least, given permission. In fact, Elihu, the last friend to speak in the narrative (Job 32-37), reminds Job that this is "the way [God] governs the nations" (Job 36:31). God rules the nations by his work in nature, through rain and lightning (Job 36:27-33). Indeed, God "commands [the lightning] to strike its mark" (Job 36:32).

God does whatever he pleases (Psalm 115:3; 135:6; Proverbs 21:1). Job confessed this in Job 42:2: "I know that you can do all things; no plan of yours can be thwarted." That confession came in the wake of God's rehearsal of his power, wisdom, and care in nature. God's rule over his creation is the critical point in God's confrontation with Job in chapters 38–41. God is the one who sends the rain, snow, hail, winds, and lightning (38:22-24,28). God is the one who leads out the stars in their constellations for the changing seasons (38:31-33). God is the one by whose wisdom the goat gives birth (39:1), the ox serves humanity (39:9), the ostrich lays her eggs (39:14), the horse exhibits strength in battle (39:19-24), and the hawk takes flight (39:26). God is not disconnected from his world. On the contrary, he is the active agent who works through what appears to us as disinterested, random nature.

The modern world removes God from his creation and distances God from natural events. The biblical picture is quite different. God is an active agent within nature. He is sovereign over his natural world. Some scientists, given the complexities of quantum physics, now speak of God's Spirit "as the enveloping supervenient power who acts in and through creation" along the analogy of "top-down causation" much like the mind is related to the body.[4] God acts through the world much as the mind acts through a body. While this analogy must not be pressed too far (as if the world is God's body so that God is incomplete without a body), it provides a model for understanding divine action through natural events. Nature is not an autonomous entity. Rather, God enlivens nature, acts through nature, and sustains nature as the mind sustains the body and acts through it. Genuine science does not divorce God from the world. Instead, it admits that it is not in the position to make a judgment about divine action. The biblical worldview sees the hand of God in natural events, even natural disasters. Job saw the "hand" of God "in the mighty wind" which "took away" his children.

The uniqueness of the situation is not the events themselves — taken individually they are quite understandable as part of the natural fabric of the world. The uniqueness rests in the cumulative effect of the seemingly coincidental occurrence of all four disasters. Yet the reader knows that these events are no mere coincidences. They are not the result of bad luck. They are not random, coincidental events. Rather, they are, in some fundamental sense, the will of God. God intended to test whether Job served God for profit. Satan intended to destroy Job's faith. God permitted Satan; he empowered Satan; and he could have stopped Satan at any time. This "evil" ultimately came from God. It was the Lord, as the narrative says, who took away his prosperity, his servants, and his children (Job 42:11).

The Second Wave of Suffering

The second phase of the trial was again brought through nature. This time the target was Job's health. Satan "afflicted Job with painful sores from the soles of his feet to the top of his head" (2:7). Of course, there was nothing obviously miraculous about these sores, that is, nothing happened to Job beyond the perceived regularities of nature. His physical suffering was nothing more than what other individuals might suffer from time to time. However, his suffering was extreme and intense. Job often reflects on this personal plague in the dialogue. There we see the cumulative effect of his own physical suffering. Anderson provides an informative summary of the disease and the symptoms from which Job suffered:

> Some kind of acute dermatitis spreading everywhere and developing infections with darkened (Jb. 30:28) and peeling (30:30) skin and constantly erupting pustules (7:5b) would manifest the pruritus and purulence

highlighted in 2:7. Other symptoms may be the results of complications in the wake of such a severe malady: anorexia, emaciation (19:20), fever (30:30b), fits of depression (7:16; 30:15f), weeping (16:16a), sleeplessness (7:4), nightmares (7:14). These and other general sufferings, such as putrid breath (9:17; cf. 17:1), failing vision (16:16b), rotting teeth (19:20) and haggard looks (2:12) are less direct clues. They add up to a hideous picture of a man tortured by degrading disfigurement (Is. 52:14) and unendurable pain, a bleak reminder that a man is flesh, made out of soil from the ground.[5]

The effects of such a degrading disease were felt socially and emotionally as well as physically. In chapters 29 and 30 Job offers an emotional lament which reflects on the difference between his past life and his present one. Chapter 29 describes his life "then," but chapter 30 describes his life "now" (30:1,9,11).

"Then" Job was blessed. He describes this blessed state in several ways. It was a time "when God watched over me" (29:2), "when God's intimate friendship blessed my house" (29:4), "when the Almighty was still with me and my children were around me" (29:5). Under those blessed conditions, Job was a civic leader (29:7), everyone listened to him (29:9,21), and everyone spoke well of his charity, righteousness, and integrity (29:11-17). Young and old alike treated him with deference (29:8). He summarized his social position in this poetic verse (29:25):

> I chose the way for them and sat as their chief;
> I dwelt as a king among his troops;
> I was like one who comforts mourners.

Job believed at one time that he would die in this condition of spiritual and social blessedness. He once thought, "I will die in my own house, my days as numerous as the grains of sand. . . . My glory will remain fresh in me, the bow ever new in my hand" (29:18,20). However, he learned differently. "*Now*," he complains, "they mock me, men younger than I, whose fathers I would have disdained to put with my sheep dogs" (30:1). *"Now,"* he cries, "I have become a byword among them. They detest me and keep their distance; they do not hesitate to spit in my face" (30:9-10). Where once "the bow" was "ever new" in his hand (29:20), *"now . . .* God has unstrung my bow and afflicted me" (30:11; cf. 30:16).

Job believed God was responsible for this transition from past blessings to present curse. His complaint is emotionally packed and genuine (Job 30:20-21, 26, 31):

> I cry out to you, O God, but you do not answer;
>   I stand up, but you merely look at me.
> You turn on me ruthlessly;
>   with the might of your hand you attack me. . . .
> Yet when I hoped for good, evil came;
>   when I looked for light, then came darkness. . . .
> My harp is turned to mourning,
>   and my flute to the sound of wailing.

The experience of suffering moved him to a new station in life. Once he looked at life from the top of the heap, but now he looks at life from the trash heap. This difference murders innocence and destroys naïveté. The old world of blessing and joy transitioned to a new world of radical evil, suffering, and loss. This is the experience of every sufferer. One day, in a single moment, the old world of peace and stability is changed into a new world of disillusionment and pain. One moment we are rejoicing, and the next we are mourning. In a single day, Job, as all who suffer, lost his innocence and his naïveté. The day of suffering colors all other days and the world is no longer the same.

The Principle of Divine Permission

The story of Job illustrates divine permission. God permitted Satan to test Job's integrity. God did not simply allow something to happen that was going to happen in the "natural course of events." On the contrary, God had protected Job and placed a hedge around him so that such events could not happen to him. In order for Satan to test Job, God had to decide to remove the hedge. Here divine permission was an active decision to empower Satan to test Job. God decided to restrict the hedge and determined the extent to which it would remain. God may not have decided exactly what Satan would do, but God gave him the freedom and power to do it.

There is no indication that God planned the evils which came upon Job. As far as the text reveals, God had not predetermined the death of Job's children. Rather, it is better to think of the future as an open reality where nothing in the human drama is predetermined (there are exceptions, of course, like the death of Jesus, Acts 2:23). There is an openness to the future though it is under the sovereign knowledge and control of God. Satan decided how he would test Job within God's limitations. There is no indication that God decided what Satan would do, but only that God gave Satan the freedom and power to attack Job. Consequently, we may speak of God's permissive will in the sense that he does not predetermine or necessarily plan every future event. History has an open future even though it is under God's sovereign control.

The story of Job seems to indicate that whatever divine permission is, it is not the relinquishment of sovereignty. Moral agents and nature do not operate autonomously in God's world. Rather, God had previously prevented Satan from attacking Job. God decided to permit Satan to test Job. Satan was not an autonomous moral agent, but rather an agent who functioned under divine sovereignty. God decided what Satan could or could not do. Satan's moral freedom did not circumscribe God. Instead, God's permission circumscribed Satan's freedom. Some version of "specific permission," where every event is at least deliberately permitted, is more consistent with the biblical evidence.

While God does not plan every future event independent of human choices and natural regularities, he sovereignly decides to permit or act with regard to every event that does take place. God's permission, then, involves a decision. It is not the action of a passive observer nor is it the powerlessness of a self-circumscribed spectator. Rather, it is the movement of an interested parent, who in the best interest of the child, decides to act or not to act; to prevent or not to prevent. Consequently, there is no event in my life about which God has not made a decision. Since he does not make decisions arbitrarily or without purpose, God has a purpose for everything that happens in my life. God can, at any moment, decide that the world should be other than it is. Consequently, it is always proper to ask, "Why did God *allow* this to happen?" "This is so," Cottrell argues, "because nothing happens without God's foreknowing it and deciding not to prevent it."[6]

Divine permission, then, means that God permits events which he neither determines nor plans. God may not have planned the death of my first wife, but he permitted it. He made a decision in response to my prayer for her health. He at least decided to permit her death. God may not have planned Joshua's genetic condition, but he permitted it. God made a decision in response to our prayers for Joshua's health. He at least decided to permit his genetic condition. If God is sovereign in such a way that he could act at any moment to change my personal history, then God at every moment decides whether or not to act. He decides whether or not to permit any given event. Therefore, when God permits something, it expresses his decision in that circumstance, and his decision, I am confident, is not arbitrary. His decision to permit arises out of some purpose or intent that he has in that circumstance. While Satan may intend any particular circumstance for evil, God intends it for good. While Satan sought to destroy Job's faith, God intended to refine it.

By way of permission, then, God is accomplishing his purposes in the world. God permitted Satan to test Job because he had *decided* to test Job. He had his own purposes for doing so. With *divine permission* Satan used both human agents and natural forces to test him. God, then, carries out his permissive will through Satanic, human, and natural agents.

The Presence of Satanic Forces

Sin is an alien force in God's good creation. It empowers Satan. In the fallen world, Satan and his cohorts are a real power. Jesus calls Satan the "prince of this world" (John 12:31; cf. 16:31). Paul refers to him as the "god of this age" who "has blinded the minds of unbelievers" (2 Corinthians 4:4). He is the "ruler of the kingdom of the air" whose spirit is "now at work in those who are disobedient" (Ephesians 2:2). "The whole world," John writes, "is under the control of the evil one" (1 John 5:19). Satan has power, influence, and dominion over the fallen age.

Satan opposes God's purposes. Satan seeks to destroy the harmony of God with his creation and to undermine God's intent of fellowship. Consequently, there is a real conflict between God and Satan. It is a contest over the hearts of people. Who will seek, love, and serve God? Satan uses his power to disrupt fellowship between God and his people as well as to enslave the hearts of the disobedient. "Like a roaring lion," Peter writes, "your adversary the devil prowls around, looking for someone to devour" (1 Peter 5:8, NRSV). The schemes of the devil are directed at the people of God. Satan is filled with anger and seeks to "make war" against God's saints (Revelation 12:12,17; NRSV). Consequently, the people of God put on God's armor in order to fight against "the powers of this dark world and against the spiritual forces of evil in the heavenly realms" (Ephesians 6:12). Satan tempts the people of God as he has opportunity (cf. 1 Corinthians 7:5). Satan schemes to tempt God's people (Revelation 2:10).

The story of Job gives us a glimpse into this cosmic battle. Satan, with God's permission, maliciously attacked Job.

Satan's intent was to destroy Job, though God's intent was to test him. The battleground, however, was whether or not Job served God for profit. Will Job curse God? Satan cannot force an answer and God, in his freedom, decided to permit Job to answer for himself. The battle was engaged and Job struggled to victory because he never cursed God. It is interesting that Satan does not appear at the end of the book as he did at the beginning. Satan played his trump card in the prologue. There was nothing more for him to say or do with regard to Job. The silence of Satan is the victory of God through Job's faith. Job's faith, then, had a cosmic significance, just as ours has.

However, the story illustrates that demonic (adversarial) forces are present in the world. Satanic influences hinder God's people or prompt, incite, and motivate evil in their hearts. Satanic influence can saturate a heart with evil. It can incite a person to commit evil without coercion. Satan "entered" the heart of Judas whom he "prompted" to betray Jesus (John 13:2,27). Satan captivates people through deception so that they "do his will" (2 Timothy 2:26). Satan can fill a heart so that it lies and attempts to deceive God himself (Acts 5:3). Satan can act to inflict an illness or destroy one's life, as in the case of the woman "whom Satan has kept bound for eighteen long years" (Luke 13:16). Indeed, it was part of Jesus' ministry to go about "doing good and healing all who were oppressed by the devil" (Acts 10:38, NRSV). Within the fallen, cursed world, God permits Satan to afflict his creation and his people. God permits the Evil One to work his own designs.

Satan's design is to create an opportunity for stumbling, to frustrate the work of God's people and to afflict God's people in order to disrupt their communion with him. For example, Paul wanted to return to Thessalonica, but "Satan stopped us" (1 Thessalonians 2:18). Nevertheless, Paul prays that God would "direct" him back to Thessalonica (1 Thessalonians 3:11, NRSV). Paul understands that there is a Satanic conflict which seeks to hinder or destroy his work (cf. 2 Corinthians 2:11), but Paul also knows who controls the world. He prays that God will over-rule Satan's hindrances and permit him to return to Thessalonica.

Satan's power, then, is controlled and limited by God's sovereign reign over the world. Satan must ask permission to act, and sometimes it is granted. We see this in the story of Job, but it is also evidenced in other texts. For example, Jesus informs Peter that "Satan has asked to sift you as wheat" (Luke 22:31). Satan seeks, and is apparently grant-ed, God's permission to tempt Peter. Another example is Paul's thorn in the flesh. Whatever the "thorn in the flesh" is, it is something that comes from Satan but under God's sovereign decision. Satan uses it to torment Paul, but God uses it to keep him humble. Both Satan and God have a hand in this "thorn," but they have different intentions. Paul prays to the Lord three times to seek relief, but each time he answers, "No." God is in control of this "messenger of Satan" (2 Corinthians 12:7). God will decide when or whether the thorn will be removed, even though it is an active agent of Satan.

Satan has his own limited freedom. He roams the earth seeking whom he may devour. He chooses his opportunities and makes the most of them (cf. Ephesians 4:27). But Satan is not autonomous. What Satan does, he does by God's permission. God binds and unbinds Satan. He puts hedges and removes hedges at various stages in history and in the personal lives of people. The classic example is Revelation 20 where Satan is bound in order to "keep him from deceiving the nations" (20:3), and he is released to deceive them once again (20:7). God is sovereign over Satan and he can do nothing except what God allows him to do.

Whatever freedom Satan may have, God controls it and believers know that God will ultimately decide whether Satan is permitted to act against them. Consequently, our prayer to the Father is "lead us not into temptation, but deliver us from the evil one" (Matthew 6:13). In our prayer, we are confident that nothing — no power, no demon, nothing — can "separate us from the love of God that is in Christ Jesus our Lord" (Romans 8:37-39). We are confident that God is sovereign over the Evil One. We may respect the power of Satan, but we do not fear him. We know that the one who is in us is greater than the one who is in the world (1 John 4:4).

The Freedom of Human Choice

Adam and Eve were created with the ability of "contrary choice." They could choose to assert their own moral autonomy, or they could choose loving fellowship with God. This is the basic choice all human beings make. We have the unique ability among God's creatures to transcend ourselves and to contemplate our own existence in relation to God. We are responsible before God, just like Adam and Eve, for our choices, particularly our most fundamental choice — whether we will find security in our own autonomy or through fellowship with God.

Scripture offers this choice over and over again. God continually offers his fallen creatures fellowship. Moses offered it to Israel at Shittim when he set before them "life and death, blessings and curses," and called upon them to "choose life" through obedience to God's covenant (Deuteronomy 30:19). Joshua offered it to Israel at Shechem when he rehearsed God's graciousness to Israel and called upon them to "choose for yourselves this day whom you will serve" (Joshua 24:15). Jesus lamented that Jerusalem had chosen to rebel against God's designs rather than seeking God's fellowship (Matthew 23:37). Human beings must choose life or death, just as they did in the Garden, and they are responsible for whatever choice they make.

Nevertheless, given the fallen nature of the world, there is a sense of inevitability about sin and human rebellion. Despite that inevitability, our choices are neither coerced nor predetermined. We are responsible for our rebellion. We have all fallen under sin's bondage and have been enslaved by its destructive power. No one is righteous (Romans 3:9-23). The fallen world is filled with fallen people. While freedom gives humanity a wonderful potential for good, it also has given humanity a horrible potential for evil. Radical evil arises out of the fallen human heart which enjoys the suffering, exploitation, and pain of others.[7] Sin abuses human freedom in a search for autonomy and independence. The fallen human heart will do anything to assert its own freedom in service to its own pride. It seeks to resolve its own anxieties by seeking its own way. Sin is rebellion against God's intention for us. It is our failure to reflect God's glory and be like him (Romans 3:23). While God intended fellowship with us in his holy communion of love, the fallen self seeks independence and its own happiness.

However, while human freedom is genuine and we are responsible for our actions, human freedom is not autonomous. It does not operate independently of God's sovereignty or beyond his control. Human beings are free to choose between contrary options (such as, to love God or reject God) but their freedom is circumscribed by God's sovereignty. God values this freedom because he values genuine love rather than coerced submission. Consequently, God permits human freedom. This permission is not a reluctant one, but a value that God expressed in creation. He created us with the ability of contrary choice. He wants us to choose. God graciously preserves the ability of human beings to make their own ultimate choice whether to seek their own autonomy or find their meaning in God's love. But God does not relinquish his sovereignty in order to provide this freedom. Rather, God provides this freedom within his sovereignty. He permits human beings to make choices contrary to his moral will. This does not mean he approves their choices, but he grounds the freedom of those choices by permitting them. In other words, he does not always prevent the exercise of moral evil (Acts 14:16; Romans 1:18-32).

Nevertheless, human freedom does not circumscribe God, but God circumscribes human freedom. For example, as Jacob prepared to flee from Laban, he explains how Laban had cheated him by changing his wages ten times. Nevertheless, his confidence in God's sovereign providence is reflected in such statements as "the God of my father has been with me" (Genesis 31:5), and, speaking of Laban, "God did not permit him to harm me" (Genesis 31:7, NRSV). Instead, "God has taken away your father's livestock and has given them to me" (Genesis 31:9). The story illustrates how God's permission restricts human freedom. God did not permit Laban to destroy or undermine Jacob's prosperity.

God's promise that he will not permit us to be tempted above our abilities involves a similar involvement of God's permission. He does not permit us to face overwhelming and irresistible temptations (1 Corinthians 10:13). This promise entails that God limits human freedom, that is, he prevents others from tempting me in ways that I cannot bear. Just as Laban was prevented from destroying Jacob, so God prevents others from tempting me above what I am able to bear. In order for humans to act, they must have God's permission.

Another illustration is the way Paul talks about his travel plans. Paul understands that his missionary travels are rooted in God's permission. He hopes to visit the Corinthians "very soon, if the Lord is willing" (1 Corinthians 4:19). He intends to spend some time with them "if the Lord permits" (1 Corinthians 16:7). Cottrell comments: "Paul recognized that he would be able to carry out his plan *only* if God permitted him to do so, because he knew that in his sovereign providence God could *prevent* such a visit if he so chose."[8] Similarly, Paul assures the Ephesians that he will return, but only "if it is God's will" (Acts 18:21). Again, Paul believes it is only "by God's will" that "the way may be opened" for him to visit Rome (Romans 1:10) and he asks Roman Christians to pray "so that by God's will" he may go to them (Romans 15:32).

Another significant text is James 4:13-16. We may plan our days, but these plans are circumscribed by the will of God. James counsels that our perspective should always be that "if it is the Lord's will, we will live and do this or that" (James 4:15). Whether we live or die, whether we do "this" or "that," is dependent upon the will of God. If God permits us to live, and if God permits us to do "this" or "that," then we will conduct our lives accordingly. But to think otherwise — to think as if God is uninvolved in our decision process — is to "boast and brag," and "all such boasting is evil" (James 4:16). Human freedom must recognize its limitations. It is circumscribed by God's permissive will.

In the story of Job the Chaldeans and the Sabeans could not have attacked Job's servants and prosperity if God had not permitted them. Previous to God's permission, the Chaldeans and the Sabeans were prevented from attacking Job. God had a hedge around him. No demonic or human freedom could climb over that hedge without God's permission. Job would only be tested if God willed it. But God permitted the perpetration of moral evil against Job in order to test him. This does not mean that God sanctified that moral evil, but only that he permitted sinful people to act freely against one of his own. God permitted evil people to commit evil acts out of their evil hearts in order to test Job. God is sovereign over evil. He decides its boundaries and he permits its existence for his own purposes.

The Chaos of Nature

What God created was "very good" (Genesis 1:31). God created this goodness out of a primordial, chaotic void (Genesis 1:2). God brought light out of darkness and order out of chaos. Whatever the void of Genesis 1:2 is, it is clear that the phrase "Spirit of God" expresses God's "control over the cosmos and his ability to impose his will upon it."[9] The creative work of God conquered chaos (the void) and transformed it into something "good."[10] However, when sin entered that world, it corrupted God's good creation. The cosmos was subjected to frustration and the ground was cursed. The present world is no longer the pure blessedness that God created. Now it is the chaos of God's curse. Chaos now operates in the fallen world along the analogy of cancer in a body. When the human couple fell, the natural world also came under the sentence of chaos (at least as it relates to human beings). God now permits chaos in his creation because of its fallen character.

As noted earlier, redemption follows the model of creation and the model of redemption illuminates creation. It is not surprising, then, to find the chaos motif in texts about redemption. When God elected Israel, God found Israel "in a desert land" which was "a barren and howling waste" (Deuteronomy 32:10). The term "waste" is used in Genesis 1:2 to describe the chaotic void. Israel was created out of chaos. Israel was a stubborn, tiny nation whose meager significance was defined by its Egyptian bondage. Nevertheless, God created them out of love (Deuteronomy 7:7-9; 9:1-6; 32:6).

However, Israel rebelled. Now, due to sin, Israel was cursed. God promised life and blessing in response to Israel's obedience, but he also promised death and cursing in response to their disobedience (Deuteronomy 28; 30:11-20). When Israel sinned and rebelled, God executed his curses, just as he did in the Garden. The curses turned Israel's land into a chaos filled with famine, locust, drought, disease, and barrenness. Nature, intended to bless Israel, cursed it. The same is true for the original creation. What was intended to bless humanity became a curse as a consequence of sin.

This imagery is beautifully pictured by Jeremiah as he applies the Deuteronomic curses to the sins of Judah (Jeremiah 4:23-26).[11] In this oracle God expresses his anguish over the sins of his people. Nevertheless Judah's punishment is something the people have brought upon themselves (Jeremiah 4:18-19). Babylon will destroy them as an expression of the Lord's wrath. Jeremiah uses the images of God's creation out of chaos to describe the return to chaos that God's curse will bring (4:23-26):

> I looked at the earth,
>> and it was formless and empty;
> and at the heavens,
>> and their light was gone.
> I looked at the mountains,
>> and they were quaking;
>> all the hills were swaying.
> I looked, and there were no people;
>> every bird in the sky had flown away.
> I looked, and the fruitful land was a desert;
>> all its towns lay in ruins
>> before the LORD, before his fierce anger.

The allusions to creation are unmistakable. Genesis 1:2 and Jeremiah 4:23 are the only places in the Hebrew text where "formless and empty" are conjoined. Further, "heavens" and "earth" are paralleled just like in Genesis 1:1. The light had vanished in Jeremiah's description. Creation had been reversed. There are no more people. The fruitful land which God created was now a desert. What God had created had been destroyed, and it was destroyed by God himself as an expression of his anger toward Judah's rebellion (cf. Jeremiah 10:10). Creation had returned to chaos in the light of Judah's punishment. This parallels the curse story of Genesis 3. The good that God created was corrupted by the consequences of sin. God cursed the ground and subjected his creation to futility. Chaos returned because sin had entered the world.

But chaotic nature does not act autonomously or independently of God's reign. On the contrary, it serves the purposes of God. It is by God's gracious presence that any order remains in the universe. Otherwise, God's creative act would have been totally reversed and all of creation would have returned to chaos. God, however, graciously sustains the world and manifests his glory through nature, just as he graciously permitted Adam and Eve to continue their life outside the Garden. But this fallen world is not the world God created. God created Eden. Our present world is not Eden. Rather, sin has entered the cosmos, and creation has become chaos. It would be total chaos if it were not for God's gracious blessings (cf. Psalm 104; 136:1-9; 148). God continues to uphold the cosmos by his power, and he sustains it by the decision of his will. Creation continues by grace even though it is presently chaotic.

God reigns over this fallen chaotic world. He reigns over darkness as well as light. He reigns over the order and the chaos. This is the message of Psalm 97:1-5. It is a proclamation of God's sovereignty.

> The LORD reigns, let the earth be glad;
>   let the distant shores rejoice.
> Clouds and thick darkness surround him;
>   righteousness and justice are the foundation of
>   his throne.
> Fire goes before him
>   and consumes his foes on every side.
>   His lightning lights up the world;
>   the earth sees and trembles.
> The mountains melt like wax before the LORD,
>   before the Lord of all the earth.

The story of Job illustrates the reign of God over nature. Natural evil does not fall outside of God's sovereignty. As famines starve children, as earthquakes kill hundreds and as hurricanes destroy cities, nature works evil in human lives. Job experienced natural evil. He suffered from lightning, mighty winds and disease. Nevertheless, God is sovereign over those chaotic forces. None of this had to happen to Job. Rather, God permits Satan to use these natural forces to test Job.

In fact, the reign of God over the chaotic cosmos is the primary theme of God's speeches to Job. Whether it is the gracious power of God to create and sustain his universe (as in Job 38–39), or whether it is the power of God to control and tame the chaotic forces in nature like the Leviathan and the Behemoth (as in Job 40–41),[12] the point is the same. Job cannot claim to control or even know about these forces, but God does. God reigns over nature, and while there is chaos, it is not beyond his control. On the contrary, that chaos is at God's command. It will do his bidding. The Behemoth is one whom no one can capture, but his maker can tame him (Job 40:19,24). The Leviathan is one whom no one can bridle, but he belongs to his maker (Job 41:11,13). No one but God can control the chaotic forces of nature. God reigns over his fallen world, and we must confess with Job, "I know you can do all things; no plan of yours can be thwarted" (42:2). God alone controls nature.

Thus, whatever we say, we must at least say that God is in such control of nature that he could prevent any event at any time. Consequently, we must at least say that every act of nature is permitted if not caused by God. God, then, permits natural evil within his universe. It is something he could otherwise prevent, but God has determined, in the light of the fall, to at least permit natural evil as a just consequence of sin. If humanity wants autonomy, then let it toil for its food from the cursed ground. Perhaps, in this way — just perhaps — it may learn to depend upon God and seek his fellowship.

Conclusion

God permits evil in a fallen world, but this raises the question of rationale. Why does God permit evil? Why did God permit Job's suffering? What reason does God have for this permission of moral (e.g., the Chaldeans killing Job's servants) and natural (e.g., the mighty wind that killed Job's children) evil? What God had previously prevented he now allowed. If God is going to test Job's integrity, why does he permit Satan to involve his family? Why does God permit Satan to kill innocent bystanders like Job's seven sons and three daughters or his servants?

But the reader knows there was meaning in this test. It had cosmic meaning. It was a contest between God and Satan (between faith and unbelief) about whether anyone, particularly Job, could love God for God's own sake; whether anyone, particularly Job, would choose fellowship with God over pride. Would Job bless God or curse him? Would he choose the tree of life — fellowship with God — or would he choose the tree of the knowledge of good and evil — moral autonomy? Job chose fellowship with God. He never cursed God though he was often impatient; he endured even though he was embittered. God permitted the test as a means of unveiling Job's heart before cosmic witnesses. Job loves God for no other reason than for God's sake, that is, for fellowship with God. God's permission served to glorify God through Job's faithfulness.

God, then, permits Satanic freedom, natural chaos, and human freedom because he seeks genuine fellowship between himself and his people. It is a fellowship that is tested in the crucible of a fallen world where God permits sin and natural evil. God permits such because it serves the purpose of generating and sustaining genuine faithfulness on the part of his people, and God is glorified by that faithfulness. Just as Job's faithful endurance magnified God's glory, so also does our faithful endurance.

But we need to say more about God's purposes. The story continues . . . .

---

[1]Whether "Satan" refers to a personal agent of evil or to the role of a particular angel in God's presence is inconsequential to my point. See Peggy L. Day, *An Adversary in Heaven: Satan in the Hebrew Bible* (Atlanta: Scholars Press, 1988) and Marvin Tate, "Satan in the Old Testament," *Review and Expositor* 89 (1992): 461-474.

[2]D.A. Carson, *How Long, O Lord? Reflections on Suffering and Evil* (Grand Rapids: Baker, 1990), pp. 199-228, discusses this problem in some detail.

³Ibid., p. 224.

⁴James S. Nelson, "Divine Action: Is It Credible?" *Zygon* 30 (1995): 279-280.

⁵Francis I. Anderson, *Job: An Introduction and Commentary*, Tyndale Old Testament Commentaries (Downers Grove, IL: InterVarsity, 1976), pp. 91-92.

⁶Jack Cottrell, *What the Bible Says about God the Ruler* (Joplin, MO: College Press, 1984), p. 407.

⁷Cf. Ted Peters, *Sin: Radical Evil in Soul and Society* (Grand Rapids: Eerdmans, 1994).

⁸Cottrell, *God the Ruler*, p. 314.

⁹M.P. Deroche, "The *ruah elohim* in Gen 1:2c: Creation or Chaos," in *Ascribe to the Lord: Biblical & Other Studies in Memory of Peter C. Craigie*, Journal for the Study of the Old Testament Supplement Series 67 (Sheffield: JSOT Press, 1988): 318.

¹⁰See B.W. Anderson, *Creation Versus Chaos: The Reinterpretation of Mythical Symbolism in the Bible* (Philadelphia: Fortress, 1987, reprint of 1967 edition); S. Niditch, *Chaos to Cosmos: Studies in the Biblical Pattern of Creation* (Chico: Scholar's Press, 1985); Ronald A. Simkins, *Creator & Creation: Nature in the Worldview of Ancient Israel* (Peabody, MA: Hendrickson, 1994); and Claus Westermann, *Genesis 1-11: A Commentary*, tr. John J. Scullion (London: SPCK, 1984), pp. 19-47.

¹¹Cf. Jack Vancil, "From Creation to Chaos: An Exegesis of Jeremiah 4:23-26," in *Biblical Interpretation: Principles and Practices*, ed. F. Furman Kearley, et al. (Grand Rapids: Baker, 1986), pp. 181-192.

¹²Many interpret the Leviathan and the Behemoth as God's control of chaotic nature which he has placed at Satan's disposal. See Elmer B. Smick, "Another Look at the Mythological Elements in the Book of Job," *Westminster Theological Journal* 40 (1978): 213-228; and J.C.L. Gibson, "On Evil in the Book of Job," in *Ascribe to the Lord: Biblical & Other Studies in Memory of Peter C. Craigie*, Journal for the Study of the Old Testament Supplement Series 67 (Sheffield: JSOT Press, 1988): 399-419.

Chapter Five

Why Does God Do What He Does in a Fallen World?

The Purposes of Divine Action

> *Remember this, fix it in your mind,*
> *take it to heart, you rebels.*
> *Remember the former things, those of long ago;*
> *I am God, and there is no other;*
> *I am God, and there is none like me.*
> *I make known the end from the beginning,*
> *from ancient times, what is still to come.*
> *I say: My purpose will stand,*
> *and I will do all that I please.*
> *From the east I summon a bird of prey;*
> *from a far-off land, a man to fulfill my purpose.*
> *What I have said, that will I bring about;*
> *what I have planned, that will I do.*
> *Isaiah 46:8-11*

Whenever God permits, he acts. He decides to permit what he could have prevented. God permits Satan, humanity, and the chaos of nature to operate within the bounds of their own freedom, yet he is sovereign over that freedom. He permits whatever happens and this is a decision of his own will. Since God's decisions are neither arbitrary nor random, he permits every act of Satanic, human and natural freedom for a purpose. Consequently, every event in the world involves a divine purpose.

The distinction between permission and action is helpful though, perhaps, ultimately shrouded in mystery. While permission still involves an act of the divine will, in that God decides not to prevent, permission remains a passive disposition. By his "passivity," God permits a natural course of events (like the path of a tornado), or he permits a human decision that involves moral evil, or he permits Satan to tempt someone. God himself is not necessarily the author of these actions in the sense of acting with specific causation. Rather, he decides to withhold countercausation, that is, he does not overrule the freedom of those causes. God's permission is passive though he is sovereign over what he permits because he could have decided otherwise. Nevertheless, God is "doing" something in that he permits for a reason. God has some purpose for his permission. Consequently, God is never passive in the sense that he is uninvolved, but he is passive in the sense that he is not the author of moral evil and he permits his free creatures to commit such evil.

In contrast to divine permission, divine action is a specific work of God which he plans and/or causes in order to accomplish his purposes. Divine permission is, in a sense, a divine action in that God permits others, in their freedom, to accomplish his purposes. But in the strictest sense, divine action is characterized by an additional dimension in which God himself is an agent in the world working through his creation as he initiates actions to accomplish his specific purposes. God does not always simply permit one nation to attack another, he sometimes plans it (as in the destruction of Judah by Babylon). God does not always simply permit Satan to tempt someone, he sometimes plans to try that person (as in the case of Abraham's sacrifice of Isaac). God does not always simply permit a king to make a particular decision, God sometimes plans that decision (as when he stirred the heart of the Assyrian king). God is not merely passive in his world (in the sense of divine permission), but he is also active.

But whether God permits or acts, what is his purpose?

God's Ultimate Intent

God's fundamental purpose in the fallen world is to fulfill his original intent in creation. Everything that God does is related to his intent to have a people for himself with whom he can live in holy communion. This was God's intention in creation, and it is his intention in re-creation/redemption. God's goal is an eschatological community among whom he can dwell as God and they as his people. He seeks fellowship with a people who will share his holy triune communion in a new heaven and new earth.

This is the key structural principle of God's story in the Bible. Everything God does and permits has this principle at its root. No matter what happens, God intends that whatever happens express this purpose and tend toward that goal.

This yields an important principle. We are often self-absorbed with our own happiness. Everything we do has the goal of happiness. If we are unhappy in our marriage, we get a divorce. If we are unhappy in our work, we change jobs. We expend a great amount of energy in recreation, escapism (drugs and alcohol) and adventures (sexual as well as thrill-seeking) in order to satisfy our deep longings for happiness or to forget our unhappiness. We promote, use, and even distort whatever we possess (power, wealth, fame, knowledge, talents, family, even religion) in the hope that we might find happiness in those things. We are restless until we are happy, and we are unhappy because we are restless.

God's goal for us is happiness, but it is not the kind of happiness which we self-absorbed, fallen humans seek. We seek our own selves, our own autonomy, and our own independence. God's goal, however, is that we find happiness in communion with him. God desires our happiness, but he also, as Creator, has defined it. Happiness is to enjoy God forever.[1]

We can benefit from the insights of anthropology on this point. It is an insight that Pannenberg calls "openness

to the world."[2] The phrase refers to the unique human ability to experience our environment in new ways. Humans
have a transcending quality about them. We are always
searching, seeking something new. We are always attempting to find our place in the world and the meaning of our
lives. We grope for happiness but never find it. We are
always seeking to create a home for ourselves, but we never
are comfortable with the home we create. Our openness to
the world is an expression of our finitude and the fact that
we are dependent upon a reality that transcends us. We
yearn for identity.

Eventually we face the truth that our fulfillment depends
upon something beyond ourselves. Consequently, we are
always open to the future. We are never complete. As
Augustine said, "Our hearts are restless until they find rest
in thee, O God."[3] Or, as Pascal is supposed to have said,
there is a God-shaped vacuum in the heart of every person.
Or, as the preacher in Ecclesisastes wrote, God has put
"eternity" in our hearts (3:11). Within the cosmos we are
the restless creatures that look beyond the material for ultimate fulfillment. We are designed to find our meaning and
identity in relation to, and only in relation to, God. The
future that God intends is eschatological communion. Only
there will we find genuine, authentic happiness though we
may experience some foretaste of that communion now.

We are designed for happiness, but we have always
looked for it in the wrong places. We seek the creature
rather than the Creator. We seek sensual pleasure rather
than communion with God. We choose the tangible over
the intangible, the seen over the unseen, the temporal over
the eternal. Adam chose Eve over God. We choose ourselves, others or things over God. We have been looking for
love in all the wrong places.

God's response to our misguided search is to initiate
redemption. God permits and acts with a view toward
accomplishing his goal. He seeks eschatological communion
with his creatures. Though he dwells in us now through his

Holy Spirit (1 Corinthians 6:19), he too yearns for a face-to-face communion. Consequently, God is more interested in our communion with him than our sensual pleasure. He calls us to faith and trust. He calls us into communion with him. God is more interested in our faith than our pleasure.[4] Our present pleasure is secondary to God's eschatological goal.

Therefore, God's intent is not to make everyone happy in the way that we want to be happy (e.g., wealth, fame, power, knowledge). God does not ensure everyone's happiness in the world by providing them with everything their fallen hearts desire. God is not Santa Claus. His ultimate goal is not temporal happiness, but an eternal one. Consequently, if our temporal pain will serve God's eschatological goal, then God may very well afflict us with pain because of his priorities. Thus, we may confess with the psalmist that it is "good" to be afflicted (Psalm 119:71). When we recognize the "goodness" of the affliction, we can also recognize its origin. God afflicted the psalmist who confessed: "in faithfulness you have afflicted me" (Psalm 119:75). The faithfulness of God was God's own commitment to his goal. God was more interested in the psalmist's faith than he was his pleasure. Consequently, when it is necessary to accomplish his goal, God may afflict us in order that we might seek him. The affliction may be the very thing that turns us from sensual pursuits to communion with him. This is at least what the psalmist thought when he wrote, "Before I was afflicted I went astray, but now I obey your word" (Psalm 119:67).

God uses troubles, tribulations, and trials to generate, strengthen or refine our faith. God is interested in our faith as a means of communion with him. As a result, he will use whatever means necessary to turn us from unbelief to belief, from distrust to trust; to turn us from the world and its sensual pleasures to the joy of communion with him. God will use the circumstances of this fallen world to accomplish his eschatological goal, and this involves the discipline, training, and testing of his people.

"Fairness" must be evaluated in the light of his goal. God is no respecter of persons (Acts 10:34) in the sense that he has the same goal for everyone. He yearns for his people and intends that all share in his eschatological communion. God does not want anyone to perish (2 Peter 3:9). But while God has the same intent for everyone, he may use different means to achieve his goal much like we treat our children differently because they have different personalities and needs. In other words, God is under no obligation to treat everyone just alike in a kind of egalitarian justice. Nor must everyone receive his deserved share of blessings and sufferings in a kind of distributive justice.[5] Egalitarian and distributive justice applied to God's dealings with human beings is more the American democratization of God than it is the biblical story.

God did not treat Ishmael like he treated Issac (Genesis 17), and neither did he treat Esau like he treated Jacob (Romans 9:9-16). God has the sovereign right to treat people differently. He may give wealth to some, but poverty to others (1 Samuel 2:7). He may give health to some, but sickness to others. "Fairness" does not mean that God treats everyone exactly the same or with an equal distribution of blessings and sufferings. It only means that he has the same intent for everyone. "Fairness" is relative to the means which will best achieve God's eschatological intent for a person. Consequently, God may use "affliction" to achieve his goal, or he may use "blessing." God disciplines, trains, and tests his people in view of what will best accomplish that goal in any particular situation.

However, not everyone turns to God or accepts his discipline. Many seek their own way and reject God's offer of communion. They glory in their own immorality. They oppress the poor. They enslave the needy. They persecute the people of God. They have chosen to seek their own way. They prefer their autonomy to God's holy communion. They seek the fellowship of sinners rather than the fellowship of the holy God.

Thus, God's holiness means that he punishes the wicked. He excludes them from his fellowship because his communion is a holy one. God does not fellowship with those who have rejected that communion. God's holiness excludes the wicked from his presence, just as he excluded Adam and Eve from the Garden. When God's holiness confronts the rebellious or ungodly, it becomes God's wrath which punishes the wicked. Wrath is the expression of God's holiness toward the ungoldly. Wrath, then, expresses God's glory as a function of his holiness (cf. Psalm 76:10).[6]

The relationship between Israel and the original inhabitants of the land of Canaan illustrates this point. Israel was a holy people dedicated to God's holiness (Deuteronomy 7:6; cf. the holiness code of Leviticus 18-20). They were given a land that had been the possession of idolaters. God destroyed these idolaters because of their wickedness. It was not because Israel was so righteous that they received the land. Rather, it is because the Canaanites were so wicked (Deuteronomy 9:4-5). God had been patient with the Canaanites since the days of Abraham. He was patient until their cup of wickedness was full (Genesis 15:16), and then he destroyed them. But their destruction, which was deserved, was also the means by which God offered Israel the gift of that good land (Deuteronomy 9:6).[7] Indeed, God's wrath against the Canaanites was also divine grace for Israel. The destruction of the Canaanites was also a warning to Israel (Deuteronomy 7:4). God patiently waited until their sinfulness was such that God's holiness was moved to action (much like in the Noahic flood of Genesis 6–9), and by that same action God's holiness expressed his love for Israel by offering them both a gift and a warning.

In summary, it is important to remember that God's actions serve his eschatological intent. Everything God permits or does has this in mind. He punishes evil because evil cannot partake of God's holy communion. He destroys the wicked, the ungoldly, and the unbeliever because they have rebelled against his holy communion. He disciplines the believer because he seeks to strengthen and test faith. He seeks eschatological communion with them so he permits and acts in such a way that maximizes their entrance into his eschatological presence. God punishes the wicked because he is holy, and he invites the believer into his presence because he is love. The holy love of God motivates and prescribes the nature of this eschatological communion. This holy love guides God's permissive and active will in the world.

God's Circumstantial Purposes

Whatever we say about the nature of "divine permission," God governs a world in which suffering is real. Whatever we say about the nature of "divine action," God has acted in the world to destroy and to discipline as well as to redeem. God is sovereign over every evil in this fallen world. Why does God have a world where he permits moral (sin) and natural (tornadoes) evil? Everyone would admit that God created such a world even though, according to some, he does not directly cause any "evil" within it. For many the broad answer to that question is "soul-making" or character development.[8]

According to this perspective, God created this world to provide an ideal environment for "soul-making" or "character-building." It is a place where humanity is challenged, where it learns and matures, and where it exercises free moral agency. It builds character and draws humanity to God without overwhelming it. Suffering functions to build that character, to provide a challenge for faith, and to give humanity a choice between loving and hating God. Suffering, then, has value because through it we grow to heights we could not otherwise reach. Human beings mature and grow to their potential through this "soul-making" process.

There is legitimacy in this perspective. God is interested in character development, but God did not create for that purpose. God created to have fellowship with a people. God did not intend natural or moral evil. He did not create a world where sin was inevitable or where natural evil was unavoidable. On the contrary, sin brought death into the world, and sin brought a curse. The circumstances of this present world are different from the original creation. God did not originally intend to use "evil" to build the character of his people. He intended to commune with them in their sinless freedom. God intended that they live with him, mature in the light of his holiness, and be his people, without the introduction of sin or natural evil in their lives. But humanity sinned.

What God created was good, but the fall corrupted it. Instead of a "good" creation he now has a fallen, cursed world. The world has been sentenced to death. Human beings are ruled by death, enslaved by Satan, and corrupted by sin. In this world human beings have no inherent claim to life. They have no rights before God. Whatever God gives, he gives by grace. Consequently, God says to Job, "Who has a claim against me that I must pay? Everything under heaven belongs to me" (Job 41:11, and quoted by Paul in Romans 11:35).

Since God always permits and acts according to the principle of his ultimate intent, in this circumstance — the situation of a fallen world — God permits and acts through the curse as well as through redemption. He builds character through discipline. He punishes the wicked who reject his communion. He "makes souls" and offers a choice between fellowship with him or autonomy. God intends either to destroy the wicked or to promote the proper choice in others. God permits evil and even acts through evil for the sake of his ultimate goal. He seeks to "make souls" through the circumstances of fallenness. God, therefore, uses death, pain, and suffering for his own purposes as he promotes his ultimate intent. God sovereignly decides (by permission or action) to put fallenness in his service, so that even evil may serve God's goal. In other words, God

acts so that ultimate good might arise even out of the most
radical evil.

The purposes of divine actions may be summarized in
three broad categories. The first is punishment where God's
holiness destroys the wicked because they have rejected fellowship with him. The second is discipline where God's
love seeks to promote communion between himself and his
creatures. The third is redemption where God reverses suffering, destroys its effects and reconciles his people with
himself.

Punishment

Punishment serves a negative purpose which involves
both retribution and deterrence.[9] It is God's response to
moral evil. It arises out of God's holiness. Suffering both
punishes evil and deters others from committing evil.

Given the fallen world, Scripture recognizes the value
of both. Indeed, God is often pictured as directly involved
in sin's retribution or deterrence. Sin deserves punishment.
God's holiness will act against it. God also discourages his
creatures from sinning and therefore attaches certain consequences to immoral actions. The fact that God punishes
evildoers deters others from sinning. Yet the consequences
attached to immoral actions are not simply issues of deterrence — they are deserved. The by-product is that they also
deter. Deterrence is best conceived as a gracious warning.
When God acts in retribution against the ungodly, it also
serves the gracious purpose of warning others about the
consequences of sin.

Just punishment is ultimately retribution. God punishes evil with suffering and ultimately death. If this premise
is removed, the whole structure of grace comes tumbling
down. Grace is so wonderful and so unexpected exactly
because we deserve punishment. If there were no wrath,
there would be no grace. Consequently, the wonder of grace
is directly related to the reality of wrath. As Berkouwer has

perceptibly noted, "only when we acknowledge the complete *reasonableness of his wrath* do we see the Gospel as a *total surprise.*"[10] Grace, then, is unexpected because it is "favor bestowed when wrath is owed."[11]

The reality of God's wrath is expressed in both the Old (e.g., Isaiah 1:24; 5:25; 13:9,13; 63:3-6) and New Testaments (e.g., Romans 1:18; 2:5,8; 3:5). This reality is both eschatological (e.g., Romans 5:9; 1 Thessalonians 1:10) and within history (e.g., Romans 1:18-31; 13:4; 1 Thessalonians 2:16). The story of God's life with Israel illustrates how God meted out retribution for their sins. God acted in history — through nature, through other nations and through individuals — to punish his people for their sins.

Amos 4:2-13 illustrates the purposes of God's actions in history. Three points are notable. First, the rebellious character of the people draws out this response from God. They go to Bethel and Gilgal to offer their worship. Both of these places were important to the history of God's people — Jacob named Bethel (Genesis 28:19) and Gilgal is Israel's first encampment in the promised land (Joshua 4:19,20). But the people, instead of remembering what God had done for them, boasted in their own sacrifices and worship. They sinned in their arrogance which expressed itself socially by their oppression of the poor and needy (Amos 2:6-7; 4:1; 5:10-13; 6:1-7). Their altars at Bethel were monuments to their arrogance just as their winter and summer houses were monuments to their social injustice. In response to this arrogance, God determined to destroy both their altars and their houses (Amos 3:14-15). God swears their punishment by his holiness. God does not dwell among an arrogant people who promote a self-styled righteousness. Therefore, God is the enemy of an arrogant people (Isaiah 63:10; Psalm 18:28; 78:21-22).

Second, Amos 4 demonstrates how God seeks to deter and discipline his people in an effort to reverse their path. God deterred sin in specific ways. He gave them empty stomachs (a famine). He stopped the rains so that they lacked water, though out of his grace he gave rain to some. Nevertheless, both hunger and thirst were pervasive. God also sent locusts and destroyed their crops. God also sent death through plagues, war, and fire. These disasters were God's actions. He acted to destroy and kill. "When disaster comes to a city," Amos asks, "has not the LORD caused it?" (Amos 3:6b). These were no mere natural disasters by God's permissive will. Rather, they were divine acts to deter his nation. God intended these disasters to restore Israel's desire to seek him. God acted, but, as the refrain says five times (4:6,8,9,10,11), "yet [they] have not returned to me." The Lord calls to the people, "Seek me and live" (5:4b) and "Seek good, not evil, that you may live" (5:14a). "Then," Amos promises, "the LORD God Almighty will be with you, just as you say he is" (5:14b). But Israel did not heed the warnings imbedded in the disasters that befell them. They continued in their sinfulness and in response God handed them over to the Assyrians.

Third, Amos 4 demonstrates the retributive justice of God. The Lord concludes his message with a declaration of his intent. Because Israel had not returned to the Lord, God announces that they should "prepare to meet [their] God" (4:12c). They will stand before God's judgment and God announces what he is about to do. They will meet the God who created the mountains and the winds, who turns day into night (cf. 5:8-9), and he will surely act against this people. "Therefore I will send you into exile beyond Damascus," says the Lord (Amos 5:27). God will punish Israel through the Assyrians, and he will destroy this sinful people. God will "stir up a nation against" Israel "that will oppress" them (Amos 6:14). God's eyes have seen the wickedness of Israel, and he has sworn in his holiness to "destroy it from the face of the earth" (Amos 9:8).

God himself punished Israel. He initiated these natural disasters. He "stirred up the spirit of Pul king of Assyria" (1 Chronicles 5:26). God influenced the king to attack Israel as an act of God's just punishment though

Pul himself acted out of arrogance and covetousness. The Lord "has strengthened Rezin's forces against [Samaria and Ephraim] and has spurred their enemies on" (Isaiah 9:11). Isaiah described Assyria as God's "club of wrath" (Isaiah 10:5), and God sent Assyria into battle against Israel in order "to seize loot and snatch plunder, and to trample them down like mud in the streets" (Isaiah 10:6). The punishment of Israel was a divine act which God accomplished through Assyria (cf. Isaiah 10:12-19).

God is patient with sinful people, but his patience ultimately wears thin with the arrogant. Eventually their cup becomes full and God destroys them. God did this during the Noahic flood. He did it during the conquest of Canaan. In Amos he proclaims his intention to destroy Israel. God will not tolerate a full cup of wickedness. Rather, in his holiness he destroys the ungodly who do not seek him. The "day of the LORD" is a time when day turns to night. It reverses creation. The day of the Lord is God's judgment upon his creatures where he destroys them because of their wickedness, just as the night destroys the day and chaos curses creation (Amos 5:18-20). God offers communion, but the rebellious reject his offer in favor of their own pride and arrogance. Consequently, God destroys them.

This purpose of God — to destroy sinful people — is not only carried out against Israel, but against all nations. It is God's work throughout history. He has punished human arrogance from the tower of Babel (Genesis 11) to the fall of Rome (Revelation 17-18), and it continues into the present. The prophet Amos spoke a message against Israel's neighbors as well as against Israel herself. The sins of Damascus (1:3), Gaza (1:6), Tyre (1:9), Edom (1:11), Ammon (1:13), Moab (2:1) as well as Judah (1:4) are the object of God's wrath. God will not turn back his wrath from these nations. He has determined to punish them. The prophets regularly offer the nations a message of judgment which often includes an offer of grace (cf. Isaiah 45:22-25). Large sections of Isaiah (13–23), Jeremiah

(46–51), and Ezekiel (25–32) are judgment oracles against the nations.

Revelation is also a message about God's judgment against the nations, particularly the Roman Empire. God announces through his prophet John that Babylon (Rome) will fall. She has been judged because of her violence, immorality, and excessive luxuries (Revelation 18:4-9,24). The people of God are called to come out of her so that they will not share in "her plagues" because "her sins are piled up to heaven, and God has remembered her crimes" (Revelation 18:4-5). Babylon the harlot will be consumed "for mighty is the Lord God who judges her" (Revelation 18:8). What God was doing among the nations in the Old Testament he continues to do among the nations in the New Testament and throughout history. God is the Lord of all nations and the Lord of all history (Acts 17:26; Daniel 4:25,35).

God is active in his world to deter and to destroy. God creates disasters (Isaiah 43:7) in order to deter, and when deterrence does not accomplish its redemptive goal (that is, to engender repentance), God then determines to punish. God's intent in deterrence is to force the ultimate choice: submission to God or rebellion against him. Will they seek him and live, or will they continue to serve their own passions? Will they seek communion with God or will they choose their autonomy? When they reject his fellowship, God excludes them from his presence (cf. 2 Kings 17:22-23).

However, we cannot leave the subject of deterrence/punishment without noting another significant point in Amos. While God will destroy the arrogant (Amos 9:10), he will nevertheless preserve a remnant. He will not "totally destroy the house of Jacob" (Amos 9:8). God will return a remnant to the land from which he removes them (Amos 9:14). Even when God proclaims destruction, his intention to have a people for himself remains. Even when his people are filled with sin, he will find a remnant with whom he can dwell. During the Noahic flood, Noah found grace in the sight of God (Genesis 6:8-9). During the Conquest of Canaan, Rahab found grace in the sight of God (Joshua 6:25). During the prophetic ministry of Amos, God promises that a remnant of grace will return to the land. Even in his wrath, God still seeks to act graciously toward his people.

Discipline

While God sometimes acts to punish sinners, not all suffering is retributive. Job is the classic example of an innocent sufferer. His suffering was not a punishment. It was a cosmic test. Humanity was on trial and Job was the focal point. Consequently, suffering does not always express God's wrath. On the contrary, it may express God's confidence in his people. God trusted Job. He was confident that Job would maintain his integrity, and that is what Job did. He never cursed God. He maintained his faith even though he struggled with impatience, bitterness, and questions.

If suffering is not always retributive, then there are some positive purposes for suffering. These include testing and education. These purposes are not positive in the sense that there is no real pain. The pain is genuine and the hurt is real. But they are positive in the sense that they yield discernible good or real benefit in a person's life. Here suffering is not intended to punish, but to refine, train, and educate. It disciplines. Believers learn to love God more than they love themselves.

Testing

God has always tested his people. By testing, God searches the heart, promotes his cause and refines the faith of his people. Even Abraham, the father of the faithful, was disciplined in this manner. The narrative of Genesis 22 begins with the simple but profound statement: "Some time later God tested Abraham." This was God's act — he decided to test Abraham's faith. He commanded Abraham to sacrifice the son of promise, his only son, Isaac (cf. Hebrews

11:17-19). It was a test to see if Abraham loved his son more than he loved God. Would Abraham seek his own means of fathering a nation or would he bow before God's agenda in submissive trust? Unlike Adam and Eve in the Garden, Abraham loved God more than he loved his own autonomy. Abraham chose God over his son. God's response was to commend Abraham's faith (Genesis 22:12).

Throughout its history, God often put Israel to the test. We not only find these tests in God's grand design for the history of his people (cf. Exodus 15:25), but also in their daily lives. For example, God provided manna for the people in the wilderness and gave specific instructions regarding its collection. "In this way," God says, "I will test them and see whether they will follow my instructions" (Exodus 16:4). Consequently, Israel went through a daily test — will they follow God's instructions or will they not? Will they hoard food to themselves or will they trust God's daily provision and take only what they need? His instructions, therefore, functioned in a way similar to that of the tree of the knowledge of good and evil in the Garden. They require a choice — will Israel seek God's presence and obey his instructions, or will they seek their own autonomy and reject God's presence? In this way, God's instructions test his people. They unveil the submissive heart.

God tests his people in order to know their hearts (cf. Deuteronomy 8:2; 13:3; Judges. 2:22; 3:4; 2 Chronicles 32:31). After God's testing of Abraham, God concluded: "Now I know that you fear God" (Genesis 22:12). In a similar way, God tests his people to reveal whether their hearts truly desire communion with him.

This is a key motif in Deuteronomy. While Israel wandered in the wilderness as a punishment for their rebellion (cf. Deuteronomy 4:26), it was also a discipline, a testing, for those who would eventually enter Canaan. The wandering was a punishment for those who died, but in Deuteronomy their children stand on the banks of the Jordan ready to cross. They too suffered through that wilderness wandering. Why did the children of these sinners suffer for the sins of the parents? Deuteronomy 8:2-5 provides an answer:

> Remember how the LORD your God led you all the way in the desert these forty years, to humble you and to test you in order to know what was in your heart, whether or not you would keep his commands. He humbled you, causing you to hunger and then feeding you with manna, which neither you nor your fathers had known, to teach you that man does not live on bread alone but on every word that comes from the mouth of the LORD. Your clothes did not wear out and your feet did not swell during these forty years. Know then in your heart that as a man disciplines his son, so the LORD your God disciplines you.

The wilderness wandering had a disciplinary purpose. He tested them to see if they had a heart to obey him. He taught them to depend upon him rather than upon their own strength. He taught them to live by the word of God rather than by bread alone. God humbled them so that he could test them, and God's intent was redemptive. God tested them so that in the end he could do "good" for them (Deuteronomy 8:16, NRSV). Through his discipline, God prepared his people for their inheritance. The discipline refined them so that they might remember that the Lord is God when they finally entered the promised land (cf. Deuteronomy 11:1-2).

God continued the testing of his people throughout their history. Judges 2 describes the cycle of rebellion and repentance which characterized Israel during the times of the Judges. The cycle runs something like this: Israel would fall into sin, God would discipline them through various means, the people would plead for help, God would raise up a judge, the people would repent and God would deliver them (Judges 2:10-19). In this context, God used the Canaanites who remained in the land to "test Israel and see whether they will keep the way of the LORD and walk in it as their forefathers did" (Judges 2:22; cf. 3:1,4). God would sometimes act "against" Israel (Judges 2:15) in order to "test" their faithfulness. God used their fallen circumstance, that is, the fact that they did not do what God commanded in exterminating the Canaanites, to test them. God uses fallenness to test the hearts of his people.

In the years preceding the Babylonian exile, God sent Jeremiah among his people as one who would test their hearts. It was a testing, however, that the people of Judah would miserably fail. Before God punished Judah, he decided to test them. He wanted to refine them rather than reject them. But God warned Jeremiah that the testing would turn out badly (6:27-30):

> I have made you a tester of metals
>   and my people the ore,
> that you may observe
>   and test their ways.
> They are all hardened rebels,
>   going about to slander.
> They are bronze and iron;
>   they all act corruptly.
> The bellows blow fiercely
>   to burn away the lead with fire,
> but the refining goes on in vain;
>   the wicked are not purged out.
> They are called rejected silver,
>   because the LORD has rejected them.

Jeremiah's message was a test for the people of Judah, but their hearts were already hard. They would not listen. Yet God continued to test. He told Jeremiah at another point, "I will refine and test them, for what else can I do because of the sin of my people?" But eventually God "will make Jerusalem a heap of ruins." After all, the Lord declared, "Should I not punish them for this?" (Jeremiah 9:7,11,9).

God also tested individuals in this manner. Hezekiah is a classic example. Previously God had struck Hezekiah with an illness because of his pride, but had delivered him from death in response to his prayer of faith (2 Kings 20:1-11; 2 Chronicles 32:24-26). After Hezekiah was cured, he received some envoys from Babylon who had heard about his healing. Hezekiah showed his guests everything in his kingdom (2 Kings 20:12-15). The Chronicler says that in this situation "God left him to test him and to know everything that was in his heart" (2 Chronicles 32:31). But Hezekiah's heart was filled with pride, and God predicted that one day the Babylonians would return only to take this wealth back to Babylon (2 Kings 20:16-19). Hezekiah failed the test.

God desires fellowship with those who reciprocate his love, who seek his communion, and trust in his promises. Consequently, God is always active in the world to test hearts. God tries the hearts of people (Jeremiah 11:20; 12:3; 17:10; Psalm 7:9; 11:4-5; 1 Chronicles 29:17). He tests them to see whether or not they truly seek his communion or their own autonomy. God tests in order to know the hearts of his people. God tests for the same reason he put the tree of the knowledge of good and evil in the Garden. In the test we discover what we love the most — God or ourselves.

Education

The classic text for God's pedagogical purposes in discipline is Hebrews 12 (the Greek verbs and nouns for discipline are used eight times in verses 5-11). The writer of Hebrews applies an Old Testament principle of discipline to the situation in which his readers find themselves. The Old Testament principles of discipline are applicable to New Testament saints. The writer anticipates that his readers will face another period of persecution as in the earlier days of their faith. He calls them to remember those early days when they "stood [their] ground in a great contest in the face of suffering" (Hebrews 10:32). They were publicly insulted and persecuted. Some were thrown in prison and others suffered the confiscation of their property (Hebrews

10:33-34). The believers persevered then, and now they must expect another contest of suffering (Hebrews 12:4).

Whatever the nature of this coming struggle, the writer interprets it. It does not come as some punishment for sin, nor does it come because God is angry with his people. Rather, it is a discipline that arises out of God's love (Hebrews 12: 7-10). The writer quotes Proverbs 3:11-12 as a "word of encouragement that address [them] as sons" (Hebrews 12:5b-6):

> My son, do not make light of the Lord's discipline,
>   and do not lose heart when he rebukes you,
> because the Lord disciplines those he loves,
>   and he punishes everyone he accepts as a son.

The term translated "punishes" literally means to "flog" (Jesus and his disciples were flogged; Matthew 10:17; 20:19; 23:34; Mark 10:34; Luke 18:33; John 19:1). Some of the previous witnesses mentioned in chapter eleven had suffered flogging (Hebrews 11:36). The readers could, perhaps, expect some of that themselves. The context here does not mean "punishment" as when God expresses his righteous judgment against a sinner, but rather refers to the pain that discipline often involves. God chastises his people; he afflicts them with pain for the sake of a higher goal. "Rebuke" is a similar idea. This rebuke does not arise out of anger, but out of a desire for God's people to reach a higher level of maturity. God disciplines his people in view of that goal. He intends to perfect his people in preparation for and as a means to eschatological communion.

The readers, therefore, should not misinterpret this new wave of persecution as a sign of God's anger. It is a sign of his fatherly love. God trains his people through this pain. He educates his people so that they are equipped to share his holiness and communion. In order to persevere through the struggle, believers need to keep their eye on the goal to which God has called them. This is the example of Jesus who models endurance. Jesus endured the cross with all its shame in order to experience the joy that was set before him, and even now he sits at the right hand of God (Hebrews 12:2). Likewise, all the faithful who have gone before witness to the power of faith. Though their faith did not receive what it hoped for in this life, nevertheless it persevered because they sought a city whose builder and maker is God (Hebrews 11:13-16,39-40; 12:1). God used struggle in their life to strengthen their faith so that it might persevere.

It is important to see God's intent here. God disciplines and he chastises (causes pain, even flogs) for a reason. The author writes (Hebrews 12:10b-11):

> God disciplines us for our good, that we may share in his holiness. No discipline seems pleasant at the time, but painful. Later on, however, it produces a harvest of righteousness and peace for those who have been trained by it.

What good does God intend in discipline? He intends that we share his holiness. The discipline trains us in such a way that it produces righteousness and peace, and the effect of this discipline is that we share God's holiness. God uses suffering and pain to produce a fruit whose purpose is communion with him.

What does it mean to share God's holiness? It certainly includes the cultivation of fruit so that when the harvest of righteousness and peace is produced, we reflect God's holiness. But there is more since "without holiness no one will see the Lord" (Hebrews 12:14). There is an eschatological dimension. Holiness is required to enter into the eschatological presence of God. We are sanctified by the blood of Christ as we persevere in faith (cf. Hebrews 10:14). If perseverance means to endure suffering for the sake of the joy set before us, that is, the joy of God's presence, then suffering is worth the goal. God uses suffering and pain — he disciplines us — in order to bring us closer to that goal. If Jesus suffered for the sake of the joy set before him, and the faithful of chapter eleven struggled for the sake of the promise, then the present people of God must expect to suffer as well. The goal of faith makes suffering worthwhile. If discipline is a means to the joy, then discipline should be endured for the sake of the joy. The joy, however, is no earthly paradise. It is communion with God and the anticipation of the eschatological city of God, the heavenly Jerusalem.

Just as the writer of Hebrews encouraged his readers to endure trials for the sake of discipline, so James encouraged his readers to "consider it pure joy . . . whenever you face trials of many kinds, because you know that the testing of your faith develops perseverance" (James 1:2-3). And James also encouraged the one who "perseveres under trial, because when he has stood the test, he will receive the crown of life that God has promised to those who love him" (James 1:12). The crown of life is worth the trials, and God disciplines us with that goal in mind. God acts, sometimes by inflicting pain, even floggings, to train and prepare us to share his holiness. God intends good even when it seems painful and senseless to us.

God's Redemptive Acts

With the exception of the eschatological exclusion from the presence of God (e.g., Hell), God's actions always have a redemptive intent. When God acted to deter Israel through various national disasters, his intent was redemptive. Discipline is occasioned by God's love for his people as a means of refining their faith, guiding their direction or awakening their hearts (cf. Haggai 1:5-14). It has a redemptive intent. He disciplines with a view toward creating a people for himself.

But God does not simply act to deter, test or educate. While all of God's acts have a redemptive intent, some of his acts are redemptive in character. God's redemptive acts are those moments when God acts to remove suffering, to overcome evil, and to destroy death. Those are the moments when God rescues, delivers, and restores his people.

While Christians understand God's act in Christ as the climactic redemptive event in the Bible because it reveals God's eschatological intent (that is, to destroy death), the Old Testament is filled with descriptions of God's redemptive acts which anticipate God's work in Christ. God acted redemptively when he called Abraham out of Ur of the Chaldeans and entered into a covenant with him to bless all nations (Genesis 12:1-3; 17:1-8). He acted redemptively when he sent Joseph ahead in order to preserve a remnant for himself (Genesis 45:7; Psalm 105:17). God acted redemptively when he delivered Israel from Egyptian bondage (Exodus 15). God acted redemptively when he raised up judges to destroy the enemies of Israel (Judges 2:18). God acted redemptively when he entered into a royal covenant with David that would ensure the messianic kingdom (2 Samuel 7:5-16). God acted redemptively when he sent his prophets again and again to warn his people (Jeremiah 7:25-26; Nehemiah 9:30). God acted redemptively when he returned Judah from Babylonian exile (Jeremiah 32:37-38). God acted redemptively when he sent Nehemiah and Ezra to rebuild the walls of Jerusalem and restore the nation's purity (Nehemiah 2:12; Ezra 7:6,28; 9:9).

The Old Testament is a history of redemption. But two redemptive events stand out as particularly significant. The first, the Exodus, is foundational and paradigmatic. The second, the return from Babylonian exile, is patterned after the first. In turn, both of these events provide the context in which Israel interprets God's redemptive work in their own lives.

The Exodus

In response to the cries of his people, God redeemed Israel from their Egyptian bondage (Exodus 3:7ff). The story of the Exodus is the story of God's redemptive love. God saw the misery of his people and heard their cries. God responded out of his compassion. The Exodus was God's redemptive act whereby he remembered his covenant with Abraham and redeemed his people from slavery (Exodus 2:23-24; 6:2-3).

God intended for his people to know him through the Exodus. When Pharaoh decreed that the Hebrews should collect their own straw, the Lord reassured Moses (Exodus 6:6-7):

> I am the LORD, and I will bring you out from under the yoke of the Egyptians. I will free you from being slaves to them, and I will redeem you with an outstretched arm and with mighty acts of judgment. I will take you as my own people, and I will be your God. Then you will know that I am the LORD your God, who brought you out from under the yoke of the Egyptians.

God revealed himself in the Exodus as the Lord, the God of Abraham, Isaac, and Jacob, and he offered himself for communion with his people. He sought them as a people and desired to be their God. The Exodus reveals God's intent to have a people.

However, the redemptive story of the Exodus is not only the story of God's compassion for his people. It is also the story of God's power over nature and the revelation of his glory to Pharaoh. God unleashed the chaos of nature through the plagues he sent upon Egypt. God redeemed Israel and punished Egypt. When God redeemed his people (Exodus 15:13-18), he also destroyed his enemies (Exodus 15:1-12). The psalmist recounts the history of God's work (Psalm 105:28-36):

> He sent darkness and made the land dark —
>   for had they not rebelled against his words?
> He turned their waters into blood,
>   causing their fish to die.
> Their land teemed with frogs,
>   which went up into the bedrooms of their rulers.

He spoke, and there came swarms of flies,
    and gnats throughout their country.
He turned their rain into hail,
    with lightning throughout the land;
he struck down their vines and fig trees
    and shattered the trees of their country.
He spoke, and the locusts came,
    grasshoppers without number;
they ate up every green thing in their land,
    ate up the produce of their soil.
Then he struck down all the firstborn in their land,
    the firstfruits of all their manhood.

The psalmist praises God for his redemptive work, including the punishment of Egypt. In order to redeem Israel he turned creation into chaos. He spoke and the locusts came. He spoke and flies swarmed over the land. He turned rain into hail and water into blood. He turned the day into night. And, as a parallel to the climatic event of creation, he turned life (procreation) into death when he took the firstborn of Egypt. God's good creation turned to chaos in order to punish Egypt. God redeemed Israel from slavery through the chaos of nature.

God was also active in the hearts and lives of people. God hardened Pharaoh's heart to accomplish his redemptive purpose for Israel. Exodus describes the hardening of Pharaoh's heart as both God's act (4:21; 7:3; 9:12; 10:1,20, 27; 11:10; 14:4,8) and Pharaoh's own act (7:13-14,22; 8:15,19,32; 9:7,34-35). God hardened Pharaoh's heart so that he might display his glory to Israel as well as to the Egyptians. At the same time Pharaoh's pride refused to submit to God's demands.

The story tells us exactly why God hardened Pharaoh's heart. He hardened it so that his miraculous signs might be the subject of discussion for generations to come within Israel — "that you may tell your children and grandchildren how I dealt harshly with the Egyptians" for the purpose that "you may know that I am the LORD" (Exodus 10:2).

God glorified himself through these miraculous signs and revealed his mighty presence in the world so that even the Egyptians would know that the Lord is God (Exodus 14:4,18). God hardened Pharaoh's heart "for this very purpose" that he might "show [his] power and that [his] name might be proclaimed in all the earth" (Exodus 9:16).

The story also tells us that Pharaoh hardened his own heart. Pharaoh refused to listen to Moses and Aaron. His pride would not submit to their demands (Exodus 8:15,32). Even when his own priests and magicians wanted to relent, his pride refused (Exodus 8:19). Whenever God relented and rescued Egypt from a plague, Pharaoh would harden his heart (Exodus 9:34). Pharaoh acted out of the motives of his own heart and in his pride he sinned.

How do we relate these two ideas? How can God harden Pharaoh's heart while Pharaoh hardens his own heart? While there is mystery here (e.g., how can God look into the future and know that he would so influence a heart that it would do his will?), there is also a simple explanation. God worked through the heart of Pharaoh to accomplish his redemptive intent, and Pharaoh's pride was a willing accomplice to God's actions. Pharaoh did exactly what he chose to do. He did what he wanted to do. God simply worked with Pharaoh's pride to accomplish his own end. God knows how to use a stubborn and prideful heart for his own purposes. Pharaoh responded to God's mighty deeds with more stubbornness, and this served God's redemptive goals.

But the bottom line here is the sovereignty of God. God will decide on whom he will have mercy and whose heart he will harden (Romans 9:18). Nevertheless, God's decisions are not arbitrary. He acts according to his redemptive intent. He has mercy on all those who approach him in faith and he rejects all those who through unbelief reject him (Romans 11:20,23). Pharaoh stumbled through unbelief and Israel was redeemed through faith. God seeks fellowship with all his creatures, but he excludes those who reject his offer of communion. Just as God hardened Pharaoh's heart, so he hardened the hearts of the Canaanites to wage war against Israel in order that Israel might exterminate them (Joshua 11:20). Just as God hardened Pharaoh's heart, so he hardened the hearts of the Jewish nation in order to bring in the fullness of the Gentiles (Romans 11:7-12; 11:25).

Whatever might be said about God's influence upon the heart of Pharaoh or the Canaanites, or the Jews in Paul's day, God accomplishes his purposes through the agency of human hearts. God is not only the Lord of nature who can turn order into disorder for the sake of his people, he is also the Lord of hearts who can accomplish his purposes through human decisions and actions. God turns hearts (1 Samuel 10:9; 1 Kings 18:37; Ezra 6:22; Psalm 105:25; Proverbs 21:1), hardens them (Deuteronomy 2:30; Isaiah 63:17; John 12:40; Romans 9:18), and opens them (Acts 16:14) according to his own purposes. Yet human beings are responsible for turning (Deuteronomy 30:17; 1 Kings 11:9; Jeremiah 5:23; 17:5; Hebrews 3:12), hardening (1 Samuel 6:6; 2 Chronicles 36:13; Hebrews 3:8,15; 4:7), and opening (2 Corinthians 6:13) their own hearts. God redeemed Israel through hardening the heart of a prideful Pharaoh, and yet Pharaoh was responsible for his own sinfulness. God gave Israel the land of Canaan by turning the hearts of the kings to wage war against Israel, but those kings were responsible for their own actions. God redeemed the Gentiles through hardening the hearts of a prideful Israel, but Israel was responsible for its own unbelief. No wonder Paul must ultimately bow before the mystery of God's works. All he can do is offer praise to the sovereign God (Romans 11:33-36):

> Oh, the depth of the riches of the wisdom and knowledge of God,
>> How unsearchable his judgments,
>> and his paths beyond tracing out!
> "Who has known the mind of the Lord?
>> Or who has been his counselor?"

"Who has ever given to God,
   that God should repay him?"
For from him and through him and to him are all things.
   To him be the glory forever! Amen.

The Return from Exile

The prophet Jeremiah interpreted the Babylonian exile as a punishment for Judah's sins. Jeremiah's "Temple Sermon" is an example of his rhetoric (7:1-8:3). Because Judah's lifestyle did not reflect God's holy presence in the temple (7:5-6,9), God determined to thrust them from his "presence" just as he did the northern Kingdom (7:15). Therefore God says, "my anger and my wrath will be poured out on this place, on man and beast, on the trees of the field and on the fruit of the ground" (7:20). God will create a "desolation" where once there was joy, fruitfulness and life (7:34). God's punishment for sin is death, exile, and a chaotic nature. "Because of your great guilt and many sins," the Lord declares, "I have done these things to you" (Jeremiah 30:15).

However, as we saw with Amos, God still yearns for communion with his people. Even in their sin, God mourns for his people and out of his love desires a remnant who will again share his presence. While God will not let their sin "go entirely unpunished," neither will he completely destroy his people as he does other nations (Jeremiah 30:11; also Hosea 11:8-11). God has determined to "restore the fortunes of Jacob's tents and have compassion on his dwellings" (30:18). Even though Ephraim and Judah have rebelled and God has punished them, God yet "yearns" for them (Jeremiah 31:20). God loves his people with an "everlasting love" (Jeremiah 31:3). Consequently, he has purposed to raise up a leader who will "devote himself to be close" to the Lord so that God might accomplish his eternal intent, as the Lord declares, "so you will be my people, and I will be your God" (Jeremiah 30:21-22). God will "fully [accomplish] the purposes of his heart" (Jeremiah 30:23-24).

Out of his eternal love, then, God redeems Judah from Babylonian bondage. He punished Babylon and destroyed them with his own might. He removed the chaos of nature and restored the fruitfulness of their land. He re-created his people. He redeemed the fallen, re-created what was desolate, and renewed communion with his people. As a result, he will glorify his name in all the earth because all the nations on the earth will hear of this work (Jeremiah 33:9).

Isaiah 40–48 describes this redemption. God prepared a way in the wilderness which leads from Babylon back to Zion (Isaiah 40:3-5). The Creator God created a path of redemption. The God of the Exodus will once again act to redeem his people from bondage (Isaiah 40). The focal point of this lengthy section is God's determination both to destroy Babylon and redeem his people through the actions of Cyrus the Great, king of Persia. God "stirred up" the heart of the Persian King (2 Chronicles 36:22, NRSV) and handed the nations over to him. But Cyrus will not accomplish this great feat. It is not his initiative and neither can he take credit. "Who has done this and carried it through, calling forth the generations from the beginning?" asks God. "I, the LORD — with the first of them and with the last — I am he," he answers (Isaiah 41:2-4).

Isaiah's message to exiled Judah is that God has chosen a servant to redeem them. But they must not mistake this changing of the guard from Babylon to Persia as merely the random course of history. Rather, it is God's work. God says of Jerusalem, "It shall be inhabited," even as Cyrus says of Jerusalem, "Let it be rebuilt." God says of Cyrus, "He is my shepherd and [he] will accomplish all that I please" (Isaiah 44:26-28). God has taken Cyrus by the hand and subdued the "nations before him," and stripped "kings of their armor" (Isaiah 45:1). God has stirred up the heart of Cyrus to accomplish his purpose (Jeremiah 51:1,11). God fulfills his promise through Cyrus. "I will raise up Cyrus in my righteousness," the Lord declares, and "I will make all his ways straight" (Isaiah 45:13).

Through Cyrus God will glorify himself among the nations. "Which of the idols has foretold these things?" the Lord asks. "The LORD's chosen ally will carry out his purpose against Babylon . . . . I will bring him, and he will succeed in his mission" (Isaiah 48:14-15). God will announce his glory to the world. He will not yield his glory to another (Isaiah 48:11). He will not permit Babylon to credit their victories to their own gods, astrologers, and stars. In its arrogance Babylon said, "I will continue forever — the eternal queen." It said about itself, "I am, and there is none besides me" (Isaiah 47:7-8,10). Consequently, God will create a disaster for it. "Disaster will come upon you, and you will not know how to conjure it away," the Lord declares (Isaiah 47:11). Just as it had trusted in its own wickedness, so God would send wickedness upon it (Isaiah 47:10-11 — "wickedness" in verse 10 is the same word for "disaster" in verse 11). God himself will create the evil (disaster) that will come upon Babylon (Isaiah 45:7). The Lord God of Israel is alone God. He is the one who has planned the destruction of Babylon for his own glory (Isaiah 46:8-11) and for the sake of his people. God will not tolerate arrogance and he will not permit his glory to be given to another. He will not permit idols to receive the glory that is due him.

Further, not only has God anointed Cyrus to destroy Babylon (Jeremiah 51:11), he has also anointed him to carry out his decree to inhabit Jerusalem. The decree to rebuild Jerusalem is God's decree, but it is given through Cyrus (Isaiah 44:24-45:7). Even though Cyrus does not acknowledge the Lord as God, nevertheless God has summoned him by name to carry out his purposes. Cyrus will do the Lord's bidding without knowing that the Lord empowers him. The Lord not only stirs the heart of Cyrus to destroy Babylon, he also stirs his heart to carry out Judah's restoration: "In the first year of Cyrus king of Persia, in order to fulfill the word of the LORD spoken by

Jeremiah, the LORD moved the heart of Cyrus king of Persia to make a proclamation throughout his realm" (Ezra 1:1; cf. 6:22; 7:27).

God, therefore, redeemed his people through the agency of the Persian king Cyrus. God defeats the gods of Babylon by raising up another nation, and he releases his people through the decrees of a pagan king. Somehow, in some way, God accomplishes these redemptive acts by Cyrus. Just as God used Babylon to punish Judah, so God used Persia to punish Babylon. It is the Lord God of Israel who has done these things and no one, not even Cyrus, should steal his glory.

Further, as God brings his people back to his land and his temple, he promises to renew his creation. When God punished Judah, he turned their land into chaos, a desolate wasteland. Now, as God redeems his people, he renews the land and re-creates its prosperity and fruitfulness. The same Jeremiah who proclaimed Judah's land a desolation (Jeremiah 4:23-26) now promises that the land will be redeemed as well as the people (Jeremiah 33:12-13):

> In this place, desolate and without men or animals —
> in all its towns there will again be pastures for shep-
> herds to rest their flocks. In the towns of the hill coun-
> try, of the western foothills and of the Negev, in the
> territory of Benjamin, in the villages around Jerusalem
> and in the towns of Judah, flocks will again pass under
> the hand of the one who counts them.

God will again bring prosperity and peace to his people (Jeremiah 33:9), and they will again plant vineyards whose fruit they will enjoy (Jeremiah 31:5). God will renew his creation, remove the curse, and overrule the chaos as his people seek him. In his redemption, "the LORD will create a new thing on earth" (Jeremiah 31:22). God has heard the mourning of his people and he has responded with redemption (Jeremiah 31:18-19).

God punished Israel, but in his compassion he redeemed a remnant. The remnant sought God in their exile, and God responded to their prayer. God will be found by those who seek him (Isaiah 55:6). Redemption flows out of God's great love whereby he seeks to share his communion with his people. God yearns for a people and he acts in the world to create a people for himself. Consequently, a time is coming, Jeremiah prophesies, when God will enter into a new covenant with Israel and Judah where, the Lord says, "I will be their God, and they will be my people" (Jeremiah 31:33b). The New Testament finds the ultimate fulfillment of that promise in the redemptive work of Jesus Christ (Hebrews 8:7-13; 10:15-18), but that is a story for another chapter.

Psalm 107

Psalm 107 is the last in a series of psalms (104–107) that proclaim God's mighty deeds. They are Psalms of praise which rejoice in the works of God. Psalm 104 recounts the works of God within his creation. Psalm 105 recounts the history of God's redemptive work in the Exodus. Psalm 106 recounts God's redemptive work from the Exodus to Israel's return from Babylonian exile. These three psalms, then, recount the history of creation, fall, and redemption in the life of Israel. They retell the story of Israel in poetic epics.

Psalms 105 and 106 offer a poetic pattern for God's redemptive work. Psalm 107 applies this redemptive pattern to the personal lives of God's people. Just as God responded to the cries of his people in Egypt and in the exile (Psalm 106:44-45), so God listens to the cries of his people in their personal crises. God's mighty works in redemptive history provide the pattern of God's works in the lives of his people. They know God hears them because he has always acted to redeem his people and he has demonstrated that he is the Lord Almighty who remembers his covenant.

Psalm 107, then, is a praise offered to God for his wonderful deeds in the personal crises of his people. It is a celebration of God's redemptive interventions. The Lord God not only acts at a national level, he also cares for his people as individuals. The psalm is a call for God's people to recognize God's "wonderful deeds" for his people and to give thanks "for his unfailing love" (Psalm 107:8). This is the refrain that is repeated throughout the Psalm (107:8,15, 21,31). The people of God must recognize that their God delivers them from their troubles and acts redemptively in their lives. He "satisfies the thirsty and fills the hungry with good things" (Psalm 107:9). He releases prisoners and saves those who cry to the Lord in their trouble (Psalm 107:10, 13-14). He saves his people from fatal sicknesses (Psalm 107:18-19). He controls the natural chaos which threatens human life (Psalm 107:23-30). He turns chaos into a fruitful land (Psalm 107:35-40). He lifts the needy out of their affliction (Psalm 107:41). Mays summarizes the importance of this psalm when he notes that these examples of redemption are:

> really open paradigms of deliverance into which any and all who have benefited from God's saving work can enter. Hunger and thirst, darkness and gloom, sin and affliction, storm and sea all belong to the general symbolic vocabulary with which the redeemed portray the trouble from which they have been saved. The psalm as a whole is the great summary song of thanksgiving for salvation by all the redeemed.[12]

God's people respond by praising him for his redemptive work — not only in the Exodus and in the exile, but also in their daily joys. They praise him with their thank offerings and by testifying to God's gracious work in their lives (Psalm 107:22). They stand in the assembly of God's people and exalt God's name (Psalm 107:32). The psalm reflects the function of *shalom* (peace, fellowship) offerings in the Old Testament (cf. Leviticus 3, 7) where individuals would come before God in order to express their gratitude through sacrifice, eat a meal in his presence (Deuteronomy 27:7), and testify to God's work before the assembly of his people (Psalm 40:9,10). Our worship, then, is not only rooted in God's mighty deeds in redemptive history, but it is also rooted in God's redemptive work in the lives of individual believers. We worship a living God who is not simply satisfied to testify to himself in past history, but is also active in the lives of his people to rescue, cure, and satisfy in the present. God's love for his people means that he remains active in their lives. Consequently, the psalmist concludes with a call for perceptive application (Psalm 107:43): "Whoever is wise, let him heed these things and consider the great love of the LORD." God's redemptive acts continue because his great love continues.

Conclusion

According to Scripture, God is active in his world. He punishes evil, deters wicked intentions, tests the righteous, trains his children, and redeems his people. God is no mere spectator. God is a player. He is at once sovereign over the world and working in it. God acts in his own freedom and by his own will according to his own purposes.

God's actions have a purpose. Nothing is arbitrary with him. He permits evil in the world, and he uses it to punish, deter, test, and educate. But he also acts to punish, deter, test, educate, and, most importantly, to redeem. What God seeks is holy fellowship with his people. Everything God does is related to that single desire and intent. God acts to accomplish his eschatological purpose — to have a people who are his own.

Consequently, the people of God trust in God's sovereignty. We know that God does whatever he pleases (Psalm 115:3), and he controls the world through his permission and actions. God is in control. Not even evil can overrule his purposes. God is sovereign over evil. He will, we trust, permit and do only what serves his eschatological goal. As a result, even when our circumstances seem dire and meaningless, we trust that God has some reason for his permission or some rationale for his action that is rooted in his eternal love for us.

---

[1] Piper, *Desiring God*, p. 11, n. 4.

[2] Wolfhart Pannenberg, *What Is Man?* trans. Duane A. Priebe (Philadelphia: Fortress, 1970). Grenz, *Community*, pp. 169-173, provides a good summary of this perspective upon which I am dependent.

[3] Augustine, *Confessions*, 1.1.

[4] It was a significant moment in my life when I grasped this point. I am indebted to Philip Yancey, "When the Facts Don't Add Up," *Christianity Today* 30 (June 13, 1986), 19, who first raised it for me.

[5] Paul Feinberg, *Deceived by God?* (Wheaton, IL: Victor Books, 1997), pp. 85-93, discusses these themes in a perceptive way.

[6] Cf. Jack Cottrell, *What the Bible Says about God the Redeemer* (Joplin, MO: College Press, 1987), pp. 175-400 and Bloesch, *God the Almighty*, pp. 137-165.

[7] On the problem of the annihilation of the Canaanites, see the classic essay by William B. Green, Jr., "The Ethics of the Old Testament," in *Classical Evangelical Essays in Old Testament Interpretation*, ed. Walter C. Kaiser, Jr. (Grand Rapids: Baker, 1972), pp. 207-235; and more recently, J.P.U. Lilley, "The Judgement of God: The Problem of the Canaanites," *Themelios* 22 (January 1997): 3-12.

[8] The most prominent has been John Hick, *Evil and the God of Love*, rev. ed. (New York: Harper & Row, 1978). See also Austin Farrer, *Love Almighty and Ills Unlimited* (Garden City, NY: Doubleday, 1961); S. Paul Schilling, *God and Human Anguish* (Nashville: Abingdon, 1977); and Thomas B. Warren, "God and Evil: Does Judeo-Christian Theism Involve a Logical Contradiction?" (Ph.D. dissertation, Vanderbilt University, 1970). Warren's dissertation was published as *Sin, Suffering and God* (Jonesboro, AR: National Christian Press, 1980), and a popular version was published as *Have Atheists Proved There Is No God?* (Jonesboro, AR: National Christian Press, 1972). For a well-reasoned response to this position, see Douglas R. Geivett, *Evil and the Evidence for God: The Challenge of John Hick's Theodicy* (Philadelphia: Temple University Press, 1993).

[9] John W. Wenham, *The Enigma of Evil: Can We Believe in the Goodness of God?* (Grand Rapids: Zondervan, 1985), pp. 50-88.

[10] G.C. Berkouwer, *Sin*, Studies in Dogmatics, trans. Philip C. Holtrop (Grand Rapids: Eerdmans, 1971), p. 371.

[11]Cottrell, *God the Redeemer*, p. 375.

[12]James Luther Mays, *Psalms*, Interpretation (Louisville, KY: John Knox Press, 1994), p. 346.

Chapter Six

How Does Faith Endure?
Job in God's Story

> *What is man that you make so much of him,*
> *that you give him so much attention,*
> *that you examine him every morning*
> *and test him every moment?*
> *Will you never look away from me,*
> *or let me alone even for an instant?*
> *If I have sinned, what have I done to you,*
> *O watcher of men?*
> *Why have you made me your target?*
> *Have I become a burden to you?*
> *Why do you not pardon my offenses*
> *and forgive my sins?*
> *For I will soon lie down in the dust;*
> *you will search for me, but I will be no more.*
> *Job to God, Job 7:17-21*

While all suffering is relative (the death of a loved one hurts more than the loss of a job; or, perhaps it is better to say that it is a different kind of hurt), the endurance of suffering levels all suffering to the same plane. The suffering that is most painful is the present one. Though we may distinguish between different kinds of suffering, the pain is emotionally and spiritually indistinguishable. The questions we all ask, the doubts we all ponder, are the same ones — no matter what the suffering.

They are also the questions and doubts of Job. Consequently, righteous Job teaches us about endurance. As we watch Job, we watch a person who passed the test. As a result, we learn something about faith. We see one whom we can emulate.

Job's trial was a struggle of faith. He blazed a trail of faith, but it was no effortless task. Job is the story of a believer who struggles with his questions, doubts, and despair. His persistent refusal to curse God is an example of faith. His trial is the trial of all believers. His victory is the victory of all believers. Therefore, it is important to watch him struggle in order to learn something about the nature of faith. The story of Job discloses the nature of faith and lament as well as our relationship with God in a fallen world.

Job addressed his questions to God. He asked the one who controls nature. As a result, the question "why" is a real and legitimate one. It is no mere emotional outburst nor venting of frustration. The question is genuine and meaningful. If God acts, if he permits, if he causes, God must have a reason. God does not act arbitrarily. Consequently, like Job, we ask, "Why?"

For some "Why?" is more an exclamation than a question. It is a declaration: "What a senseless and meaningless thing to happen!" For Job, "Why?" is a real question for the sovereign God. While it is an exclamation, it also asks, "Why has God done this?" It asks, "Why did God permit or cause such a senseless and meaningless thing to happen?" It asks, "What is the meaning of this suffering?"

Job as Faithful Lamenter

In his opening lament (3:1-26) Job does not directly address his friends or God as he does in the ensuing dialogue. Yet it is for the benefit of both. Job vents his despair. His poetic complaint implicitly addresses God.[1]

Job laments that he was not stillborn (3:1-8). The day of his birth should have never dawned. It has become to him a day without joy (3:7). Even though his mother carried him to term, it would have been better to have been stillborn than to suffer the present trouble (3:9-10). Job wants to die since in the grave he can rest. "There," Job says, "the weary are at rest" (3:17). Exiles can enjoy release from captivity in the grave, and slaves can enjoy freedom from their masters (3:18-19). But God continues to give light to those, like Job, who are miserable. Job will rejoice at death (3:20-22) because it will be a release from suffering. He asks, "Why is life given to a man whose way is hidden, whom God has hedged in?" (3:23). Life has nothing more to offer Job. He has "no peace, no quietness" and "no rest, but only turmoil" (3:26). His only resolution is death. Only there can he find peace and rest. From the vantage point of the trash heap, it would have been better had he never seen life than to have suffered as he has. Job reverses the saying, "It is better to have loved and lost than never to have loved at all." Job believes it is better to never have loved than to have loved and lost. This is the depth of Job's grief.

The attitude of complaint is clear in the constant questioning. The most significant and expressive word for any sufferer is repeated five times (NIV, NRSV) in this short lament.[2] It is the word "why." "*Why* did I not perish at birth?" (3:11a). "*Why* were there knees to receive me and breasts that I might be nursed?" (3:12). "*Why* was I not hidden in the ground like a stillborn child?" (3:16a). "*Why* is light given to those in misery, and life to the bitter of soul?" (3:20). "*Why* is life given to a man whose way is hidden, whom God has hedged in?" (3:23). Job equates life with misery and bitterness. Since the womb did not shut its doors, "trouble" is now before his eyes (3:10,20). Death and darkness in Sheol (grave) are better than misery and trouble.

Job asks a real question. He wants to know "why," and he knows that God has the answer. Job's question is the lament of a despairing person — one who believes death is better than his troubled existence. "My eyes will never see happiness again," he laments (7:7). Death is Job's best prospect. Yet death does not come (3:21).

In a twist of irony, Job believes that God has "hedged" him in (3:23) when, in fact, God has simply constricted the "hedge" that protected him (1:10).[3] The nature of the hedge depends on one's perspective. For Job, God has come crashing down on him. This is the perspective of every sufferer. He is right, of course, in that God does bear responsibility for his condition. The prologue sees God's hedge as his protection. Satan is restricted. God has hedged Job's life — he will not permit Satan to take it. But from Job's perspective that is no protection at all. Rather, it prolongs the suffering. Ironically, Job wants even that hedge removed. Job wants relief. He wants death. Yet that is the very thing that God will not permit. The very hedge which God has around Job is the thing Job wants removed. Job, consequently, is frustrated, troubled, and grieved.

Job's lament reflects his present suffering. He expresses his pain, disillusionment, and hopelessness. Sufferers wonder "why" they suffer. They think about how it used to be, and whether it was worth being born at all. They think about how death — as horrible as death is — would be better than what they presently feel. There is no quiet rest for the sufferer in the moment of suffering. As believers sit on the trash heap, their only response is faithful lament which waits for God to speak comfort.

The Problem: The Unfairness of Suffering

Job knows he is innocent. He also knows that God's hand has done this. The problem is fairness. God does not seem to be playing by his own rules. Job's friends could draw the conclusion that Job is an arrogant hypocrite. The friends think that God is punishing Job for his sins, but Job knows better. He cannot succumb to such a simplistic answer. To do so would deny his own integrity.

As readers, we understand Job's problem. Job knows, and we know, his integrity. He is God's righteous servant (1:1,8; 2:3). Yet he suffers the fate of the wicked. He has no option but to wonder about God's fairness. He cannot dismiss what has happened to him as mere coincidences or "bad luck." He cannot believe God was totally uninvolved. But neither can he deny his own integrity. He wonders about the "evil" that has come upon him when such trouble only belongs to the wicked. After all, it is the "fate" of the wicked that he now suffers (27:13). Job has tradition behind him: people reap what they sow. Yet either his traditional interpretation of that principle or his traditional understanding of God must be adjusted. In the midst of his suffering, it is difficult for him to adjust either. Consequently, his faith leads him to lament rather than to precise theological diatribes. It evokes lamentation rather than sophisticated theological discussion.

Job initially asks the question that all sufferers ask: "Why?" The question arises out of intense agony and disillusionment. All sufferers can empathize. The question gropes for meaning. Job thinks, as do we, that knowing why will lessen the pain and provide the motivation for endurance. That is part of his disillusionment. Is there really any finite reason which can justify the suffering that Job endures? Is there any human reason that can make sense of the death of his children? Job can see no good reason. As a result, he questions. If the end of his life is this kind of suffering, Job asks "why" he was even brought out of the womb (10:18)? If this is the nature of his suffering, he wants to know "why" God has made him a target for his arrows (7:20)? If he is innocent and does not deserve this suffering, Job wants to know "why" God has become his enemy (13:24)? The question "why" underscores the perplexity that Job feels. He is bewildered. He is a righteous person who is suffering terribly. If he could just know why, if he could just know the reason, then perhaps he could understand and endure the burden. But his ignorance generates confusion and disillusionment.

His constant questioning of God receives no answer except the stinging attacks of his would-be comforters. They know why — Job has committed some great sin. But Job cannot accept that answer. He knows differently. Yet he receives no answer from the one to whom he has addressed the question. God does not reply. He is silent, and this increases Job's frustration. Job becomes impatient, and his questions become bitter complaints.

In response to Eliphaz, he adamantly roars that he will not sit in meek silence. Job cries, "I will not keep silent; I will speak out in the anguish of my spirit, I will complain in the bitterness of my soul" (7:11). When Bildad asserts that God does not reject a blameless person but punishes the wicked (8:20), Job's deeply felt questions become frustrating affirmations. He responds, "I loathe my very life; therefore I will give free rein to my complaint and speak out in the bitterness of my soul" (10:1). When Eliphaz holds out the hope of restoration after repentance (22:22-30), Job will not relent and give up the only thing he has left — his integrity. He asserts, "Even today my complaint is bitter" (23:2a).

In these three texts (7:11; 10:1; 23:2) where "complaint" and "bitterness" are combined to express Job's feelings (the only places in the Hebrew canon where they occur together), Job vents his frustration. As he rethinks his relationship with God, his only resort is to lodge a complaint against him. This complaint is shrouded in bitterness. To "forget" the complaint does not rid him of the suffering (9:27,28). He would gladly give up the complaint if God would only relieve him of the suffering, or at least explain it. But the pain combined with God's silence pushes him to press his complaint even further.

Job finally begins to accuse God of injustice. Is it really fair that Job should suffer this way? What reason could

God give that would justify this treatment? Since Job cannot avoid the question "Why?" and he can see no good reason for the suffering, he can only struggle with the impossible thought that God is unjust. He questions God's fairness. Of course, Job knows better than to call God's justice into question, but from the vantage point of the trash heap Job can fathom no other alternative. He agrees with Bildad who asks the rhetorical questions, "Does God pervert justice? Does the Almighty pervert what is right?" (8:3). No, he does not. Job agrees. But Job is confused. He is righteous but he is suffering. Job must think the unthinkable. Is it possible that God is unjust and is amusing himself with the misery and confusion of his creatures? Where is the God of justice in the suffering of Job?

Job realizes that he cannot dismantle the justice of God. God is "not a man like me that I might answer him, that we might confront each other in court" (9:32). If Job wishes to question God about his justice, "who will summon him" (9:19)? Who will justify himself before the Pure One and dispute his justice (14:3,4a)? The answer is, "No one!" (14:4b). Yet, despite Job's theological recognition that he is no match for the Almighty, his suffering drives him to vent his frustration and his anger by raising unthinkable questions. These are the questions no one dares to ask, but which everyone does ask.

In chapter nineteen Job becomes particularly frustrated with both his friends and with God. He accuses his friends of betrayal. In this painful explosion, he expresses his disappointment (19:5-7):

> If indeed you would exalt yourselves above me
>> and use my humiliation against me,
> then know that God has wronged me
>> and drawn his net around me.
> Though I cry, "I've been wronged!" I get no response;
>> though I call for help, there is no justice.

Here Job is responding to Bildad's question, "Does God pervert justice?" (8:3). Job responds that God has "wronged" him so that he receives no "justice." The verb "wronged" (translated "pervert" in 8:3) and the noun "justice" are the same terms Bildad used. Given his experience, Job knows that Bildad is wrong. God's justice does not mean that only the wicked suffer. Job himself is an innocent sufferer.

"There is no justice" rings in the ears of all sufferers. Everyone can empathize with this exclamation. We have felt it even if we have not voiced it as boldly as Job does here. Job, like all of us, sees a serious problem with the justice of God in relation to innocent suffering. His experience affirms what he knows is theologically impossible. The existential moment of the sufferer is a far more powerful thing than the intellectual reflection of happier times. In this context, and as the dialogue reaches a climax, Job, in the framework of an oath, emphatically states that God "has denied me justice" (27:2).

The sufferer, and Job is a primary example, can see no good reason for his suffering. Where he can find a good reason, there he would acknowledge God's hand as punishment or discipline, or even redemption. But finding good reasons is rarely achieved in the moment of suffering. We may find it in hindsight, but even then a good reason is often elusive, and rarely found. There are some things, many things, which seemingly defy any hope of finding "good reasons." The moment of suffering, however, cannot discern them even if they are there. The natural frustration of the believer, then, is vented in complaint to God. Even righteous Job could not escape those feelings. In the moment of pain, in the heat of the dialogue, Job sees no alternative other than to conclude that God has denied him justice.

The different literary genres within the speeches by Job reflect this bewildered orientation. Not only does Job lament, but he enters into a polemical or controversial dialogue with his friends and with God, in which he argues for his own vindication.[4] He is righteous. His suffering, he insists, is undeserved. These protestations are particularly seen in his assertions or "asseverations" of innocence (cf. 6:28-30; 16:17; 23:10-12; 27:2-6),[5] an innocence which God himself verified in the prologue (cf. 1:1,8; 2:3). Such protestations lead him to utilize another genre in his speeches: the legal metaphor. It is particularly important in Job's climactic speech in chapter 31. Job's last words to God prior to God's speeches (38–41) are legal in character. He prosecutes a lawsuit against God and asks God to explain his justice. Job seeks a trial in which God would give his list of particulars — where God would hand down the indictments (cf. Job 31:35-37).

Job's first question is "Why?" His second question is "Is it fair?" His questions were accompanied with pleas and requests. Finally, his pleas became demands. He demands an audience with God himself. He wanted a list of charges and a trial to vindicate him.

The Legal Metaphor: Innocence Affirmed[6]

Job, in fact, was already on trial. Köhler has suggested that the whole dialogue (Job 3–27) exhibits the formal proceedings of a legal assembly at the gates.[7] It is as if the city elders are debating the righteousness of Job. Wisdom clearly distinguishes the consequences of righteous and wicked living. Their evidence is what God has done to Job. The three friends and others who are nearby (like Elihu in chapters 32–37) are engaged in a grand legal discussion which is tailored to answer one question: Why has Job suffered so much? The legal argument proceeds along these lines: (1) Only the wicked suffer the loss of their children (among other things); and (2) Job has lost his children (among other things); (3) therefore, Job is one of the wicked. The friends conclude that Job must have done something to anger God. Job, armed only with his own integrity, seeks to rebut the charge.

Satan's accusation was continued by his own friends. Job is fed up with his friends, and he knows his only recourse is to present his case to God. He tells his friends, "What you know, I also know; I am not inferior to you. But I desire to speak to the Almighty and to argue my case with God" (13:2,3). The friends must be quiet, and he will present himself before God if God will summon him. He challenges the friends, "Can anyone bring charges against me? If so, I will be silent and die" (13:19). Job wants to speak, and then he wants God to reply (13:22). He wants the list of sins he has committed which have resulted in this trouble. "How many wrongs and sins have I committed?" he asks. "Show me my offense and my sin" (13:23). He asks God to remove his "hand" from him and to "stop frightening" him with "terrors" (13:21). He calls upon God to summon him into his presence so that he may speak and hear God's reply (13:22).

Of course, both Job and God, as well as the reader, know that there is no list of sins. God has no indictment against Job. Satan is the accuser and God is the defender. God refutes Satan's accusation through Job's faith. God has confidence in his servant.

Job believes that, given his day in court, "there an upright man could present his case before him," and he would be "delivered" (23:7). Lest we misunderstand, we should note that Job's confidence is his integrity, not his sinlessness. Job admits the "sins of [his] youth" (13:26). But he protests his innocence in the light of his integrity before God. This is the crux of the test — God seeks authentic hearts that reach out to him in faith. Even in the midst of his suffering Job remains God's disciple who treasures his words and keeps his commandments. Even though he suffered under the burden of God's hand (23:1), he remains committed to God. His credo is steadfast (23:10-12):

> But he knows the way that I take;
>> when he has tested me, I will come forth as gold.
> My feet have closely followed his steps;
>> I have kept to his way without turning aside.
> I have not departed from the commands of his lips;

> I have treasured the words of his mouth more
> than my daily bread.

Rebuking Eliphaz's implication that Job had turned his back on God's instruction (22:22), Job replies that he has never rejected God's words. On the contrary, he has always treasured them more than bread itself (cf. Deuteronomy 8:3; Matthew 4:4). Job is confident that when God has finished testing him in this darkness, he will come out of the fire like gold. In the midst of his trial, suffering did not push Job over the edge into accepting the counsel of his friends to profess a false self-incrimination (19:4-6) or the counsel of the wicked to admit that serving God is unprofitable (21:16).

Job's problem is that he cannot find God. In God's presence he could state his complaint and have it acted upon, but where is God in this suffering? Everywhere he looks, God is not there (23:8,9). God does not answer him. In fact, Job is perplexed by God's hiddenness. "Why," he asks, "do you hide your face and consider me your enemy?" (13:24). "Why," he questions, "does the Almighty not set times for judgment? Why must those who know him look in vain for such days?" (24:1). In other words, why does not God act so as to set the world aright and repair the world's injustices?[8] God's silence makes him appear apathetic, both to the tragic circumstances of his saints (like Job) and the prosperity of the wicked. When the poor are oppressed and starve (24:4-5), God is silent. When the children of the poor are seized for debt payments (24:9), God is silent. When murderers, thieves, and adulterers pillage humanity (24:14-15), God is silent. "God charges no one with wrongdoing" (24:12).

Even though God is silent, Job will not remain so. He invokes a curse upon the wicked and calls upon God to judge them.[9] Even though God is silent, Job is confident that God's "eyes are on their ways" (24:23), just as God knows Job's "way" (23:11). Job curses the wicked in the hope that God will no longer be silent. God, in the final analysis, is the only one who can rectify the situation. He alone can condemn the wicked and redeem the righteous (24:22). Job, therefore, seeks an audience with God to discuss the fallen nature of his universe. He seeks an explanation as to why he is treated as though he were wicked and why the wicked are treated as though they were righteous. Of one thing Job is certain: God "does whatever he pleases" (23:13). Why, then, does he not do what is just?

After his friends have fallen silent and given up on Job's conversion, Job gives an extended declaration of his case. Chapters 29–31 function as Job's legal brief in the divine courtroom where he makes his own case for his integrity. It is his legal complaint. The climax is this bold plea (31:35-37):

> Oh, that I had someone to hear me!
> I sign now my defense — let the Almighty answer me;
> let my accuser put his indictment in writing.
> Surely I would wear it on my shoulder,
> I would put it on like a crown.
> I would give him an account of my every step;
> like a prince I would approach him.

Job has presented his case. His circumstance has moved from blessing (29) to suffering (30). He has affirmed his ethical lifestyle (31). Now he wants God to hand down the indictment. He wants to know the exact charges against him. What is the sin that permits God's justice to cause this suffering? If there is no such sin, then Job should be acquitted. But the acquittal of Job is the indictment of God. If Job does not deserve his suffering, what right did God have to lay it upon him? Job is confident about his case. He knows his integrity. He will approach God "like a prince" because once he knows the charges, he is confident he can answer them. He is confident of his acquittal. Job's problem is not self-righteousness, but ignorance. Job knows his own integrity, but he does not know the prologue. He knows his integrity, but he does not know the purposes of God or how he works. Job is innocent but he does not understand the mysterious ways of God.

The Victory of Faith

Job's questions are neither simplistic nor illusory. They are hard and real. His despair is no momentary pitfall, but the bottom of a deep ravine. Suffering has evoked depressing thoughts (God as an enemy, 19:11), severe accusations (God attacks him in anger, 16:6), and bitter complaint (7:11). Job has lost hope of ever seeing happiness again (7:7). He despairs over the loss of all his dreams and goals (17:11). He yearns for the grave where he can find peace and rest (17:13ff). Yet this is "patient" Job! He is not patient in the sense of some kind of sentimental self-imposed acquiescence. In fact, Job admits his own "impatience" (21:4). Rather, he is patient as one who continues to trust in God. Job is an example of endurance (James 5:11). But can a person of faith accuse God? Can a person of faith despair? Can a person of faith lose the hope of joy in this life? Job did all three.

Job struggled to believe despite his circumstances. He trusts even when there seems to be no reason to trust. Job's wife thought the best resolution was to curse God and die (2:9). But this was the essence of the test. Will Job believe even when he has no reason to believe? Will he maintain his integrity where there is no gain or profit? Everything was taken from him materially, physically, and emotionally. Will Job maintain his integrity, his fear of God, even in this desperate circumstance? The answer throughout the book's dialogue is "Yes!"

Throughout his vacillations between despair and anger, between doubt and terror, Job maintained an implicit trust in God. Job would not deny his integrity, but neither would he curse his God. Several texts offer a window into Job's faith.

Job 13-14

In chapter 13 Job rebukes his friends for speaking wickedly on God's behalf. His friends showed "partiality" to God, or spoke "deceitfully for him" (13:7-8). Job demands their silence since they would not fare any better than he were God to examine them (13:9-12). They must be silent, but Job must speak. He cannot suppress his fears and misapprehensions. He must approach God (13:13-14,16). This is a terrifying prospect — to stand before God and defend one's integrity. Yet lament as prayer often becomes the means by which the faithful vent their feelings, doubts, and frustrations. Lament cries out to God about the fallenness of the world, and often complains about the suffering of the righteous. Job affirms his faith through the prayer of lament. He confesses (13:15-16):

> Though he slay me, yet will I hope in him;[10]
> I will surely defend my ways to his face.
> Indeed, this will turn out for my deliverance,
> for no godless man would dare come before him!

Faith and hope belong together. Indeed, "hope" is sometimes translated trust. The verb simply means to wait or tarry, and here it clearly carries the sense of trust/hope/faith. Job is determined to state, even defend, his case before God. He knows that a possible outcome is death, or expulsion from the presence of God (the term "slay" is God's act against the wicked, as in Psalm 139:19). But his faith will still rest in God. He will wait on God. He trusts God no matter what. "This speech," Anderson comments, "expresses the strongest confidence of Job in both his innocence and God's justice."[11] Even if God should act in what appears to be an unjust manner, that is, to slay him, Job will still put his hope in God. When all is lost, who else can he trust? Who else is there to trust? As Peter said to Jesus, "To whom shall we go? You have the words of eternal life" (John 6:68).

Job's deep faith is seen again in that same speech (chs. 12–14). Job hopes in God's fellowship with him after death. Job is ready to go down into the grave without vindication (14:13), but he expects to receive "renewal" or "release" (14:14) when God calls him and takes care of his sins. God will seal up his transgressions in forgiveness (14:17). Then he will receive vindication. Yet Job recognizes that he must "wait" (same word as in 13:15) for that time to come (14:14). After God's testing is past, God will renew fellowship and restore relationship with Job. God will call and Job will answer. This is the language of personal relationship, of a "renewed communion" between God and Job.[12] It may be that Job expects some kind of eschatological vindication here. He certainly expects a day when he would, in the words of Alden, "experience 'renewal' (v. 14), converse with God, and have his sins forgiven and forgotten."[13]

Job believes that justice must find expression somewhere. God will again consider him his friend. At some point God must set the world right. At some point, God will vindicate Job. There is a such a finality to death that Job does not expect to come back to his community after death (14:7-12). He does not expect his vindication to be a resuscitation that returns him to his prior blessed existence. Nevertheless, he does not expect his death to be the final act in God's drama. He believes that after death, God will vindicate him. The final act in Job's story will be vindication and restoration, even if he dies in his current condition. Job will wait on God for this renewal. He expects it because he trusts him.

Job 16-17

Chapter 16 also contains an expression of faith that transcends the despair of the moment. Job has rejected his friends as "miserable comforters" (16:2). They cannot empathize with him. Job's pain intensifies when he reflects on how God has attacked him like a lion tearing apart its prey (16:6,9). God has turned him over to evil people (16:11), devastated his household (16:7), and made him the bullseye of his target (16:12-13). The result is that Job is in bitter mourning (16:15), and he cries, "My spirit is broken, my days are cut short, the grave awaits me" (17:1). Job does not believe he will live to experience his own vindication before his peers (17:13-16). Nevertheless, he has not sinned in his grief — his prayer is pure (16:17). He is committed to the way of the righteous (17:6-9). Despite appearances to the contrary, Job believes that he has a "witness" in heaven or an "advocate" who will intercede for him (16:18-21):

> O earth, do not cover my blood;
>> may my cry never be laid to rest!
> Even now my witness is in heaven;
>> my advocate is on high.
> My intercessor is my friend
>> as my eyes pour out tears to God;
> on behalf of a man he pleads with God
>> as a man pleads for his friend.

Earlier Job had asked for a mediator who would reconcile God and himself (9:33). Here, however, he expresses the confidence that he has an intercessor who pleads his case. He has moved from requesting an impartial arbitrator to his confidence in an intercessor. Whoever this intercessor is, Job rests his hope in him. His doubts and questions do not bring him to the point of ultimate despair. He despairs but he hopes. He complains, but he is confident that God will commune with him again.

His cry in 16:18 is a cry for vengeance over spilled blood, much like when the ground cried out for vengeance for the blood of Abel (Gen. 4:10), or the saints under God's altar cried out for vengeance for the blood of the martyrs (Revelation 6:10). Job's blood must not be covered up. On the contrary, this tragedy must be reversed. Justice must be done, and only the one who is "in heaven" can carry out this vengeance. Whom does Job have in mind here? Hartley answers the question well:

> Considering the various passages in which Job thinks about arguing his case before God, the best candidate for the defender that can be found is God himself. . . . . Here Job appeals to God's holy integrity in stating his earnest hope that God will testify to the truth of his claims of innocence, even though such testimony will

seem to contradict God's own actions. Such risking is the essence of faith. For a moment Job sees God as his steadfast supporter. In this plea he is expressing the trust that God had expressed in him in the prologue because he is pushing through the screen of his troubles to the real God. He is not essentially pitting God against God; rather he is affirming genuine confidence in God regardless of the way it appears that God is treating him. Since Job, in contrast to his friends, will not concede that truth is identical with appearances, he presses on for a true resolution to his complaint from God himself.[14]

In this moment, as he pours out his tears to God, he knows God will be his friend and his intercessor. God, who knows the facts, will testify to his innocence, as, in fact, God did in the prologue (2:3) and will again in the epilogue (42:7). God, in the end, will show himself friendly to Job even though present appearances are to the contrary (and this is what happens in the epilogue). Though Job vents his laments with talk about God as his enemy, in the depths of his heart Job knows that God is his friend.

Job 19

In chapter 19 Job complains that his friends treat him like an enemy. In this context, Job offers the most laudable expression of faith in the book. Here, clearly and decisively, we see the person of faith. The Job who refuses to deny his integrity also refuses to deny his God. He is unable to integrate how the two fit together because he does not understand why God has permitted this suffering. That tension generates lament, but it also generates hope. Though he lives without hope of a future joy in this world, he does not live without the ultimate hope of his vindication. His confidence is rooted in God the redeemer (19:25-27):

> I know that my Redeemer lives,
>   and that in the end he will stand upon the earth.
> And after my skin has been destroyed,
>   yet in my flesh I will see God;

> I myself will see him
>> with my own eyes — I, and not another.
> How my heart yearns within me!

This is a crucial text. Some have seen Job's confidence in a "Redeemer" as fulfilled in Jesus Christ who is the mediator between God and humanity (cf. 1 Timothy 2:5).[15] Others see his "Redeemer" as his own innocence and righteousness; that is, Job is his own legal advocate.[16] Such a chasm of interpretation underscores the difficulty of the text. But despite its difficulties, the expression of confidence is clear.

This text evidences three important points about Job's faith. First, he is confident of redemption. His redeemer lives, and he will act on Job's behalf. The redeemer, the one who stands as the deliverer of his people (cf. Exodus 6:6; 15:13; Psalms 74:2; 77:16), is the Living God.[17] Job is confident that the God who appears to be his enemy is also the God who will redeem him. Second, he believes in his ultimate vindication by the resurrection, or at least a restoration of communion with God after death.[18] Job understands that the future involves some kind of encounter with God, whether resurrected or not, in which communion with God will find its fullest expression. Job expects to "see" God. Indeed, at the end of the book, Job does "see" God (42:5). Third, he yearns for a relationship with God. Whatever the difficulties of the text, this is a cry of faith. It expresses his trust. This cry does not deny his God. Rather, he yearns to see him. This does not arise out of arrogance or self-righteousness. Job yearns to commune with God and to experience his friendship again.

Job has no illusions about his present state. He believes that God is angry with him, has made him his enemy, and will never restore restfulness in this life. He calls for, even demands, a hearing. Yet his only real confidence is that in death God will redeem him and restore this relationship. God, as his Redeemer, will encounter him after death, and there Job will see God.

But his suffering has clouded his perception of his relationship with God — he perceives God as his enemy when God is really his friend. Suffering has colored Job's outlook. It colors everyone's. Suffering does not permit us to see things clearly. While Job doubts and despairs about his present life, he has no doubt about his ultimate life with God. He knows that his Redeemer lives. He knows that he has a witness and advocate in heaven. Even if God slays him, Job trusts God. Job may have been knocked off balance by his suffering, but he was not toppled.

Job's faith endured. He did not curse God. He maintained his integrity. He retained his hope. However, his enduring faith was mixed with doubt, despair, disappointment, and sharp accusations. Yet it was still faith. It was a struggle of faith, but it was a victorious faith. It was a faith that answered Satan's accusation: Does Job serve God for profit? The answer is "No." Indeed, when Job puts that question in the mouths of the scoffers he rejects it as the "counsel of the wicked" (21:16). Job does not serve God for profit. Rather, he trusts his God even when there appears to be no reason to trust him. That is the endurance of faith. Genuine faith is a faith that ultimately trusts and hopes in God even though it struggles through doubt and despair. Job teaches us that genuine faith is not perfect faith. Rather, genuine faith is a faith that retains its integrity through the struggle.

God Encounters Job

Throughout the dialogue, Job first addressed his friends and then turned to address God. Both aspects of his speeches were full of complaint and accusation. The three friends answered Job until they concluded that Job was too full of arrogance to be won by argument (32:1). For twenty-four chapters the friends attempted to answer Job's questions. They were answering, but God was silent. God's silence disturbed Job. Did God not see his anguish? Did God not hear his prayers? Would God not answer?

Job had no illusions that if God spoke that he somehow would be able to escape the misery of his present life. But he wanted a word from God even if it were a word of condemnation. Job simply wants to know something even if it is not what he wants to hear. He wants to know the charges against him (10:2; 13:23). He wants to understand the seeming moral chaos of the universe where the wicked prosper and the righteous suffer (21:7-26; 24:1-12). If God charges the wicked with evil and judges them, "Why must those who know him look in vain for such days?" (24:1). Job challenges God, "Let the Almighty answer me" (31:35). Will God speak? Will he explain?

No doubt to the shock and surprise of all the participants, God does speak. He comes to Job out of the whirlwind (38:1; 40:6). God is no longer silent, but does he answer? He speaks, but does he explain? That God spoke is one surprise, and what he said is yet another.

The text records two separate speeches by God (38:2–40:2 and 40:7–41:34), and gives two corresponding responses by Job (40:4-5; 42:1-6). Each of God's speeches has a similar pattern. First, God approaches Job with a challenge (38:2-3; 40:7-14). Second, God poses a series of questions to Job about the natural order and design of the world (38:4–39:30; 40:15–41:34). Third, God closes the first speech with a summary challenge (40:1-2). It is the first and third parts which reflect the approach that God takes to Job. How does God view Job? Does he regard him as a boisterous, self-righteous sinner who must be crushed by God's power, or does he regard him as an ignorant sufferer whose misery has pushed him to the brink of rivalry with God? I think he sees Job in the latter perspective. God confronts Job, but in mercy and grace rather than in wrath or anger. He confronts him with tough questions out of tough love, but Job is also God's servant and God graciously appears to him.

But God's answer is no answer. It does not answer Job's questions. Why is life given to those in misery (3:20)? God does not answer. Why has God made Job his target (7:20)? God does not answer. Why did God hide his face from Job and count him as an enemy (13:24)? God does not answer. Why do the wicked prosper (21:7)? God does not answer. Why does God not set a time for judgment (24:1)? God does not answer. God does not provide an explanation for his moral government of the world and neither does he explain to Job why tragedy befell him.

Instead, God engages Job in a personal dialogue that focuses on two primary points which parallel the two divine speeches. The first speech concerns God's transcendent wisdom and care, and the second concerns God's sovereignty over his creation, particularly over evil.

The first speech (38:1–40:2) is a series of questions about God's role as transcendent creator in contrast to Job's finitude and ignorance. Job had spoken about things he did not know, so God questions him about his role in the universe. "Where were you when I laid the earth's foundation?" (38:4). God poses question after question, all reflecting his role as the creator and sovereign Lord of the cosmos. And with question after he question he prods Job to reflect on his own limitations. "Tell me, if you know all this" (38:18). The questions force Job to admit his own ignorance and remember his finite role in the cosmos.

But these questions also point to God's wisdom and care. These are not simply questions about power. Their function is not simply to remind Job of God's power, but also to remind him of God's wisdom and care. The questions are not arbitrary; they move from God's creative work when he laid the foundations of the world (38:4-7) and controlled the chaotic waters (38:8-11) to his transcendence over the chaos of the wicked and death (38:12-21), control over the waters (snow, rain, rivers) of the earth (38:22-30, 34-38), and his regulation of the stars and seasons (38:31-33). The questions then move to the animal kingdom and God's management of his living creation. The questions are not just about knowledge but about care. God asks if Job "knows" (e.g., 39:1), but he also asks whether Job can manage this creation and care for it the way God does. Does Job hunt for the lion (38:39), feed the young ravens (38:41), give the wild donkey his home (39:6), use the wild ox in his service (39:9-12), care for the ostrich even though she has no sense (39:12-18), and give the horse his strength (39:19). God asks, "Does the hawk take flight by your wisdom" (39:26) or "does the eagle soar at your command?" (39:27). Through his power God manages his creation with wisdom and care. God's creation is not the playground of his power but the nursery of his care. The world is not out of control; God is managing it quite nicely.

The second speech (40:6–41:34) is a series of questions about God's control over chaotic forces. God challenges Job to manage this chaos and evil better than he does. "Do you have an arm like God's?" (40:9). If so, then "unleash the fury of your wrath, look at every proud man and bring him low" (40:11) and "crush the wicked where they stand" (40:12). If you can manage evil in the world better than me, then "I myself will admit to you that your own right hand can save you" (40:14).

The animals "behemoth" (40:15) and "leviathan" (41:1) represent evil and chaos in the world. The former is a large land animal, but the latter is some kind of aquatic creature. The language here is highly poetic and serves the point about God's management of chaos and evil. Job cannot "crush the wicked" or bring the proud low, but God can. God controls even the behemoth which no one else can capture (40:19,24). God controls the leviathan which no else can handle (41:1-10). No creature can control these animals. The behemoth is the "first" among God's works (40:19), and the leviathan has no equal and "is king over all that are proud" (41:33-34). Evil reigns in the world. Chaos fills the earth. But God is still in control and everything belongs to him (41:11).

But how do these speeches answer Job's questions? In one sense they do not. They do not address the particulars of Job's situation. God does not tell Job about the heavenly wager described in the prologue. The speeches do not address the issue of distributive justice and moral balance. God does not explain why the wicked prosper while Job suffers. The speeches do not address Job's specific questions about suffering and justice. Rather, they address something more fundamental. They address the critical issue that was raised in the prologue and assumed throughout the dialogues: trust in God's management of the world. Do we believe God is wisely managing his creation? This is what Job doubted, and this is what gave rise to the questions and accusations of his laments.

When evil surrounds us and chaos fills our life, then we begin to doubt God's sovereignty (is God really in control?) or we doubt his goodness (does God really care?). We wonder whether God knows what he is doing or whether he can do anything at all. This occasions lament. We believe in God, just like Job, but the chaos of our lives creates doubt, despair, and disappointment. So, we, like Job, complain, question, and accuse.

God's answer is: I am in control, I care and I know what I am doing. Can you trust me? If I controlled chaotic waters in creation, can I not manage the chaos of your life? If my care feeds the lions and the ravens, will I not care for you? If I can tame the leviathan who crushes the proud, can I not crush chaos and evil in your life? God's answer is his transcendence, but it is not a naked transcendence. It is not a sheer assertion of power. Rather, it is a loving, caring transcendence which manages the chaos of the world for benevolent purposes. The question is whether Job can trust God's management of his creation.

Job saw an answer in God's answer. It was not the answer he sought, but it was sufficient for his needs. He confesses God's transcendence and his own ignorance. Indeed, he offers God his praise. He confesses that there are things too "wonderful" for him to understand. The world is incomprehensible to him, but it is not to God. While God's providence is unknown to him, he knows that no divine plan "can be thwarted" (42:2). Job responds to God's dialogue with praise. He confesses the wonder of God's providence and the inscrutability of his designs. Job's lament turns to praise. He no longer questions or doubts. Through his encounter with God, he moves from complaint to praise.

Does Job "repent" and thus repudiate all that he has said in his laments? Does Job now retract all his questions? I do not think so. While the standard translation of Job 42:6 is something like the NIV, "Therefore I despise myself and repent in dust and ashes," this is not the best rendering. The term translated "despise" may also mean "melt." It may refer to Job's humility before God. The verb has no object in Hebrew so that it probably means something like "I humble myself before you." The term translated "repent" means to "change one's mind" or "reverse a decision about something" (Exodus 32:12,14; Jeremiah 18:8,10; Amos 7:3,6).[19] It does not mean to feel remorse about sin, or to confess guilt. Indeed, Job does not confess sin or regret. In fact, God judged that what Job had said was correct and that what the friends had said was erroneous (42:7). Instead of repenting of some sin, he changes his mind — he changes from lament to praise. He changes his approach to God. He gives up his lament. Job is saying, "I am comforted" or "I will no longer lament." He will give up his "dust and ashes" — the "dust" of mourning (2:12) and the "ashes" of his tragic lament (2:8).

Job is comforted by his encounter with God.[20] The Hebrew term translated "repent" (NIV) occurs seven times in Job (2:11; 7:13; 16:2; 21:34; 29:25; 42:6,11). In every instance, unless 42:6 is an exception, it refers to comfort or consolation. In fact, Job's three friends visit him for the purpose of offering comfort (2:11), but they are miserable comforters (16:2; 21:34). After God revealed himself, his friends and family again sought to comfort him (42:11).

But in the midst of his tragedy Job could find no comfort, even in his nightly sleep (7:13). Job found no comfort until he encountered God. Job 42:6b perhaps should read something like "I am comforted by your presence in my dust and ashes" or "comforted over my dust and ashes."

This parallels what happens in the lament Psalms. In response to a divine encounter, or a salvation oracle, the lamenter confesses *"now* I know . . ." (cf. Psalm 20:6; 59:9; 140:12; 41:11; 135:5). If Job is a "dramatic lament," as Westermann argues, then the divine speeches are the "salvation oracle" and God encounters Job so that "now" Job sees God and submits to his presence. Job turns from lament to praise:

> 42:5 contains the "solution" to the "problem" of Job. There is no other. God has answered Job. God has met Job. Insofar as Job attests to this, he attests to the reality of God in its wholeness. Now he knows God, and no longer just one aspect of God's activity.[21]

When God came near, when he engaged Job by his presence and by his revelation of himself, then Job was comforted. Job ceased his lament. The difference is the experience of God himself. While previously Job had only "heard" of God, now he had seen him (42:5). Job was comforted by God's presence and he "repented of his dust and ashes," that is, he ceased his mourning and his heart turned to praise. Job had a "sanctuary experience," and just as in the laments of Psalms, Job was moved by God's presence to turn from lament to praise.

What is missing from the divine speeches is exactly what Job demanded. There is no list of charges. There is no indictment. There is no explanation of the suffering. There is no reasoned discussion of the seeming chaotic state of moral justice in the world. What answer can Job find in these speeches? How can we find our answer in God's speeches?

If the speeches do not answer our questions, perhaps the problem is not the divine answer but the human questions. Or, more precisely, perhaps the divine answer is intended to underline the finite and limited character of the human questions. Perhaps God displays his knowledge in order that we might sense our ignorance and our finitude. Perhaps the answer is: "You're not able to understand at this level, but you are capable of understanding my goodness and my sovereignty — so trust me." Perhaps the answer is: "You cannot understand the answer I am capable of giving — so trust me."

Human misery will always raise questions. It cannot help but do so. The emotional and spiritual lows of suffering will ask the questions. The intensity of suffering will bear the fruit of prolonged agony. It will ask, "Why?" It will wonder, "Where is God?" It will doubt, "Does he really care?" God does not condemn the questions. He does not even condemn the answers we often vent in the midst of suffering. God is patient with his people. But the answer lies in recognizing the distinction between God and humanity — between his character and our questions. God's answer to Job is: "I understand your questions, but recognize your finitude; I understand your frustration, but recognize my faithfulness and care." God's answer to Job is his overwhelming but comforting presence. Now Job "sees" God, and this is enough.

Throughout our questions, doubts, and pointed accusations, we must recognize that we speak from our finitude. We speak from the bottom of the bowl. We cannot see the full range of life and meaning. We do not have the perspective from which to judge all events. Our finitude is limiting. Our ignorance is debilitating. What must shine through, as it does in the words of Job, is an underlying trust in God's goodness and faithfulness.

In recognizing our limitations we understand that our perceptions of God are conditioned by our finitude and limited by our ignorance. The same can be said for the world around us, and especially God's relationship to it. Thus, God did not humiliate Job or "blow him away" with his wrath which is what the friends expected. In this sense, Job himself was vindicated because the God who appeared to him was not the God his friends had imagined. On the contrary, God revealed himself as the transcendent God who wisely cares for his creation. Job encountered the transcendent God and bowed in humble submission before him as he confessed his own limitations. He encountered the living God and worshiped him.

We must learn to live by revelation rather than reasoned judgments about the relationship between God and humanity. We must learn to live by faith and not by sight. For in revelation God is not silent. He speaks, and he reveals himself in ways that assure us of his faithfulness and love. There we find the God who cares, loves, and reigns. There we find God's comforting presence. Only in the knowledge, contemplation, and experience of that God can we come to endure misery with faith, integrity, and hope.

Conclusion

> For what hope has the godless when he is cut off,
>   when God takes away his life?
> Does God listen to his cry
>   when distress comes upon him?
> Will he find delight in the Almighty?
>   Will he call upon God at all times?
>   Job 27:8-10.

Will believers continue to call upon God even when there is distress in their lives? The ungodly will stop praying when distress comes. They have no other option than to sit in silence and face the nothingness. However, when believers are distressed, they cry to God. Indeed, this is one reason why believers sometimes experience distress or trouble. God wants them to call on his name. The ungodly will reject God's discipline and refuse to call on his name. But believers, like Job, will continue to call upon God and offer their prayers, though their prayers may be filled with questions, bitterness, and doubt. God's faithful people cry out to him day and night (1 Kings 8:59: 2 Chronicles 6:20; Lamentations 2:18; Nehemiah 1:6; Jeremiah 9:1; Psalm 32:4; 42:3; Revelation 4:8; 7:15).

After the exile Zechariah interpreted the meaning of the wars that had engulfed Judah. God declared that two-thirds of the land would perish, and that the remaining third would be left in the land. God stated his intention for this third (Zechariah 13:9):

> This third I will bring into the fire;
> I will refine them like silver
> and test them like gold.
> They will call on my name
> and I will answer them;
> I will say, "They are my people,"
> and they will say, "The LORD is our God."

God tested his people and refined their faith through the exile. Those who were left in the land were put to the test through the distress of a devastated land. The people then cried out, and the Lord answered by renewing his covenant of love. God fulfilled his creative intent by again dwelling among his people as their God and they as his people. God tests his people to see if they will cry out to him in faith or whether they will rebel against his intentions and curse him. God tests his people to see what is in their hearts.

What God expects of his people is that they constantly and consistently engage him in prayer. He expects his people to persistently call on his name, and God's loving faithfulness means that he will respond in a manner consistent with his eschatological goal. God intends to have a people for himself and he himself is faithful to those goals, but the question is whether we will persist in prayer. When God's eschatological goal is accomplished, "when the Son of Man comes, will he find faith on the earth" (Luke 18:8)? Will the people of God continue to engage God in persistent prayer with the confidence that God will act on behalf of his people who "cry out to him day and night" (Luke 18:7)?

Believers, when they are burdened with the fallenness of this world, turn to God and make their burdens known. They petition, they cry for help and they ask questions. Believers turn to God in faith while the ungodly curse God and seek their own way. Believers pray even when it seems as though God has become their enemy (Psalms 6, 44, 74, 88, 90).[22]

---

[1]Robert Alter, *The Art of Biblical Poetry* (New York: Basic Books, 1985), pp. 76-84, provides an excellent literary discussion of Job 3 to which I am indebted.

[2]The Hebrew word for "why" only occurs in 3:11,20, but the word is implied by the construction and context in 3:12,16,23.

[3]Job 1:10 and 3:23 use different Hebrew terms but the concept is the same.

[4]See James L. Crenshaw, "Wisdom," in *Old Testament Form Criticism*, ed. John H. Hayes (San Antonio: Trinity University Press, 1974), pp. 228, 254.

[5]Claus Westermann, *The Structure of the Book of Job: A Form-Critical Analysis*, trans. Charles A. Muenchow (Philadelphia: Fortress, 1981), pp. 97-99.

[6]Michael Brennan Dick, "The Legal Metaphor in Job 31," *Catholic Biblical Quarterly* 41 (1979): 37-50; "Job 31, the Oath of Innocence, and the Sage," *Zeitschrift für Alttestamentliche Wissenschaft* 95 (1983): 31-53; Sylvia Hubermann Scholnick, "The Meaning of *Mispat* (Justice) in the Book of Job," *Journal of Biblical Literature* 101 (1982): 521-529; "Poetry in the Courtroom: Job 38–41," in *Directions in Hebrew Poetry*, ed. Elaine Follis (Sheffield: JSOT, 1987), 185-204; J.J. Roberts, "Job's Summons to Yahweh: The Exploration of a Legal Metaphor," *Restoration Quarterly* 16 (1973): 159-165; and Norman Habel, *The Book of Job: A Commentary*, Old Testament Library (Philadelphia: Westminster Press, 1985), pp. 54-57.

[7]Ludwig Köhler, *Hebrew Man*, trans. P.R. Ackroyd (Nashville: Abingdon Press, 1957), pp. 134-139.

[8]Gerald Janzen, *Job*, Interpretation (Atlanta: John Knox Press, 1985), pp. 168-169.

[9]John E. Hartley, *The Book of Job*, The New International Commentary on the Old Testament (Grand Rapids: Eerdmans, 1988), pp. 352-353.

[10]This is a notoriously difficult verse to translate. The NIV footnote gives the alternative "He will surely slay me; I have no hope — yet I will . . . ." The difficulty lies in the Hebrew construction. Does it mean "I have no hope" or "I will hope in him"? I have opted for the NIV text

which Anderson, *Job*, p. 166, defends. In either event, Job is confident about his vindication. The NIV footnote would mean something like: Whether God kills him or not, whether he has hope for future prosperity or not, he is certain that his innocence will be confirmed (cf. 13:18).

[11]Anderson, *Job*, p. 166.

[12]David J.A. Clines, *Job 1–20*, Word Biblical Commentary (Dallas: Word Books, 1989), p. 333.

[13]Robert R. Alden, *Job*, New American Commentary (Nashville: Broadman Press, 1993), p. 168.

[14]Hartley, *Job*, p. 264.

[15]Roy B. Zuck, *Job*, Everyman's Bible Commentary (Chicago: Moody Press, 1978), p. 92; and Alden, *Job*, p. 207.

[16]Clines, *Job*, pp. 459-460.

[17]Hartley, *Job*, pp. 293-295.

[18]That Job speaks of a resurrection is controversial in contemporary scholarship. I will not take the time to defend this understanding except to point the reader to the fine explanations of Janzen, *Job*, pp. 142-145.

[19]Dale Patrick, "Job's Address of God," *Zeitschrift für die Alttestamentliche Wissenschaft* 91 (1979): 279-281. See his earlier article, "The Translation of Job XLII 6," *Vetus Testamentum* 26 (1976): 369-371; Habel, *Job*, p. 583; and Gustavo Gutiérrez, *On Job: God-Talk and the Suffering of the Innocent*, tran. by Matthew J. O'Connell (Maryknoll, NY: Orbis Books, 1987), pp. 82-87.

[20]David Wolfers, *Deep Things Out of Darkness* (Grand Rapids: Eerdmans, 1995), p. 461, translates 42:6 as "I am comforted." See also D.J. O'Conner, "Job's Final Word — 'I Am Consoled. . .'" (42:6b), *Irish Theological Quarterly* 50 (1983/84): 181-197.

[21]Westermann, *The Structure of the Book of Job*, p. 128.

[22]Ingvar Fløsvik, *When God Becomes My Enemy: The Theology of the Complaint Psalms* (Saint Louis: Concordia Academic Press, 1997).

Chapter Seven

How Does Faith Question?
Lament in God's Story

For I envied the arrogant
  when I saw the prosperity of the wicked. . . .
This is what the wicked are like —
  always carefree, they increase in wealth.
Surely in vain have I kept my heart pure;
  in vain have I washed my hands in innocence.
All day long I have been plagued;
  I have been punished every morning.
If I had said, "I will speak thus,"
  I would have betrayed your children.
When I tried to understand all this,
  it was oppressive to me
till I entered the sanctuary of God;
  then I understood their final destiny.
                    Psalm 73:3,12-17

My Experience

I remember the moment of prayerful communion which comforted my lament over Joshua. From the first day Joshua saw a school bus, he wanted to ride one. He wanted to be like his older sister. She rode the bus, and so would he! Whenever a bus came into view, he would shout, "I wanna ride!" Finally, his day came. Every morning I would take him out to wait for the bus at a place near my office. When he saw it coming, he would jump and scream for joy. He knew he was going to ride. It was "my bus," as he would say.

But one day, for some reason, he did not want to get on. I took him by the hand and gently led him up the steps of the bus, and he got on. But he was whining, hesitant, and reluctant. I thought perhaps he was just having a bad day, but as the bus drove away I learned why he was hesitant, and I heard words that tore my heart. It was as if a knife had been stuck into my gut and twisted. His schoolmates were ridiculing him. The older children were calling him names. They ridiculed his need for diapers and mocked his use of them the previous day. As the bus drove off I could hear the mockery, and I could see my son stumble down the aisle as he looked for a seat.

Anger grew inside me. All morning I wanted to take some of those older kids aside and heap some abuse of my own on them. Let them see how it feels! Let them know what it's like to be hurt, ridiculed, and mocked. Maybe I should talk to the bus driver, or to the school principal, to the teachers, or to the parents! My helplessness increased my frustration.

Finally, I took my anger and hurt to God. I went to my office and poured my heart before him. I held nothing back. I complained bitterly, and then I complained some more. There was plenty to complain about. Why was my son born with this condition? Why are others permitted to inflict pain upon the innocent? Why hadn't God answered our prayers for a healthy son? Why couldn't Joshua ever fulfill the dreams we had for him and honor the name which we gave him as a leader among God's people? Why hadn't the sovereign God of the universe blessed him with health?

Somewhere in the middle of that complaint, in the middle of that lament, I became intensely aware that my complaint had been heard. I did not hear a voice or a whisper. I did not have a vision or feel the wind blow across my face. Rather, I sensed God's presence, and I came to understand his own pain. In the middle of my lament over my own son, I became aware that God understood. God empathized with me. It was as if God had said to me, "I understand — they treated my Son that way, too." In that moment God provided a comfort that I cannot yet explain but one that I still experience in my heart.

Now, only now, do I have some sense of the pain that a father has when his son is ridiculed. Only now can I begin to appreciate the pain of my heavenly Father as he watched his Son be ridiculed. In that moment of prayerful communion the death of Jesus became more than a historical fact; it became real to me in a deeply emotional and religious moment. It was an experience that cut across my pain and led me into an awareness of God's presence. It was a "sanctuary" experience.

My prayer that morning turned from complaint to praise. It turned from anger to joy. Oh, I was still angry and frustrated, but my anger and frustration were overcome by a sense of awe, a sense of reverence, a sense of wonder — an awareness of God's comforting presence. God understands. He knows the pain of a father who mourns over his son.

In that moment of prayer — a moment of communion — God engaged me and reassured me of his love and empathy. God comforted me. My lament turned to praise not because I had received an answer to my "why" questions, but because God gave me the answer I needed. He came near to me in the power of the Holy Spirit and created hope, peace, and joy in my heart by his own hand (cf. Romans 15:13). Through lament we enter the sanctuary of God, and he answers with his comforting hand. We do not always receive the answers we seek, but we receive the very thing we need — God's presence.

We live in a fallen world filled with sin, despair, and death. Yet it is God's world and he is sovereign over it. The combination of these two ideas — fallenness and sovereignty — generates some fundamental questions for the people of God. How can a good God be sovereign over a fallen world? Why does he permit this fallenness? Is God fair? In the light of innocent suffering, how can God be just? How long must people of faith endure this fallenness? These kinds of questions fill the prayers of God's people as they suffer under the weight of the world's darkness. These kinds of prayers are called laments. They are prayers of faith because they express the questions of faith to the God whom faith trusts. They ask God the questions that only he can answer.

Just like Job, the people of God expect answers. Prayer does not simply function as a vehicle for venting. It is the cry of faith. It hopes for a sympathetic ear and a resolution to the despair of lament. However, like Job, we do not always get the answer we seek, but we often receive the answer we need. What Job wanted was an explanation, and what he got was the comforting, reassuring presence of God. Our laments ask real questions and God offers himself in communion, and by the power of the Holy Spirit he creates hope, comfort, and peace in the midst of our lament (Romans 15:13).

Job's experience was my experience. No longer had he only "heard" of God, he had now "seen" him. The psalmist's experience was my experience. The sanctuary reorients our vision of the world (Psalm 73). This is the experience of the people of God throughout Scripture. They question their God, and God answers them by the gift of his presence.

The Prayers of Habakkuk

By the last decade of the seventh century B.C., Babylon had replaced Assyria as the supreme imperial power. Babylon defeated Egypt at the battle of Carchemish in 609 B.C. and besieged Jerusalem in 605 B.C. As a result, Jehoiakim, King of Judah (609–598 B.C.), became the servant of Nebuchadnezzar, the King of Babylon (2 Kings 24:1). Nevertheless, Jehoiakim resisted the Babylonian king and allied himself with Egypt. His policies would ultimately lead to a second siege in 597 B.C. and the imprisonment of his son, Jehoiachin, in Babylonian captivity (cf. 2 Kings 24:12).

Habakkuk prophesied during the reign of Jehoiakim (2 Kings 23:37) which overlaps Jeremiah's prophetic ministry. Jeremiah prophesied during the reigns of the last kings of Judah: Josiah, Jehoiakim, Jehoiachin, and Zedekiah (Jeremiah 1:2-3; 626 to 586 B.C.). The book of Habakkuk, however, is set in the reign of Jehoiakim sometime after the rise of the Babylonians to power and before the first siege of Jerusalem, that is, between 609 and 605 B.C. The Babylonian power is relatively new to Habakkuk, but he knows their ruthlessness and idolatry (Habakkuk 1:6,15-17).

Habakkuk appears as a prophet who speaks to God for the people rather than a prophet who speaks to the people for God. While Habakkuk clearly delivers a word from God through two prophetic oracles (1:5-11; 2:2-20), these oracles are answers to the two laments which the prophet offered on behalf of the people (1:2-4; 1:12–2:1). The final chapter is Habakkuk's response to God's last oracle as he offers a prayer of faith and invokes God's promises (3:1-19).[1] The structure of Habakkuk may be pictured like this:

Lament One: How long before you judge Judah (1:2-4)?
   Answer One: Not long; Babylon is coming (1:5-11).
Lament Two: Why Babylon (1:12-2:1)?
   Answer Two: There is an appointed time for Babylon as well (2:2-5).
      Woe Oracle: The sins of Babylon are many (2:6-20).
Praise: Rejoice in God's saving judgment and his faithful presence (3:1-19).

Habakkuk stands among the people and offers two communal laments. He addresses God as one of the people in order to hear God's answer. He stands before God as one of God's people to question, complain, and petition the Sovereign Lord of Judah.

Lament One (1:2-4)

Habakkuk's opening lament is a succinct but powerful questioning of God. It contains the two classic questions of lament: "How Long?" and "Why?" It asks God to judge Judah's fallen society.

> How long, O Lord, must I call for help,
>   but you do not listen?
> Or cry out to you, "Violence!"
>   but you do not save?
> Why do you make me look at injustice?
>   Why do you tolerate wrong?
> Destruction and violence are before me;
>   there is strife, and conflict abounds.

> Therefore, the law is paralyzed,
> and justice never prevails.
> The wicked hem in the righteous,
> so that justice is perverted.

The moral collapse of Judah occasions Habakkuk's lament. In previous years, under the good King Josiah, Judah had prospered (2 Kings 23:25). However, Jehoiakim did not imitate his father's good example. Instead, Jehoiakim's reign was characterized by violence and injustice (cf. Jeremiah 22:13-17). Jehoiakim ordered the death of the prophet Uriah (Jeremiah 20:20-24). He refused to listen to the warnings of Jeremiah, even burning one of his scrolls (Jeremiah 36). God warned Jehoiakim through Jeremiah, but his pride would not listen (Jeremiah 22:21). Consequently, his arrogant path ultimately led to his destruction.

Habakkuk complains that Jehoiakim has filled the land with violence and destruction, with injustice and strife. The righteous, including the poor, are extorted, oppressed, and killed. Jeremiah echoes the same words as Habakkuk: "Violence and destruction resound in [Jerusalem]," and "it is filled with oppression" (Jeremiah 6:6-7). Just like Habakkuk, Jeremiah wants to know when God is going to judge the wicked. "O LORD Almighty, you who judge righteously and test the heart and mind," Jeremiah prays, "let me see your vengeance upon them, for to you I have committed my cause" (Jeremiah 11:20; cf. 20:12). Jeremiah prays for the destruction of the wicked and calls for the punishment of the city. Jeremiah can ask, along with Habakkuk, "Why does the way of the wicked prosper? Why do all the faithless live at ease?" (Jeremiah 12:1). Why does God not judge the sinfulness of his people and call the wicked to account?

Habakkuk's lament is a complaint about evil, but it is also an implicit imprecation. He asks, how long will God refrain from punishing the wicked? It is a cry for help and it is also a plea for God's justice. When will God act? When will God answer? Justice is perverted and the wicked abuse the righteous. Why does God tolerate this situation? How long will God continue to remain passive and refuse to act? Habakkuk wants God to do something.

God answers Habakkuk's prayer (1:5-11). There is no indication as to how much time elapsed between the lament and its answer. It may have been immediate or it may have been years. Indeed, it may be that the cry of Habakkuk's lament had been the cry of God's righteous people for several years, perhaps ever since the death of Josiah. Nevertheless, God does answer.

God will punish the wickedness of Judah. He will bring down the prideful rulers of Jerusalem. He is beginning a new work in the world through the "ruthless and impetuous" Babylonians (1:6). Habakkuk is told to watch the surprising work of God (1:5). God will raise up the Babylonians who will "sweep across the whole earth to seize dwelling places not their own" (1:6). They will "promote their own honor" (1:7) and devour everything in front of them like a vulture (1:8). "They deride kings and scoff at rulers," the Lord says, and they will capture fortified cities (1:10). Their military power will be so overwhelming that they will make their own strength "their god" (1:11).

Habakkuk received a positive answer to his lament. He asked for justice, and God responded. God will punish the wicked, destroy the city of Jerusalem, and remove its king. Just as Jeremiah announced, God has determined to punish Judah for its sins (Jeremiah 11:1-17; 18:13-17). When the severity of the judgment is announced, even the prayers of Jeremiah — even if Moses and Samuel stood as intercessors (Jeremiah 14:19–15:4) — cannot avert God's avenging destroyers. God has seen the injustice of his land and he has heard the cry of his prophet, and consequently God will purge the land.

Lament Two (1:12–2:1)

Habakkuk acknowledges that the Holy One has determined to "execute judgment" and "ordained [the

Babylonians] to punish" his people (1:12). This was the major burden of Jeremiah's message. God had determined to hand Judah over to the Babylonian King (Jeremiah 20:4; 22:25; 27:6; 32:3,28,36; 34:2). In fact, Jeremiah pictures the Lord as summoning the King to do battle for him. The Lord calls Nebuchadnezzar "my servant" (Jeremiah 25:9). When Babylon invades Judah, God will work through his servant. God has decreed Judah's punishment.

Habakkuk questions the justice of the invasion. He does not doubt that Judah deserves punishment. But he wonders how the Holy One of Israel can involve himself with such wicked invaders as the Babylonians. How can the righteous God use such wicked people? Does not this dirty God's holy hands? How can God use evil people to achieve good? Habakkuk questions God (1:13):

> Your eyes are too pure to look on evil;
>   you cannot tolerate wrong.
> Why then do you tolerate the treacherous?
> Why are you silent while the wicked
>   swallow up those more righteous than themselves?

If God cannot tolerate evil, how can he ordain evil people (the Babylonians) to punish those who are more righteous (the Judeans)? God has so ordered the world in this circumstance that the nations are like fish which the Babylonians catch with their nets. The Babylonians take pride in their catch and they rejoice over their victories (1:15). They even worship their nets (idolatry) and live in luxury from the spoils of their catch (1:16). Will God continue to tolerate this evil? Babylon makes a living by destroying other nations. How long will God tolerate this? "Is [Babylon] to keep on emptying his net, destroying nations without mercy?" (1:17).

Habakkuk is no theological amateur. He raises real questions. He does not doubt that Judah deserves judgment. In fact, he has prayed for it. But it seems as if God is not playing fair, and that he is not playing according to the rules he himself has given his people. Just as one should not be silent in the face of evil (Leviticus 5:1) neither should God be silent when the Babylonians swallow up the Judeans (1:13). God had swallowed the wicked in the past, but now he will empower the wicked to swallow up his own people (cf. Exodus 15:12; Numbers 16:30-34; Psalm 106:17). The wicked, in fact, do swallow up God's people through the exile (Jeremiah 51:34; Lamentations 2:2,5,16).[2] Even more, how can God be responsible for raising up such a wicked hoard to punish his people? Is not the evil of the Babylonians greater than that of the Judeans? Why punish the lesser offender with a greater one? Is that authentic justice? Harris summarizes the point well:

> The lament does not seek an answer to the problem of evil or why the innocent must suffer. Neither does it cavil at the just punishment of the wicked. What he complains about is that something has gone wrong with the just government of the world. Why does God act in a self-contradictory way by taking upon Himself the responsibility for the evil now rampant?[3]

Has God used an unjust means to achieve a just end? Why does God not destroy the evil of the Babylonians? Why does God tolerate them he if will no longer tolerate Judah?

Given Habakkuk's first lament, it is difficult to understand Habakkuk's response to God's first answer. What had Habakkuk expected God to do? Perhaps Habakkuk thought that God might raise up a good king, like Josiah, to destroy the evil in Judah. Perhaps Habakkuk thought God would install a righteous Davidic king on the throne in Judah and get rid of Jehoiakim. He did not imagine that God would use an evil imperial power to punish Judah. It is incredulous to Habakkuk that God could use such an evil nation to destroy his own people. Yet this is exactly what God tells him he is going to do. So, Habakkuk complains again. How can the holy God use such unholy people in such an unfair way?

Habakkuk now ascends a watchtower to hear an answer to his lament (2:1). He has offered his complaint and now he waits for God's answer. Some translations identify the complaint as God's prospective answer to Habakkuk (NIV), but it is better to understand Habakkuk's lament as the complaint (NRSV). The term "complaint" has a semantic range that includes argument, rebuke, admonition, correction or reasoning (see the use of this term in Proverbs 1:23,25,30; Job 13:6; 23:4). Habakkuk has entered a complaint against God's handling of this circumstance. In effect, he rebuked God. Now he will wait to hear God's answer to his rebuke.

In his response God recognizes a difference between the wicked and the righteous. While the righteous live by faith (faithfulness), the wicked are puffed up in their pride and do not desire righteousness (2:4). The crucial distinction between the righteous and the wicked is the distinction between faith and pride. The righteous live by a steadfast trust in God while the wicked die because of their arrogance.[4] The Babylonians are "arrogant" and they are as "greedy as the grave" (2:5). They will seek out their own pride, capture all the peoples of the earth and still be unsatisfied. They will die. They will ultimately experience the "Woes" that are described in the prophetic oracle (2:6-20). God will destroy them because of their bloodshed (2:8,12,17), unjust gains (2:9), abuse of the earth (2:17), and idolatry (2:18-19). But a remnant from Judah will live by faith. They will wait patiently for the Lord's judgment upon Babylon, and they will glory in the Lord's work. The prophet is assured that God will act: "Though it linger, wait for it; it will certainly come and will not delay" (2:3). The righteous will trust God's certain word and the arrogant will perish through the woes that God will bring upon them (Jeremiah 50:15,29-32).

God's answer to Habakkuk is that the Lord Almighty can use evil to destroy evil; he can use evil to punish evil. God is sovereign over evil in the world and he will use it for his own purposes, but he will not permit evil to go unpunished. God does not explain how he can sovereignly do this, but it is sufficient that the oracle reveals the ultimate end of the Babylonians. God will not tolerate evil forever. The holy God will destroy unrighteousness but the people of God must wait for him to do so (2:3) and trust his wisdom, as "the righteous will live by his faith" (2:4).

Prayer of Faith

The superscription of Habakkuk 3:1 categorizes chapter three as a prayer. This Hebrew term is a general one. It appears thirty-two times in Psalms, often in the first verse (cf. 4:1; 17:1; 55:1; 61:1; 86:1; 102:1; 143:1) or in the superscription of the psalm itself (90; 102; 142). In its present form, Habakkuk's prayer is intended for temple worshipers. It has musical notations for the director of music (3:1,3,9,13,19; cf. Isaiah 38:20). It is an "intercessory prayer designed to be sung by the congregation or by one representing the congregation" in the temple worship of Israel.[5] It is a communal prayer which Israel utilizes in its temple assemblies. It is not simply Habakkuk's faith, but the faith of Israel as they sing their praise to God and celebrate God's ultimate victory over his enemies.

The psalm is a victory song which calls upon God to enter history on behalf of his people. The psalm celebrates the expected outcome of that redemptive act.[6] It is not a lament, but a petition. It is not a cry of despair, but an assertion of confident faith. Habakkuk has poured out his laments and he has received God's answers. Habakkuk now expresses his confidence in God's future action. Habakkuk will wait patiently for God to act. He will entrust himself to God's promises. The psalm expresses the confidence of a worshiper who trusts the word of his God.

The beginning of the prayer reminds the reader of 2:2-5 and petitions God to act according to his promise. Habakkuk remembers God's past redemptive acts, trusts in God's new promise, and petitions God to act (3:2):

> LORD, I have heard of your fame,
> I stand in awe of your deeds, O LORD.

> Renew them in our day,
>> in our time make them known;
>> in wrath remember mercy.

Habakkuk remembers God's mighty deeds. The God of Judah is the God of the Exodus, the God of the Conquest, and the God of the Davidic Kingdom. Habakkuk knows who God is from his past acts, and given his past redemptive acts and the oracle he has just announced, Habakkuk offers his victory song. He petitions God to renew his mighty deeds in his day.

The particular mighty moment Habakkuk remembers is Sinai. The language of 3:3 is similar to Deuteronomy 33:2 which describes God's descent from Sinai. It is the language of God's presence. God, as a divine warrior, is marching up from Sinai, his holy mountain, in order to act on behalf of his people (cf. Judges 5:4-5; Psalm 18:7-15; 68:4-10,32-35; 77:16-19; Micah 1:3-4; Isaiah 30:27-33). Habakkuk describes a divine theophany where God does battle for his people. He overcomes nations (3:7,12-13) and defeats the chaos of the mighty waters (3:8-10,14-15). He delivers his people and crushes the "leader of the land of wickedness" (3:13). God is Israel's Redeemer. He delivers them from the chaotic evil of an invading empire.

This theophanic vision, then, emboldens Habakkuk's faith. He has been assured of God's redemptive act. He remembers the past and he hopes for the future. He is confident that God will act. In this context Habakkuk offers one of the most stunning expressions of confidence found in Scripture (3:16-19):

> I heard and my heart pounded,
>> my lips quivered at the sound;
> decay crept into my bones,
>> and my legs trembled.
> Yet I will wait patiently for the day of calamity
>> to come on the nation invading us.
> Though the fig tree does not bud
>> and there are no grapes on the vines,

> though the olive crop fails
> and the fields produce no food,
> though there are no sheep in the pen
> and no cattle in the stalls,
> yet I will rejoice in the LORD,
> I will be joyful in God my Savior.
> The Sovereign LORD is my strength;
> he makes my feet like the feet of a deer,
> he enables me to go on the heights.

Habakkuk's response to the theophany is speechlessness. He had earlier offered his own complaint and this is God's response to it (2:1). He had rebuked God just as Job had (Job 13:3,6; 23:4). But the theophany has changed Habakkuk's attitude. He received a vision of God as a divine warrior set for the redemption of his people. God will act against Babylon and now Habakkuk waits for that "day of calamity" to come. While once Habakkuk intended to engage God in argument, now, in the presence of God through this theophany, Habakkuk submits to God's agenda and decides to "wait patiently for the day of calamity to come on the nation invading us" (3:16).

"I will wait patiently" (3:16) translates a Hebrew term which evokes images of security, restfulness, and confidence. Isaiah used the term to describe the rest God had given his people when he delivered them from Egyptian bondage (Isaiah 63:14). David used the term to describe the rest that God had granted his people through his presence among them in the Jerusalem tabernacle (1 Chronicles 23:25). The word expresses Habakkuk's confidence, his peace and fellowship with God despite the circumstances that surround him.

Even when life falls apart and fallenness envelops God's people, they gain confidence from God's past redemptive acts and in his future promises. The confidence of God's people is rooted in what God has done and what he has promised to do. When God's people encounter God in worship, then they commune with him and God emboldens their confidence. Even in the midst of dire circumstances, God's people can rejoice in the God of their salvation. Even in the midst of tragedy, God's people can find a restful peace that engenders genuine joy. But this peace is only found in worship, prayer, and communion with God. Peace comes through God's presence, and God's presence is found in prayer and worship. God's peace is found in his sanctuary, and we enter that sanctuary through the boldness of prayer. When God is acknowledged as the sovereign Redeemer who enters into communion with his people, and his people approach him in trusting humility as the one whom they worship, then genuine joy is discovered in the peace that only God can give and faith finds endurance in the strength that only God can supply.

The chaos of nature and the effects of war cannot destroy this genuine joy and enduring faith. Even if famine invades the land so that there are no figs, olives, or grapes — no harvest of any kind — Habakkuk will still rejoice in the God of his salvation. Even though there are no sheep in the pen and no cattle in the stalls, Habakkuk will still rejoice in the God of his salvation. Even though Babylon may devastate the land and turn God's good land into chaos, Habakkuk will not lose his confidence in God's redemption. Even though Habakkuk recognizes that God is responsible for the devastation that Judah will receive, he nevertheless trusts that God's wrath will turn to mercy, that God's punishment will become God's redemption for those who trust in him. The just will live by faith while the proud are destroyed. Faith is sustained by the reassuring presence of God even when questions remain.

The Lament Psalms

The Psalms mirror the soul and give expression to intense feelings of praise and worship. They express confidence in God (Psalm 23), a desire to worship him (Psalm 100), and a devotion to his ways (Psalm 1). But they also express our deepest moments of despair, doubt, and questioning. They confess sin (Psalm 51), question God about his faithfulness (Psalm 44), and call down God's wrath on enemies (Psalm 94). The Psalms are a collection of diverse hymns and prayers which reflect the continuum of Israel's life with God. They move from confidence to lament to praise. They retell the history of God's people, pray for God's deliverance, and offer thanks for God's redemptive acts. The Psalms are the hymnbook and prayer book of Israel. They have sustained the people of God through triumph and despair, through good times and bad.

Brueggemann provides a helpful typology for categorizing the psalms.[7] He divides the psalms into three groups: (1) Orientation, (2) Disorientation, and (3) New Orientation. Orientation psalms are written in the context of "satisfied seasons of well-being that evoke gratitude for the constancy of blessing." They "articulate joy" in the light of God's creation and governing law. They are faithful professions of faith. They confess confidence in God's presence, law, and creation. They rejoice in God's faithful goodness. These are psalms about God's creation (8, 19, 33, 104, 145), or law (1, 15, 19, 24, 119), or wisdom (14, 49, 112), or they express a confidence in God's enduring presence (11, 16, 23, 46, 121, 131, 133).

Disorientation psalms are written in the context of "seasons of hurt, alienation, suffering, and death" which "evoke rage, resentment, self-pity, and hatred." The sense of well-being, so evident in the orientation psalms, is overwhelmed by the fallenness of the world. These psalms face reality and seek to bring this fallen reality before the throne of God. They boldly enter God's presence with questions, doubts, and despair. They respond to the hurt and pain caused by the fallenness of the world. They are offered in the middle of suffering, persecution, sickness, and prospective death. The people of God are bewildered, confused, and angry, so they cry out to their God who is sovereign over fallenness. In Scripture, these are the psalms of lament

(3, 7, 9, 13, 22, 38–43, 52–57, 86, 88, 90, 123, 126, 129, 143), penitence (6, 32, 38, 51, 102, 130, 143) or imprecation (35, 48, 69, 82–83, 94, 109, 137). Through these prayers, they lament their suffering, confess their sinfulness, and call for God's justice in the world.

New orientation psalms are written in the context of the surprising works of God where the people of God "are overwhelmed with the new gifts of God." God has responded to the laments of his people. The petitioners are transformed by his response. This transformation evokes praise and thanksgiving. God intrudes into the fallenness of the world to work new, surprising things so that joy breaks through the despair. All these prayers and songs bespeak the redemptive action of God to give life to a world where death reigns. God is praised, honored, and blessed because he has transformed the fallen world for the sake of his people who have petitioned him. These psalms express praise (66, 68, 95, 113–114, 146–150), thanksgiving (18, 21, 30, 75, 92, 107, 116, 118, 124, 129, 138), retell the story of God's redemptive acts (78, 105–106, 135–136), exult in God's promise to dwell among his people in Zion (e.g., the Songs of Zion, 46, 48, 76, 84, 87, 121–122) and rejoice in God's promise to the royal house of David (e.g., 2, 29, 45, 95–99, 101, 110, 132, 144). They celebrate the redemptive works of God.

Given the current makeup of our hymnals, it surprises most people to discover that almost half of Psalms is lament. The emphasis in modern worship falls heavily upon orientation and new orientation songs, that is, upon confidence, praise, thanksgiving, and joy. Little appears in our hymnals that is genuinely lament or disorientation, except for some penitential or confessional hymns.[8] Modern Christians are uncomfortable with lament. It is too bold, too daring, and involves God too intimately with his world. It is a cry to God about fallenness and modern Christians want to keep God at a distance from fallenness. God must not get his hands dirty. Yet approximately half of the psalms are laments and the largest single grouping of psalms is individual lament. When fallenness breaks into the lives of God's people, they call upon their God. They invoke God's faithfulness, steadfast love, and sovereignty in order to complain to him, petition his action and ultimately praise him.

Psalm 13 is a typical lament that moves from complaint (vv. 1-2) to petition (vv. 3-4) and then to praise (vv. 5-6). It beautifully illustrates the "typical structure" of lament psalms.[9] I will use this psalm as the framework for the following discussion. The psalmist prayed:

> How long, O LORD? Will you forget me forever?
>> How long will you hide your face from me?
> How long must I wrestle with my thoughts
>> and every day have sorrow in my heart?
>> How long will my enemy triumph over me?
> Look on me and answer, O LORD my God.
>> Give light to my eyes, or I will sleep in death;
> my enemy will say, "I have overcome him,"
>> and my foes will rejoice when I fall.
> But I trust in your unfailing love;
>> my heart rejoices in your salvation.
> I will sing to the LORD,
>> for he has been good to me.

Complaint

Laments are complaints about enemies and tragic circumstances. Lamenters are confused by God's hiddenness or anger. They complain that their enemies persecute them (7:5; 31:15; 71:10; 143:3), triumph over them (41:11; 42:9; 56:2), and mock their faith (25:2; 35:19; 55:3; 69:4; 80:6; 102:8). They complain about sickness, death, and disease (9:13; 16:10; 22:15; 35:7,13; 38:3; 40:2; 56:13; 69:15; 88:4; 109:31). They complain that God has hidden his face or turned away from his people (10:1; 27:9; 44:24; 55:1; 69:17; 88:14; 89:46; 143:7), or that God has forsaken or forgotten his people and his promises (22:1; 42:9; 44:24).

Primarily these complaints come in the form of questions, like the questions of Psalm 13. They ask their Sovereign Lord, "Why?" and "How Long?" They complain to the only one who truly cares, and the only one who can redeem. They voice their frustrations, hurt, pain, anger, and disappointment to their covenant God. Consequently, they ask God not to hide his face, but to remember his covenant (27:9; 55:1; 69:17; 102:2; 143:7); not to forsake them, but to act out of his steadfast love (10:12; 27:9; 38:21; 71:9; 74:19; 138:8). The laments are grounded in God's covenant relationship with his people. They are not offered to just any God, but the cry of the lamenter is "my God" (7:6; 22:1,10; 63:1; 102:24; 140:6). They can ask these questions because they are God's people and he is their God. Laments are expressions of faith.

Psalm 13 asks God four questions, each of which begins with "How long?" The first two questions address God's involvement. How long will God continue to "forget" his servant and "hide" his face from him? The psalmist understands that God controls his universe, and he attributes his present circumstances to God's action or inaction. There must be a real answer. The psalmist assumes that God is responsible for the circumstances of his suffering and so he addresses him. The second two questions address the fallen circumstance in which the psalmist finds himself. In particular, he asks how long sorrow and pain must fill his heart while his enemies triumph over him. The questions are a complaint about God's inaction and the psalmist's sorrow. Where is God? What is he doing? Why does he not act?

Psalm 13 does not reveal the psalmist's particular problem. It speaks in generalities though it was occasioned by some painful event. However, as it appears, it speaks to all disorientation. It speaks honestly and boldly to God about the fallenness of the world. It is an honest appraisal that something is not right with the world. Lament functions to bring the fallenness of the world into the throne room of God and to question God about it. It is the means by which

God's people bring real questions about real pain into the real presence of God.

The psalms are filled with the question, "How long?" It is the cry of God's people under the weight of suffering. It is a cry to a sovereign God who can release them from their suffering. God sets the boundaries of time and he determines the length of suffering. The sovereign God can answer the question which his people ask. It is not a mere expression of despair, but a genuine longing to know. It is a call upon God to act and end the suffering of his people.

> Psalm 6:3, "My soul is in anguish. How long, O LORD, how long?"
>
> Psalm 35:16-17, "Like the ungodly they maliciously mocked; they gnashed their teeth at me. O LORD, how long will you look on? Rescue my life from their ravages, my precious life from these lions."
>
> Psalm 74:10-11, "How long will the enemy mock you, O God? Will the foe revile your name forever? Why do you hold back your hand, your right hand? Take it from the folds of your garment and destroy them!"
>
> Psalm 79:5, "How long, O LORD? Will you be angry forever? How long will your jealousy burn like fire?"
>
> Psalm 80:4, "O LORD God Almighty, how long will your anger smolder against the prayers of your people."
>
> Psalm 89:46, "How long, O LORD? Will you hide yourself forever? How long will your wrath burn like fire?"
>
> Psalm 90:13, "Relent, O LORD! How long will it be? Have compassion on your servants."
>
> Psalm 94:3, "How long will the wicked, O LORD, how long will the wicked be jubilant?"
>
> Psalm 119:84, "How long must your servant wait? When will you punish my persecutors?"

When God's people suffer, even under the weight of God's punishment, as in the Babylonian exile, they cry, "how long?" Even as Jeremiah prophesied the destruction of Judah, his question for God was, "How long must I see the battle standard and hear the sound of the trumpet?"

(Jeremiah 4:21). Zechariah saw a vision where even the angel of the Lord asked the sovereign God, "LORD Almighty, how long will you withhold mercy from Jerusalem and from the towns of Judah, which you have been angry with these seventy years?" (Zechariah 1:12). The martyred Christian souls under the heavenly altar also asked, "How long, Sovereign Lord, holy and true, until you judge the inhabitants of the earth and avenge our blood?" (Revelation 6:10). Even saints in the presence of God still offer lament.

When the Sovereign Lord permits suffering or acts to afflict his people, it is natural to ask "why?" Sometimes the answer is obvious as the history of God's people illustrates. Sometimes they suffered because of their sins. Nevertheless, the cry of "why?" often arises from the lips of God's people. The longest lament in Scripture, while it recognizes the reason for God's devastation of Jerusalem, also ends with this questioning, "Why do you always forget us? Why do you forsake us so long?" (Lamentations 5:20). Whenever Israel faced disaster, "why?" always rung in God's ears as his people lamented.

When Israel was required to gather their own straw, Moses asked, "O Lord, why have you brought trouble upon this people?" (Exodus 5:22). When Israel lost the first battle of Ai, Joshua asked, "Ah, Sovereign LORD, why did you ever bring this people across the Jordan to deliver us into the hands of the Amorites to destroy us?" (Joshua 7:7). When the tribe of Benjamin was on the verge of extinction, Israel cried out, "O LORD, the God of Israel, why has this happened to Israel?" (Judges 21:3). When the Philistines defeated Israel at Aphek, the elders of Israel asked, "Why did the LORD bring defeat upon us today before the Philistines?" (1 Samuel 4:3). When Babylon destroyed Judah and carried them off into captivity, the people asked, "Why, O LORD, do you make us wander from your ways and harden our hearts so we do not revere you?" (Isaiah 63:17). In the midst of that disaster, the people of God asked, "Why has the LORD our God done all of this to us?"

(Jeremiah 5:19; cf. Jeremiah 13:22; 16:10; 22:8; 1 Kings 9:8; 2 Chronicles 7:21). Even Jeremiah asked the Lord, "Why have you afflicted us so that we cannot be healed?" (Jeremiah 14:19). Further, Jeremiah expressed his own lament over the situation of his people by cursing the day of his birth (much like Job 3), "Why did I ever come out of the womb to see trouble and sorrow and to end my days in shame?" (Jeremiah 20:18).

The question seeks some purpose or meaning in the suffering. Certainly it is an emotional outburst, a frustrating exclamation; but it is also a genuine question. Every sufferer wants to know "why," and the people of God, who sustain a covenantal relationship with their Lord, want an answer. The lament psalms ask this question.

> Psalm 10:1, "Why, O LORD, do you stand far off? Why do you hide yourself in times of trouble?"
>
> Psalm 22:1, "My God, My God, why have you forsaken me? Why are you so far from saving me, so far from the words of my groaning?"
>
> Psalm 42:9, "I say to God my Rock, "Why have you forgotten me? Why must I go about mourning, oppressed by the enemy?"
>
> Psalm 43:2, "You are God my stronghold. Why have you rejected me? Why must I go about mourning, oppressed by the enemy?"
>
> Psalm 44:23-24, "Awake, O LORD! Why do you sleep? Rouse yourself! Do not reject us forever. Why do you hide your face and forget our misery and oppression?"
>
> Psalm 74:1, "Why have you rejected us forever, O God? Why does your anger smolder against the sheep of your pasture?"
>
> Psalm 79:10, "Why should the nations say, 'Where is their God?' Before our eyes, make known among the nations that you avenge the outpoured blood of your servants."
>
> Psalm 80:12, "Why have you broken down its walls so that all who pass by pick its grapes."

Psalm 88:14, "Why, O LORD, do you reject me and hide your face from me?"

The suffering is real, so the questions are real. The sovereignty of God is an assumed premise, so the questions are meaningful. Consequently, in the midst of suffering, lamenters seek his presence and question him. Who else can they question? The Lord God Almighty is the Sovereign King. The faithful lamenter asks God because there is no one else to ask. Faithful lament turns to God and appeals to him. Indeed, God invites the lamenter into his presence, and these psalms are present in Scripture as models for faithful lament. God will patiently listen.

Petition

Lament psalms contain a wide range of petitions, but they may be categorized into three types: (a) invocation; (b) redemption; and (c) imprecation. Invocation calls upon God to hear the prayers of his people. Redemption petitions God to deliver his people from their fallen situation. Imprecation asks God to destroy their enemies. Petition, then, appeals to the covenant God to deliver his people for the sake of his steadfast love and to destroy his enemies for the sake of his righteous judgment.

Psalm 13 illustrates these three petitions. Three times the psalmist invokes the name of God and the covenant relationship that exists between them. He uses the name of God, Yahweh, twice (13:1,3) and affirms that Yahweh is his God ("my God," 13:3). He then offers three petitions: "look on me," "answer," and "give light to my eyes." These redemptive petitions call for God to notice his suffering servant, to answer his pleas and to redeem him from the darkness. The psalmist may fear that his death is near which would delight his enemies (13:3-4). The petitioner wants redemption. There is also an implied imprecation. God must not permit his enemies to rejoice over the demise of God's servant. The honor of God is at stake if one of God's people dies. The petition arises not only out of the human need of the moment but also out of a zeal for God's holy name. Psalm 13, then, has invocations, redemptive petitions, and an implied imprecation. This is characteristic of lament psalms in general.

The *invocation* is rooted in the covenant relationship between God and his people. Lament invokes the name of Yahweh, the Lord of the covenant. The invocation assumes that God dwells among his people, that he is their God and they are his people. The lament addresses God as the one who loves his people. In Psalms this personal address ("O LORD," or "O God") occurs 320 times (NRSV) and is abundantly present in the lament psalms (e.g., Psalms 3–7). While some laments portray God as hidden, the invocation — present in every lament — appeals to God's covenantal presence. It assumes that God hears and that he will answer. While God may appear to have forsaken his people or forgotten them, the invocation calls upon God to turn his face toward his people. It appeals to God as their God. It invokes his presence (10:1; 27:9; 55:1; 143:7). Faithful lament addresses God. Lament invokes God's presence according to his steadfast love.

The petition for *redemption* (deliverance, salvation, rescue) is rooted in the steadfast love of the Lord. The psalms reflect God's constant action on behalf of his people to deliver, save, rescue, and redeem. The Hebrew words with this semantic range (*yasa', nazal, padah*) are used 136 times in Psalms. They are used in the past (18:17-18; 34:4,6,17, 19; 106:43; 107:6), present (22:20; 40:13; 72:12; 109:21), and future tenses (18:3; 24:5; 34:18; 55:16). They remember past deliverances, expect future redemption or request present salvation. The laments ask for God's deliverance. The following petitions utilizing these Hebrew terms appear in the following individual laments. Thirty-two times the psalmist cries "redeem me" or "deliver me" or "save me." Here are just a few:

Psalm 7:1, "O LORD my God, I take refuge in you; save and deliver me from all who pursue me."

Psalm 25:20, "Guard my life and rescue me; let me not be put to shame, for I take refuge in you."

Psalm 31:2, "Turn your ear to me, come quickly to my rescue; be my rock of refuge, a strong fortress to save me."

Psalm 59:1, "Deliver me from my enemies, O God; protect me from those who rise up against me."

Psalm 70:1, "Hasten, O God, to save me; O LORD, come quickly to help me."

Psalm 71:2, "Rescue me and deliver me in your righteousness; turn your ear to me and save me."

Psalm 109:26, "Help me, O LORD my God; save me in accordance with your love."

Psalm 143:9, "Rescue me from my enemies, O LORD, for I hide myself in you."

The petition for redemption is motivated by God's own glory and/or by the steadfast love of the Lord. The petitioner asks for redemption on the ground of God's covenantal relationship with him. Both of these themes reflect God's intention to commune with his people, and God's people ask him to be faithful. Psalm 109:21 combines both motivations: "But you, O Sovereign LORD, deal well with me for your name's sake; out of the goodness of your love, deliver me."

When God redeems his people, he redeems them for his own honor and out of his steadfast love (17:7; 31:16; 44:26; 57:3; 69:13; 109:26). The two thoughts are intertwined because God intends to have a people for himself through whom he can display his glory. Thus, the communal lament of Psalm 85:7 asks, "Show us your unfailing love, O LORD, and grant us your salvation." The individual lament of Psalm 6:4 asks, "Turn, O LORD, and deliver me; save me because of your unfailing love." Further, Psalm 79:9 appeals to God's honor: "Help us, O God our Savior, for the glory of your name; deliver us and forgive our sins for your name's sake." Consequently, knowing God's intent to have a people for himself and knowing his faithful love, the people of God petition him through lament to act on their behalf. The motivation of the petition is not some kind of self-pity, but the honor of God who manifests his steadfast love when he redeems his people. It is a zeal for the honor of God and a desire for restored communion between God and his people.

The petition for *imprecation* (curse, destruction) is rooted in the righteous justice of the Lord.[10] The petition for deliverance often involves the destruction of enemies. The individual lament of Psalm 3 ends with this petition, "Arise, O LORD! Deliver me, O my God! Strike all my enemies on the jaw; break the teeth of the wicked. From the LORD comes deliverance. May your blessing be on your people" (3:7-8). Or from another individual lament, "My times are in your hands; deliver me from my enemies and from those who pursue me" (31:15). This is a consistent theme throughout Psalms (7:1; 18:3,17,48; 54:7; 59:1; 69:18; 71:11; 106:10; 138:7; 142:6; 143:9). This appeal is rooted in God's righteousness. For example, Psalm 71 is an individual lament against the petitioner's enemies (71:9-11), but what he asks for is God's justice, not personal vengeance. He requests, "Rescue me and deliver me in your righteousness" (71:2). God saves according to his righteousness (36:6). God will defeat his enemies for the sake of his name, for the honor of his righteousness, and for the love of his people. It is on this threefold ground that Psalm 143 makes its final plea to God (143:11-12):

> For your name's sake, O LORD, preserve my life;
>> in your righteousness, bring me out of trouble.
> In your unfailing love, silence my enemies;
>> destroy all my foes,
>> for I am your servant.

The petitions are made to a sovereign God by a people who belong to him. "Blessed are the people of whom this is true; blessed are the people whose God is the LORD," the psalmist declares (144:15). God's people rest upon God's covenant, his sovereignty, and his steadfast love. As God's people, they are confident that God will answer their petitions. God can save (54:1; 124:8; 130:7). God is faithful to his covenant (119:170). God saves so that his name might be glorified (106:47; 79:9). God redeems his servants out of his steadfast love (6:4). When they call, he will answer (18:6; 34:17; 50:15; 55:16).

Praise

With some exceptions (Psalms 44, 88), all laments end with some kind of praise. It is either a declaration of praise itself (like 6:8-9; 10:17; 22:24; 28:6; 31:7) or a vow of praise (27:6; 54:6; 74:21; 79:12-13; 80:17-18). This praise arises out of the petitioner's confidence in God's past redemptive acts, God's continued steadfast love, and the present covenantal relationship. The petitioner praises God or vows to praise God in the light of what God has done or will do. He praises God because God has heard and he knows his God will answer.

The praise section of the lament psalms may contain four different types of confident expressions. It may, for example, rejoice in the past works of God, and consequently expect a new work of God to deliver the psalmist from the fallen situation (5:11; 35:9; 40:16). It may either contain a declaration of praise or a vow to offer praise to God in the light of redemption (9:13-14; 22:22,25; 26:12; 57:9; 71:18). It may also express the quiet confidence of waiting for God's response (25:3,5,21; 27:14; 37:9,34; 39:7; 40:1; 130:5). It may also express the fundamental trust that the petitioner has in God's gracious purposes despite the circumstances (13:6; 31:6,14; 52:8; 55:23; 56:4,11; 119:42; 143:8).

Psalm 13 illustrates this classic move in lament psalms from complaint and petition to praise and thanksgiving. Westermann has called this the *"waw* adversative" in individual laments.[11] In other words, as the psalmist laments, there comes a moment in the psalm where the writer shifts from complaint to praise. This transition is marked in Hebrew by the "*waw* adversative," signaled in English by the word "but." Psalm 13 moves from complaint to petition, and then introduces praise by declaring, "But I trust in your unfailing love" (13:5). The psalm of lament, then, ends in praise. It ends with confidence and trust. It rejoices in the God who provides salvation and deliverance. What occasioned this mood swing? Why does the tone of the psalm change from lament to praise?

Westermann and Brueggemann, among others, have argued that we need to envision an "oracle of salvation" which offers a response to the lament.[12] In other words, the psalmist offers his complaint and petition as in 13:1-4, and then waits for a divine response. Once he receives this response, he then writes 13:5-6. This may have been enacted within the liturgy of the temple worship where a spokesperson for God would respond to the lament and the worshiper would then offer his vow of praise or affirm his trust in God. There can be little doubt that this sometimes happened. Indeed, we find both Job and Habakkuk responding to divine theophanies or oracles. They offered their laments and then in response to the divine theophanies they humbled themselves before God and expressed their ultimate trust in his purposes. There are also examples in the writings of the prophets (cf. Isaiah 59:3ff; Joel 2:1ff; Jeremiah 51:36ff). It is possible that this is what is envisioned here.

However, some psalms may be translated with a "nevertheless" rather than a "but." Instead of hearing a word from God that engenders this praise, the vow of praise may arise out of the confidence of faith. Despite the dire circumstances of the lament, the petitioner through prayer experiences the reassuring presence of God. The change is not just a change in mood but is the experience of God's presence which moves the heart from lament to praise. It is a sanctuary experience

— an experience of God's presence which gives rise to praise. The petitioners' confidence in God's steadfast love moves them to praise God when just moments ago they were complaining to him. But the complaints and the praise arise out of the same attitude — faith in God's loving presence. They complain to God because they believe, and they learn to praise God through their lament. Through prayer and lamentation petitioners move to a new understanding of faith, a deeper appreciation of God's grace and the assurance of God's presence. God has already begun to act. He is present to comfort his people and he will ultimately vindicate them. "My comfort in my suffering is this," the psalmist writes, "Your promise preserves my life" (119:50). Even though he asks in lament, "When will you comfort me?" (119:82), he knows his comfort is found in God's steadfast love (119:76). Prayer as lamentation moves the people of God to a deeper understanding and a relational experience of that love. God offers his people a "sanctuary" experience in the midst of lament.

Conclusion

Job continued to pray, but his friends did not. Job never stopped praying, never gave up his faith, never cursed God. But he questioned, complained, and vented his bitterness about his situation. When Habakkuk encountered an unjust situation, he lamented it. He complained and doubted. He approached God with his questions. The psalmists approach God with questions, despair, and lament. They ask God "why?" and "how long?" They seek his face. They seek his communion. They desire God's presence and his deliverance. But they ask their God questions.

The continuity here is that the people of God have always approached God boldly with their questions because they know he is the Sovereign Lord who can redeem. Prayer moves us into the presence of God where we are awed by his wisdom, power, and love. God is present to us through prayer, through lament, through worship. In worship, in a sanctuary experience, we find God's strength by which our faith is empowered to live through the lament and ultimately to break out in praise. God acts to comfort his people through their laments. God provides "songs in the night" as we engage him in prayer. God invites us to lament and he responds in grace.

The longest lament of the Bible is the book of Lamentations. The poem does not doubt the reason for the suffering of Jerusalem. God has punished Judah for her sins (1:5). Lamentations offers a vivid description of this punishment along with expressions of repentance and sorrow for the sin that brought it. Nevertheless, in the middle of this lament there is hope. It is a hope rooted in God's steadfast love. Within the lament there is room for praise because God still seeks a people for himself and we trust in his unfailing love. The central stanzas of the lament encapsulate the meaning and function of lament itself (Lamentations 3:19-26):

> I remember my affliction and my wandering,
>> the bitterness and the gall.
> I well remember them,
>> and my soul is downcast within me.
> Yet this I call to mind
>> and therefore I have hope:
> Because of the LORD's great love we are not consumed,
>> for his compassions never fail.
> They are new every morning;
>> great is your faithfulness.
> I say to myself, "The LORD is my portion;
>> therefore I will wait for him."
> The LORD is good to those whose hope is in him,
>> to the one who seeks him;
> it is good to wait quietly
>> for the salvation of the LORD.

---

[1]Michael E.W. Thompson, "Prayer, Oracle and Theophany: The Book of Habakkuk," *Tyndale Bulletin* 44.1 (1993): 33-53.

[2]O. Palmer Robertson, *The Books of Nahum, Habakkuk and Zephaniah*, The New International Commentary on the Old Testament (Grand Rapids: Eerdmans, 1990), p. 160.

[3]J.G. Harris, "The Laments of Habakkuk's Prophecy," *Evangelical Quarterly* 45.1 (1973): 29.

[4]On this understanding of Habakkuk 2:4, see Robertson, *Nahum, Habakkuk, Zephaniah*, pp. 174-185.

[5]Ralph L. Smith, *Micah-Malachi*, Word Biblical Commentary, 32 (Waco, TX: Word Books, 1984), p. 114.

[6]Theodore Hiebert, *God of My Victory: The Ancient Hymn in Habakkuk 3*, Harvard Semitic Monographs, 38 (Atlanta: Scholars Press, 1986): pp. 118-120.

[7]Brueggemann, *Message of Psalms*, pp. 16ff. The following paragraphs are heavily dependent upon his work.

[8]Lester Meyer, "A Lack of Laments in the Church's Use of the Psalter," *Lutheran Quarterly* 7 (1993): 67-78; David N. Duke, "Giving Voice to Suffering in Worship: A Study in the Theodicies of Hymnody," *Encounter* 52 (1991): 263-272; and Resner, "Lament," 133.

[9]W.H. Bellinger, Jr., *Psalms: Reading and Studying the Book of Praises* (Peabody, MA: Hendrickson Publishers, 1990), p. 45. Westermann, *Praise and Lament*, p. 52, has a similar structure: address, lament, confession of trust, petition, vow of praise.

[10]My notes on imprecatory psalms are available on the web at *www. collegepress.com/jmhicks/imprecat.htm.*

[11]Westermann, *Praise and Lament*, pp. 71ff.

[12]Westermann, *Praise and Lament*, pp. 59-64; and Brueggemann, *Message of Psalms*, pp. 57-58.

Chapter Eight

"If I Should Die before I Wake"?
The Death of Children in God's Story

> *How long will you say such things?*
> *Your words are a blustering wind.*
> *Does God pervert justice?*
> *Does the Almighty pervert what is right?*
> *When your children sinned against him,*
> *he gave them over to the penalty of their sin.*
> *Bildad to Job, 8:2-4*

A Dialogue

"There is no one to blame," said Joy, a pediatric nurse. "These things happen. The human genetic structure is not perfect. Joshua's condition is no one's fault. It was merely the combination of a series of coincidences."

"I understand there is no one to blame," Barbara replied. "It's not the doctor's fault, it's not our fault. But there is this nagging feeling that something could have been done differently. I don't blame anyone. But that feeling leaves me pretty empty."

Overhearing the conversation, Rita interjected a question. "Is there really no one to blame? Is no one responsible?"

"What do you mean?" Joy asked.

"Things like this are not just a matter of chance or luck," Rita explained. "I believe God is responsible for this world, and he uses these kinds of things to discipline, even punish, people. It's God's way of saying, 'Pay attention to me.'"

Raising Barbara's ire, she asked: "Are you saying that Joshua was born with a genetic defect because God wanted to punish me?"

"That's a ridiculous idea," Joy blurted out. "What a terrible view of God! Isn't God supposed to be loving rather than vindictive. God is not responsible for Joshua's condition. He had nothing to do with it."

"Wait a minute, Joy," Barbara answered. "I'm not sure I want to say that God had nothing to do with it. I prayed that Joshua would be healthy, but Joshua isn't healthy; he's dying. God answered, "No." Would you rather me believe that God did not answer at all, or that his answer was, 'Well, I'm sorry, I can't do anything about that'?"

"That's my point," Rita exclaimed. "God gave Joshua this genetic condition. God protects those who love him, and . . ."

"And he did not protect Joshua, right?," Barbara interrupted. "Why? Because of some sin in my life? Is God going to take away my son because of my sin?"

Rita replied: "That might be exactly what he is doing. Submit yourself to God's discipline and he will reward your faith. Acknowledge your sin and he will renew your joy. He might even heal Joshua if you really turn to him in faith."

"This is getting out of hand," Joy said with some exasperation. "I see cases like Joshua every day. These children are not acts of God. No one is to blame, not Barbara, not God."

"I agree I'm not to blame," Barbara responded. "Though I'm not perfect, I have no great sin in my life that deserves this discipline. God is not punishing me. But neither can I absolve God of responsibility when my prayers assume God has something to do with what goes on in my life. Don't I pray for protection? Don't I pray for health? Don't I pray for the life of my child? What is God saying to me when he answers, 'No'?"

"He's not saying anything at all," Joy shouted. "There is no 'No,' and there is no 'Yes.' He has nothing to do with it! We shouldn't even be praying for those sorts of things as if God were some giant Santa Claus."

"Barbara, don't listen to Joy," Rita interjected. "She doesn't believe God works in his world anymore, but I believe God is speaking to you through your suffering. God is saying to you, 'Get your life right; change your ways, and I will bless you.' Don't reject him."

"Is there no other choice?" Barbara questions. "You two have painted me into a corner. I either admit I am a sinner deserving the death of my child, something which I do not believe, or I stop praying to God as the one who can really do something in my life. I either lie about my integrity or I shut God out of the world. I can do neither. But I am confused by a God who is responsible for my son's condition. I doubt his compassion and question his justice. I still believe in God, but wonder about what kind of God he is. Why has God given me a terminally ill son?"

This fictional dialogue between Joy, Rita, and Barbara is typical of many conversations between a secularist, a believer, and a caught-in-the-middle sufferer. The secularist presses the deistic perspective or at least one which removes God from responsibility for the daily events of his world. The believer presses a theological perspective of reward and blessing which makes easy judgments about why health and wealth are given to certain people and not to others. The suffering believer is caught in the middle. Barbara is distressed not only by the experience of suffering itself, but by the dialogue that swirls around her. The sufferer is forced into potential theological camps which have dire consequences for her faith. Does she accept Joy's perspective and stop praying for anything concrete in her life? Or, does she accept Rita's perspective and acknowledge a sin which she does not know? The first choice undermines what she believes about prayer, and the second undermines her integrity. The first relegates God to the periphery of human existence so that there is no real relationship with God in the concrete world, and the second transforms her relationship with God into a *quid pro quo* transaction where God gives one thing in exchange for something of equal value. Barbara, caught between Joy and Rita, finds the dialogue almost as distressing as the suffering. Barbara finds herself sitting on the trash heap with Job, and like Job, she listens to the "counsel" of her friends. Barbara becomes, like Job, an impatient sufferer with a questioning faith.

The setting which occasions Job's impatient questioning faith is the "comfort" of his friends. The central charge made by Job's friends is that Job now shares the fate of the wicked. What happened to him can only happen to the wicked. The most chilling argument for their case is the fact that Job is childless. As indicated by the quotation from Bildad which heads this chapter, this is a sure sign of God's justice. When Job's children died, they died because of sin, either Job's or their own. Job's sin is most clearly revealed and God's judgment most obviously announced in the death of his children. The community knows that Job is godless because he is childless.

The death of a child is still one of the most gut-wrenching and heartbreaking realities of the fallen world. It cries out for explanation. The friends had their explanation, but Job had none.

The Theodic Problem

Theodicy is an attempt, as Milton put it, to justify "the ways of God to man." Theodicy is God's defense attorney. We defend God's actions against the charges of a fallen humanity. Believers marshal biblical, philosophical, and rational evidence in order to make a case for God's fairness, justice, and blamelessness.

Such an attempt appears rooted in human arrogance. It assumes an optimistic view of human reason which is deluded into believing that it can speak for God. Ultimately God does not need our help as the book of Job demonstrates. God did not need the help of Job or his friends to explain himself. In fact, God offers no explanation but asserts his sovereignty, wisdom, and care (Job 38–42). Nevertheless, we seek explanations. We want to inspect God's reasons for suffering and judge them for ourselves.

While the discipline of theodicy is often helpful, it can also be seriously misleading and subversive.[1] It tends to set up its own standards of behavior by which to judge God. It tends to delimit God's sovereignty. It tends to put God in a box for inspection, standing over rather than submitting to him. It assumes that finite, fallen human rationality can sit in judgment on the infinite, holy divine purpose. Even in the midst of our theodic attempts we sense how overwhelmingly arrogant the attempt is. Nevertheless, we seek an explanation. We want to know God's reasons and we want to debate their legitimacy.

The death of a child creates a moment of theodic tension. The innocence of the child and the grief for a life unlived create a crisis of faith for the believer. How can God justify this? How can we justify God in the light of this? Why does he permit — or, dare we say, even cause — such suffering?

The Charge against God

At the center of Dostoevski's nineteenth century novel *The Brothers Karamazov* is the meaningless death of children. This theme runs throughout the book. It begins with the story of a mother who desperately visits one monastery after another hoping for a vision of her dead child and ends with Captain Snegirev's lament over the death of his son Iljusta. At a climactic point in the novel Ivan Karamazov, a modern nihilist comparable to Nietzsche, argues that God cannot be the center of meaning if children suffer pointlessly. As evidence Ivan offers the examples of Turkish atrocities in Bulgaria where children are cut from their mothers' wombs and infants are impaled on bayonets. Ivan protests that even if their suffering was a "necessary payment for truth" then that "truth is not worth such a price." Would you erect a building, Ivan asks, on the foundation of such suffering? Would you "consent to be the architect" if human happiness meant "that it was essential and inevitable to torture to death" babies? How, then, could God do so?[2]

Elie Wiesel, the Holocaust survivor, has also made the suffering of children a major theme. In *Night*, the powerful account of his suffering in Nazi concentration camps, he recalls the night he first saw the flames of Auswitchz. The flames which consumed innocent children "consumed [his] faith forever" and "murdered [his] God."[3] In fact, Wiesel took God to court in his play *The Trial of God*.[4] The witnesses against God include a million children who were butchered in the Holocaust. "Let their premature, unjust deaths," the prosecutor Berish demands, "turn into an outcry so forgetful that it will make the universe tremble with fear and remorse!"[5] God cannot be defended; he cannot be justified in the face of this evil. The prosecutor, near the end of the trial, shouts his protest and tells God that "He's more guilty than ever!"[6] The blood of a million children is on the hands of God. God is responsible for his world. Wiesel understands this. But the modern believer shrinks back from that thought.

The modern world understands the question. Indeed, the seeming horror of the possible answer drives some to deism (where God allows the world to run much like we watch a clock tick), and drives others to revise their concept of God (perhaps he is not as powerful or loving as we thought). Can God really be responsible for this world where radical evil is so pervasive? The modern believer seeks to absolve God, to justify him by removing him from involvement in the world or by understanding ("forgiving") God's limitations. We want to isolate God from the problem; we want to back him into corner where we can justify him. We must defend God; or, at least, we must make excuses for him. There is only so much God can do. He has his limitations. God does the best he can do with the world he has made. He does the most he can do.[7] We must understand God's predicament. We must forgive him. Wiesel will have none of this coddling of God. God is responsible or he is not God.

What do we say when we are faced with the startling fact that innocent children suffer and die? Some die from the cruelty of others as in the Holocaust. Others die in earthquakes and tornadoes. Others die from debilitating genetic and infectious conditions. The suffering and eventual death of children, for whatever reason they may die, is the most lamentable event in human experience. It is an eventuality that we would all prevent if we could. Why does not God? God could heal Joshua, but he has not yet. God could have prevented the slaughter of innocents in the Holocaust as he did in the days of Esther, but he did not. God saved Moses, but what about the other children in Egypt? God saved Jesus, but other infants in Bethlehem were slaughtered. Is the death of children something God begrudingly permits when he could prevent it? Why would God permit such evil?

The Complexity of a Fallen World

Human existence is intertwined with fallenness. Nothing escapes it. Everything is tainted. Pain, mourning, and death reach into every aspect of human experience. Unlike angels, when human beings fell from their pristine life in the Garden, all of humanity was affected. Because in Adam all die, so all human beings know fallenness. Because we are united with Adam in this earthly existence — we all bear the image of the earthly Adam (1 Corinthians 15:49) — we are all united in death together.

Human solidarity means that human experience, whether innocent or not, is bound over to death and the consequences of sin. Human solidarity means that the sin of one has consequences for another. When an alcoholic father abuses his children, it has a dramatic effect on his grandchildren. When a teenage young man fathers a child outside of marriage, it affects the future life of that child. One person's sin is another person's suffering. This is the way human beings and communities are bound together. They share a common experience and a common life so that what one does affects the other. No one is an island.

When Adam sinned, the whole world was plunged into death. When a family gives itself to evil, the consequences of that evil reverberate for generations so that God can even speak of "punishing the children for the sin of the fathers to the third and fourth generation" (Exodus 20:5). When the wicked reign, the nation is punished and innocents suffer. Even though Habakkuk and Jeremiah were God's righteous prophets at the time of the Babylonian siege of Jerusalem, they too suffered the disgrace, pain, and displacement of that tragedy.

Because human existence is bound together in this solidarity, when God acts against sin, the innocent are often entangled in sin's consequences. Because of human solidarity, when God acts against evil, it affects children. When Isaiah describes the overthrow of Babylon, he describes it in the most horrendous terms. Not only will the rulers and people "fall by the sword," but "their infants will be dashed to pieces before their eyes" (Isaiah 13:15-16). The invaders will "have no mercy on infants nor will they look with compassion on children" (Isaiah 13:18). Even though Babylon boasted in its pride that it would neither become a widow nor lose children because of its power, God promises that "both of these will overtake you in a moment, on a single day: loss of children and widowhood" (Isaiah 47:8-9).

In these punishment texts, God uses the death of children as evidence of the world's fallenness. When God flooded the earth in the days of Noah, many children died. When God destroyed Sodom and Gomorah, many children died. When God conquered the Canaanites, many children died. When God used the Syrians, the Assyrians, and the Babylonians to punish Israel, many children died (Hosea 9:12-17; Jeremiah 6:11,21; 9:21; 13:14). When God sends famine, beasts, and plague, children die (Ezekiel 5:17; Jeremiah 18:21). The death of children is a consequence of the fall. Human solidarity means that we cannot escape that consequence. Innocents die along with the guilty (Lamentations 2:19-20; 4:4,10) and the son suffers the consequences of his father's wickedness (Lamentations 5:7; Jeremiah 32:18).

The death of children is one of the most profound and powerful statements of fallenness. Children die because the world is fallen. They do not die because they are sinful. The death of children is not the cause of fallenness but is one of its many consequences. In fact, it epitomizes fallenness. The death of children, more than any other thing, testifies that the world is not the way it is supposed to be. It testifies to brokenness, heartache, and despair. When we see the picture of a dead child carried in the arms of a fireman, we sense how evil the world really is. When we see AIDS babies struggling for life in a hospital, we sense how fallen the world really is. When we experience the death of our children, we know that this is not the way it is supposed to be.

But how does God feel about these deaths? Does God take pleasure in the death of children? Absolutely not! God grieves over his people.[8] When children die, God mourns their deaths. God himself offers a lament for his people (Amos 5:1-3; Ezekiel 2:9-10; 19:1-14). He leads the funeral dirge. God weeps over death, even of the wicked (Isaiah 15:5; 16:9,11; Jeremiah 48:36-38). He takes no pleasure in the death of the wicked, much less in the death of children (Ezekiel 18:32; 33:11). God's eyes become a fountain for tears (Jeremiah 8:21–9:3; cf. 9:8-10; 12:7-12; 15:5-9). God himself weeps over the death of children. God never intended children to die. Indeed, he wanted to fill the earth with children. But now, due to sin, the world is fallen, and children die.

Their deaths seem so unfair to us. We find the death of aged adults more acceptable. We understand their deaths better. We sense that they have lived their lives and they have had the opportunity to enjoy life, raise children, and serve the common good. They lived their "natural life span." However, when the lives of children are cut short, we mourn their loss of opportunity. There is something unfair about that lost potential. Children, we think, have a right to a "life story."[9] Children have a right to their own story. No one, it seems, not even God, should steal that from them. But, as Hauerwas points out, no one has his own story. Everyone is born into the story of God. We are not autonomous agents in the world to create our own story. Rather, we are "all, adults and children alike, born into a narrative not of our own making — that is, we are creatures of a gracious God who discover that precisely because we are such, we do not have to 'make up' our lives."[10]

The loss of a potential life is a cause for lamentation, but it is not a matter for adjudication before the bar of human fairness. Our lives are not our own. We are God's creatures. More than that, we are fallen creatures who can make no claim on God. Everything belongs to him, and he is not in our debt (Job 41:11; cf. Romans 11:35). God has graciously given us a story, and it is the story of his fellowship and love. Fallen humanity wants to make up its own story. As we seek our own way, we find death and alienation. As we accept God's story, and live out our lives in the light of his grace, we praise the God who seeks communion with us.

What claim will we make upon God for the lives of our children? What story will we write in order to preserve our sense of justice and fairness? Perhaps the story of those children is part of God's story for our own lives. Perhaps they are there to create love, remind us of love, and offer the hope of love. Perhaps they are there to point us to the greatest love of all — the love God has for his children. Perhaps those children are there to witness to the mystery of God, life and death.

Diane Komp is a pediatric oncologist who teaches at Yale University School of Medicine. She describes her medical education as one which "derailed" her early religious convictions. If she were going to believe, "it would require the testimony of reliable witnesses without culturally determined expectations about death."[11] She found her reliable witnesses in dying children. The death of Anna functions paradigmatically for Dr. Komp:[12]

> Today many children with leukemia are cured, but this was not the case when Anna first became sick. Her therapy brought her periods of time when she was dis-

ease-free over the five years she received treatment, but she faced the end of her life at age seven. Before she died, she mustered the final energy to sit up in her hospital bed and say: "The angels — they're so beautiful! Mommy, can you see them? Do you hear their singing? I've never heard such beautiful singing!" Then she laid back on her pillow and died.

Her parents reacted as if they had been given the most precious gift in the world. The hospital chaplain in attendance was more comfortable with the psychological than with the spiritual and he beat a hasty retreat to leave the existentialist doctor alone with the grieving family. Together we contemplated a spiritual mystery that transcended our understanding and experience. For weeks to follow the thought that stuck in my head was: Had I found a reliable witness?

This experience, Dr. Komp wrote, "opened a window for me that had long been tightly shuttered. I recognized a pattern in their stories that helped me re-examine systems of belief that lay on the other side of the window."[13] Dying children, according to Dr. Komp, witness to the reality of God's loving care. It is not their death that offers this witness. Rather, it is their peace, confidence, hope, and experience of God that witness to God's care and love. Little children, even in their dying, testify to the Kingdom of God.

As horrible as it seems, the reality is that the death of children — even the death of my Joshua — shapes and refines our characters in ways that perhaps they could not have been otherwise. It is difficult to conceive of any other experience that would have driven me to God's throne or shaped my vision of God or molded my character more than the terminal illness of my son. As horrible as it seems, my son's terminal illness has had a powerful, formative, and positive impact on my life and on the life of my family.

It has provided the opportunity for lives to bear witness to the grace, compassion, and faithfulness of God. It has provided a testimony to the community of faith in which we live, and it has provided the community of faith the opportunity to share its life with us. Our experience has shaped the life of the church in which we live, and the life of the church has shaped our experience of Joshua's condition. It has shaped me, my wife, my children, and my community in ways that I cannot imagine, nor can I imagine any other way in which those good things could have been produced (though if I had the choice, I would not knowingly make this one). My family understands what it means to love one who cannot love back. My family empathizes with the hurts, pains, and trials of handicapped families. My family has been equipped for ministry with hurting families. My family knows the comfort of God and how to share it with those who hurt. Given the fallen character of the world, we would suffer loss if there were no dying children. But everything in my heart protests against that truth.

We gave our son the name "Joshua" because we wanted him to mature into a leader of God's people. We wanted him to serve God's people as Joshua had served Israel. We have been crushed by the loss of those dreams, but perhaps those dreams live on. Because Joshua has shaped my family, my church, my students, perhaps that is the leadership that Joshua provides. Perhaps Joshua has done more good in the world and brought more praise to God's glory through his illness and the character-formation that he has produced in God's people than he could have ever otherwise. Perhaps Joshua's illness really does serve the glory of God. But if it were left to me, I would choose another way and trade everything for the life of my son.

Is God Active in the Death of Children?

In chapter four I categorized God's purposes in the world as: (1) punitive, (2) disciplinary, and (3) redemptive. God sometimes punishes evil in the world, sometimes he tests his people and sometimes he redeems them. All of these actions serve God's ultimate purpose, and God is involved in the world to bring to fruition that purpose in the lives of his people. But is God active in the death of children?

The Story of Job (Job 1)

Because of my experience with Joshua, the story of Job reads a bit differently now. When I read that God protected Job's health in the first test, and then his life in the second test, I wonder why God did not protect Job's children? Why did God not keep his hedge around Job's children just as he kept it around Job's life? The power was in God's hands. He determined the kind of power he would put into the hand of Satan and he determined the limits of that power (1:12; 2:6). God bore the ultimate responsibility for the evil that came upon Job because it did not have to come at all (cf. 2:10; 42:7). God could have kept the "hedge" in place or he could have prevented what Satan sought to implement. God could have refused Satan's request. God extended his hand to permit Job's suffering (1:11; 2:5). Though Satan may have been the direct agent, God was responsible. He was at least responsible both in the sense that he gave Satan the *permission* and in the sense that he gave Satan the *power*! God could have refused Satan's challenge; he could have restricted Satan further than he did. He could have said, "Satan, you can destroy his property, but not his children." God sovereignly decided to test Job in the context of Satan's question, "Does Job fear God for nothing?" (1:9). God decided to open up Job's children for attack in order to answer Satan's question.

After the first disaster, Job responds, "The LORD gave and the LORD has taken away; may the name of the LORD be praised" (1:21). Job attributes the giving and taking of his children to the Lord. The Lord is praised for giving his blessings, and the Lord is praised for taking them away. Job, in the clearest of terms, asserts God's responsibility for his predicament. The Lord gave, and the Lord took away. God is as active in the taking as he is in the giving. According to

Job, people of faith must be willing to accept both. This acceptance for Job meant the acceptance of the death of his children. God is sovereign and Job is still a person of faith. But that acceptance did not come without questioning, doubt, and despair. As we read through the dialogues we find Job often impatient, bitter, and accusatory. Nevertheless, we find a person of faith. He will not curse God or give up his faith commitment.

The friends who come to comfort Job, however, find a negative message in the death of Job's children. Bildad speculates that the children were sinners like Job. Protesting that God does not "pervert justice," he confidently asserts, "When your children sinned against him, he gave them over to the penalty of their sin" (8:4). The cruelty (and falsity) of such a statement is apparent to the reader of the prologue. Eliphaz implies that if Job had been more righteous, his children would still be with him (5:25). Indeed, one consequence of a person's wickedness, according to Bildad, is that "he has no offspring or descendants among his people" (18:19). The loss of his children, according to Bildad, is a sign of Job's wickedness. "Surely," Bildad concludes, "such is the dwelling of an evil man; such is the place of one who knows not God" (18:21). Again, the reader of the prologue knows that this is not true. But it, no doubt, stung Job's heart.

The readers understand that this is not the reason at all. Job saw to the spiritual needs of his children (1:5), and the death of his children had nothing to do with them *per se*, but with Job. The meaning of the death of Job's children is found in the testing of Job. Job's children die as part of a trial where Job's faith is put in the dock. The story of Job reflects God's permissive activity. God actively decided to permit Satan to kill Job's children. He gave Satan a range of freedom, and certainly God was aware how Satan might use that freedom. He gave Satan a restriction — do not harm Job personally. As such, he placed Job's children at Satan's discretion. God was not ignorant of what Satan might do and he could have excluded the lives of Job's children. But he did not. Instead, God permitted the death of Job's children.

The nature of the trial is crucial here. The radical nature of the test implied the destruction of all that Job cherished as a blessing from God. The question is: "Does Job fear God for nothing?" (1:9). If the test is to be thorough (not only for Job but for all who would later read his story), if it is to address the question fully, then every profit for serving God, every blessing, must be removed. If anything remained, especially his children, these might be considered props for Job's faith. They would be the blessings which remained. If any blessing remained, then in it Job would find the reward of his faith. If his children were still alive, if his wife were supportive, if he could sell his sheep to feed his family, then Job could look to each of these "goods" as God's blessings. This is why the test had to extend to even Job's health, since it would still have constituted the one blessing which would prop up his faith. In order to fully test Job's faith, every prop was removed.

The necessity for the radical character of the test is indicated by Satan himself. After the first test, Satan concluded that Job was even more selfish than he had initially thought. Job was really only concerned about himself. "Skin for skin," Satan asserts (2:4). Job did not really care about his servants, his property or his children. He only cares about himself, his own skin. "Strike Job himself — in his own skin," Satan predicts, "and then he will curse you." The suffering was radical because the test went to the heart of faith. The radical nature of the test demanded a severe testing. Will Job fear God even when he has no vested interest (no family, no property, no security, no health, no benefit) in fearing God? Will Job fear God despite his radical suffering? Philip Yancey has focused the issue well:

> Do human beings truly possess freedom and dignity? Satan challenged God on that count. We have freedom to descend, of course — Adam and all his offspring have proved that. But do we have freedom to ascend,

to believe God for no other reason than, well . . . for no reason at all. Can a person believe even when God appears to him as an enemy? Is that kind of faith even possible? Or is faith, like everything else, a product of environment and circumstances? These are the questions posed in the Book of Job. In the opening chapters, Satan reveals himself as the first great behaviorist. Job was *conditioned* to love God, he claims. Take away the rewards, and watch faith crumble. Job, oblivious, is selected for the great contest.[14]

Job himself saw this point though he was unaware of the dimensions of the test. I believe one of the clearest expressions of faith in Job is found in his response to Zophar's tirade that God punishes the wicked and that their prosperity is short-lived (20:5). The fate of the wicked is God's wrath (20:28-29), according to Zophar. But Job is impatient with such an explanation and he complains, "Why do the wicked live on, growing old and increasing in power?" (21:7). More pointedly, "They see their children established around them, their offspring before their eyes. Their homes are safe and free from fear" (21:8-9a). And, "They send forth their children as a flock; their little ones dance about" (21:11). The wicked spend their lives in prosperity and they go to the grave in peace (21:13). Where is the suffering of the wicked? Their children are alive, their homes are safe, and "the rod of God is not upon them" (21:9b). Where is God's wrath? It is not there, so, Job responds, "how can you console me with your nonsense? Nothing is left of your answers but falsehood" (21:34).

Yet in this context Job rejects the counsel of the wicked. The wicked, according to Job, seek only profit from faith. They ask, "Who is the Almighty, that we should serve him? What would we gain by praying to him?" This is the critical question. What practical value is there in serving God? What advantage does one gain by praying? These are the accusations of Satan. People serve God only for what they can get from him. They serve God for profit. But Job will have none of this. "But their prosperity," he comments, "is not in their own hands, so I stand aloof from the counsel of the wicked" (21:16).[15] Job does not serve God for profit. He will not join the chorus of the wicked, but he will maintain his faith-commitment even when his questions are not answered, his doubts are still present and his pain is overwhelming. Job's faith-commitment in 21:16 does not answer the questions of 21:17-33. Nevertheless, his commitment remains. It is Job's version of the father's plea to Jesus, "I believe; help [me overcome] my unbelief" (Mark 9:24, NRSV).

In the aftermath of their children's death, religious parents generally respond with one of three bereavement theodicies: blame God ("God is unjust"), blame themselves ("God is punishing me") or seek some hidden purpose in the event ("This has happened for a reason").[16] Interestingly, the book of Job reflects all three perspectives. Job questions the justice of God, the friends blame Job's sin, but the narrator sees purpose and meaning in their death. The fundamental meaning of the death of Job's children was to test (not punish) Job's faith. It answers the question, "Does Job serve God for profit?" The answer was "No, he does not." Job serves God because he loves God.

The Story of David and Bathsheba (2 Samuel 12:15-24a)

The adulterous union of David and Bathsheba produced a child. They had tried to cover their sin by arranging a sexual encounter with Bathsheba's husband, Uriah the Hittite. When that failed, David arranged Uriah's death and then married Bathsheba who bore him a son. But God sent Nathan the Prophet to expose David's sin and announce his punishment. David confessed his sin, and the Lord forgave him, but the punishment remained. God did not punish David with death, but because David showed "utter contempt" for the Lord (2 Samuel 12:14, NIV footnote; NRSV), Nathan announced that his son would die. The death that

David deserved for his adultery would be exacted from his son. His son would die as a consequence of David's sin.

The Lord "struck" David's child. The language is clear, unmistakable, and direct. This exact phrase "the LORD struck" occurs four other times in the Hebrew Bible. Once it refers to the plague God sent because of the golden calf (Exodus 32:35), and in another place the text says, "the LORD struck Nabal and he died" (1 Samuel 25:38). The two other instances refer to God's defeat of national armies (Judges 20:35; 2 Chronicles 14:12; cf. Isaiah 19:22). The plain language of the text is that God killed David's son because of David's sin. God punished David through his son. This same language describes how God struck down the Egyptians when he took the lives of their firstborn (Exodus 12:23,27), how God struck down Jeroboam (2 Chronicles 13:20), and how God struck down Jehoram and his family (2 Chronicles 21:14,18). By whatever means, this language describes God's active role in meting out punishment. That God punished David by killing his son sounds rather harsh, but it is nevertheless the clear point of the narrative.

David responded to Nathan's announcement with prayer, fasting, and lament. He pleaded with God to spare his son. Just as Hezekiah prayed for his own life (Isaiah 38:1-2), so David prayed for the life of his son. Just as Daniel prayed for the release of the exiles (Daniel 9:3), so David prayed for a reprieve of his punishment. David threw himself before the Lord in self-humiliation and tears. He would not eat, sleep or groom himself. He refused any comfort. David humiliated himself before the Lord in the hopes that God might spare his son.

Even though David had received a word from God through the prophet, David still believed there was some possibility that God might renew his mercy and spare his son. No one knows the mind of God, and David believed that if he humbled himself before the Lord, God might change his mind even though he knew he could not manipulate God. Thus, David sought the Lord's grace. It seems as if David is praying for something he does not really expect to happen though he knows God may do whatever he pleases. David pleaded for his son and held out the hope that God would respond graciously. But ultimately God answered, "No," and the child died.

What do we do when God answers, "No"? When we pray for the life of a child, and we enter God's throne room through intercession and petition, but the child dies, how do we respond to God's answer? After grooming himself, David went into the house of God and worshiped. This is a profound moment in David's life. When his child died, David worshiped (as Job did). David understood that he had received an answer to his petition and the answer was no. David's response to God's answer was to worship. He had previously lamented and petitioned, but now he goes before the Lord to praise him. He accepts God's answer and begins life again. He eats again and comforts his wife.

But was it fair to strike David's son in order to punish David? How can God punish the son for the sins of his father? The text is clear that the son dies as a consequence of David's sin. God killed the child. But what rationale permits God to act in such a way? Our answer can only be provisional and limited. It is inappropriate for fallen human beings to ultimately judge the legitimacy of a divine rationale even if the rationale were known to us. Yet theodicy tends to invent a rationale in order to justify God's actions for those who believe there can be no legitimate rationale. Nevertheless, our hearts cry out for an explanation.

God punished David through the death of his son. God did not punish the son; he punished David. God disciplined David, not the child. While we sense that the child is mistreated because he was not given the opportunity to live out his life, God's goal is focused on David in this narrative. David must learn a lesson from his sin. After the child dies, David ceases his lament — he grooms himself, worships in the tabernacle, and eats. Rather, he trusts that he will one day be reunited with his son in God's communion.

David learned the seriousness of sin that day. When we seek our own way, it only leads to death. When we stake out our own moral autonomy, we choose death rather than life. Death entered David's family through sin just as death entered the world through Adam's sin. The child died to teach David that lesson. David experienced fallenness that day; he experienced the tragedy of death because of his adultery with Bathsheba. He existentially experienced the fall of Adam in his own life. Through his own sin, death entered his world. God cursed David's house just as he cursed his creation after the fall.

God's intent, however, is not vindictive. God hates death, just as he hates sin. His purpose is ultimately redemptive. David is led into a deeper, more intimate relationship with God through the experience of fallenness in the child's death. God uses the death of the child to bring David into closer communion with him.

The death of a child forces believers to seek the face of God in worship, lament, prayer, and petition. There is nowhere else to turn. It is God's ultimate act, whether as punishment (David's case) or as testing (Job's case), to engender or strengthen a relationship between himself and the sufferer. What is ultimately important is fellowship with God, and the deaths of children may serve that end.

Even in the narrative, God is neither malicious nor vindictive. God does not hold a grudge against David and Bathsheba. In fact, God acts redemptively to continue David's house through Bathsheba. God gave them another son whom they named Solomon, but whom the Lord named "Jedidiah" which means "loved by the LORD" (2 Samuel 12:25). God would ultimately enter the world through this lineage which included Bathsheba who "had been Uriah's wife" (Matthew 1:6). Even in the midst of fallenness, God acts to redeem his people and to ensure his redemptive victory over sin and death.

The Story of Jeroboam's Son (1 Kings 14:10-13)

Jeroboam, the first king of the Northern Kingdom, had led Israel into sin through his rebellious establishment of worship centers, including the erection of golden calves at Dan and Bethel (1 Kings 12:28-30). Further, he joined the idolatrous worship of the Lord with the Canaanite practice of Asherah poles as if God needed a female counterpart (1 Kings 14:15-16). In addition, he set up high places for idolatrous worship and appointed priests for them (1 Kings 13:33-34; 14:9-10).

"At that time," the narrative says, "Abijah son of Jeroboam became ill" (1 Kings 14:1). The illness was so serious that Jeroboam sought to ask the prophet Ahijah what would ultimately happen to the boy (1 Kings 14:2-3). He sent his wife under disguise to ask. The prophet announced that because of Jeroboam's sin his whole family would be destroyed and his descendants would be cut off. The destruction of the house of Jeroboam would be so complete that every male would die and none of them would receive an honorable burial. The house of Jeroboam would come to an ignoble end, except for Abijah.

The text does not say how old Abijah is, but we may surmise that he is a young child. He is described as a *na'ar* (1 Kings 14:3,17) which usually refers to a young adolescent or teenager though it has a wide range of meaning, including an infant (as Bathsheba's baby in 2 Samuel 12:16 or the infant Moses in Exodus 2:6). Another term used to describe Abijah is *yaled* (1 Kings 14:12) which usually refers to a very young child (1 Kings 17:21-23) or an infant (2 Samuel 12:15,18-19,20,22). The noun is derived from the verb which means to give birth. Consequently, it is best to think of Abijah as no more than a teenage adolescent or perhaps even younger. Whatever his age, the parents are frantic. As a result, they seek out the Lord's prophet.

The prophet announces Abijah's death, but it is not announced as punishment but as gracious redemption. The prophet distinguishes between punishment and redemption. Jeroboam's punishment is that every one of his male descendants will be killed and bear the shame of a dishonorable death. The sins of Jeroboam will be punished by the cessation of his royal line and by the disgrace of his line's end. However, though Abijah will also die, his death at this moment is a sign of God's grace because "he is the only one in the house of Jeroboam in whom the LORD, the God of Israel, has found anything good" (1 Kings 14:13).

This is an astonishing statement. Abijah dies in the way he does, at the moment he does, because God sees "good" in him. That does not mean that Abijah was perfect. God also found "good" in Jehoshaphat because he had set his "heart on seeking God" even though he had helped the wicked and loved those who hated God (2 Chronicles 19:2-3). Whatever the "good" is that God saw in Abijah — we might surmise that it had something to do with his heart as in the case of Jehoshaphat — God gave Abijah an honorable death. He was buried and "all Israel mourned for him" (1 Kings 14:18). The death of Abijah had a gracious meaning. Through this death God redeemed Abijah from the fate of his family. They would suffer dishonor, indignity, and desecration, but Abijah would receive honor, dignity, and entombment because God graciously willed his death.

Abijah's example seems clear. The death of a child can be an expression of God's redemptive grace. Abijah's death is something that God intended as a good. It was good for Abijah though it caused considerable pain for his parents. His death was a good, however, in a relative sense. It was better to die as he did than to die like his siblings would die.

Can the death of a child ever be good? It is never an absolute good. God never intended death, but given the fallenness of the world, God uses death to accomplish his purposes. Consequently, it can be a relative good in that it carries out the purposes of God. Is the death of a child always an evil? It is always evil in the sense that it is part of the fallenness of the world. But it may also be a good because the child enters the fullness of God's life. Though there is the loss of a life unlived, there is also the gain of a fellowship previously unknown and never to be diminished.

It was good for Abijah to die when he did. It is difficult to accept the idea that the death of a child might be "good" in that relative sense. It seems so much like an absolute evil. But the death of a child is good if it serves God's purpose of eschatological communion with a people.

Summary

These three biblical stories illustrate God's sovereignty over the death of children. Job offered sacrifices for his children, but they died. David petitioned the Lord to heal his son, but he died. Jeroboam's wife sought the Lord through the prophet Ahijah, but her son died. God was sovereign over each of these situations. The Lord chose to give Satan the power to destroy Job's children, the Lord struck David's child, and he willed the death of Jeroboam's son. God could have changed any one of these events and spared the lives of all these children, but he did not. He sovereignly acted in such a way that resulted in their deaths. He could have acted differently, but he did not.

However, we must not collapse the meaning of these deaths into one purpose. The Lord had a different reason for each of them. His intent in each circumstance was different. Job's children died to test Job. David's child died to punish David. Jeroboam's child died so that Abijah might escape the humiliation of Jeroboam's punishment. God's purpose in Job's circumstance was to discipline, refine, and test. God's purpose in David's circumstance was to punish and deter. God's purpose in Jeroboam's circumstance was gracious.

Consequently, the death of children serves three different functions in these three narratives. It parallels the previous discussion of God's actions in the world. God acts sometimes to punish (as in the death of David's child), sometimes he acts to educate or test (as in the death of

Job's children), and sometimes he acts to redeem (as in the case of Jeroboam's son). But at every moment and at every level, God has a purpose which undergirds these three. Each of these, in its own way, serves God's ultimate intent for his creatures. God desires communion with Job, David and even Jeroboam. Each death is calculated to serve that end, whatever the specific purposes and circumstances may have been.

Conclusion

As I reflect on the eventual death of my own child, I draw comfort and meaning from the story of Job and his children. I know God is not punishing me for some great sin in my life, but I do believe he is refining my family, testing us to see the nature of our faith-commitment. Like Job, I believe God "knows the way that I take, [and] when he has tested me, I will come forth as gold" (23:10). But also like Job, my prayers are often impatient, occasionally accusatory and sometimes bitter. Nevertheless, I do not, if I know my heart, serve God for profit.

What "truth" is worth the price of our children? My heart protests, "No truth is worth that price." But the story of God reads differently. I trust that somehow and in some way there is a truth that is worth that price. Perhaps that "truth" is the reality of one's fellowship with God on the ground of God's sovereign, loving grace rather than through some profit received as remuneration or merit. I will entrust my Joshua to God's loving care, and, like Job (1:21), I hope to praise the name of God when Joshua dies. My faith, I pray, does not depend upon whether Joshua lives or dies. My faith, I pray, rests in my relationship with the God who seeks communion with me and the God who will one day wipe away every tear. The day will come when God will remove the death shroud from the face of his people (Isaiah 25:7). The hard reality is that such a relationship — an eschatological community which includes innocent children like my Joshua — is worth the death of my child. It was worth the death of God's own child. But it is a truth against which I often protest and over which I weep daily. "O Lord," I cry, "I believe, but help me overcome my unbelief."

---

[1]I offer my own "theodicy" on the web at *www.hugsr.edu/Hicks/theodicy. htm.*

[2]Fyodor Dostoevsky, *The Brothers Karamazov*, trans. Alexandra Kropotkin (Garden City, NY: Literary Guild of America, 1949), pp. 179-180.

[3]Wiesel, *Night*, p. 44.

[4]Elie Wiesel, *The Trial of God*, trans. Marion Wiesel (New York: Random House, 1964).

[5]Ibid., p. 130.

[6]Ibid., p. 156.

[7]Tupper, *Scandalous Providence*, p. 75; see pp. 78-81, 116-119.

[8]See Terence E. Fretheim, *The Suffering of God: An Old Testament Perspective* (Philadelphia: Fortress Press, 1984), pp. 127-137.

[9]Stanley Hauerwas, *God, Medicine, and Suffering* (Grand Rapids: Eerdmans, 1990), pp. 65-67, reflects on this unfairness.

[10]Ibid., p. 126.

[11]Diane M. Komp, *A Window to Heaven: When Children See Life in Death* (Grand Rapids: Zondervan, 1992), pp. 24-27.

[12]Ibid., pp. 28-29.

[13]Ibid., p. 36.

[14]Yancey, "When the Facts Don't Add Up," 20. See his *Disappointment with God: Three Questions No One Asks Aloud* (Grand Rapids: Zondervan, 1988), pp. 155-246.

[15]This a difficult text to translate, but the sense is generally clear.

[16]Judith A. Cook and Dale W. Wimberley, "If I Should Die Before I Wake: Religious Commitment and Adjustment to the Death of a Child," *Journal for the Scientific Study of Religion* 22 (September 1983): 228-230. Although infrequent, some explain the event in terms of coincidence, accident or the course of nature (p. 228). That thought never occurred to the author of Job.

Chapter Nine

Where Is the Victory?
The Story of God in Jesus

Since the children have flesh and blood, he too shared in their humanity so that by his death he might destroy him who holds the power of death — that is, the devil — and free those who all their lives were held in slavery by their fear of death. For surely it is not angels he helps, but Abraham's descendants. For this reason he had to be made like his brothers in every way, in order that he might become a merciful and faithful high priest in service to God, and that he might make atonement for the sins of the people. Because he himself suffered when he was tempted, he is able to help those who are being tempted.

Hebrews 2:14-18

While God is sovereign over the world, the primary quality of God's character is not his almightiness or omnipotence. On the contrary, it is his holy love. God's power serves his holy love rather than vice versa. He disciplines out of his holy love. He rules the universe out of his holy love. God exercises his power in order to fulfill his intent to share his triune fellowship with his creation.

Greek thought focused on the supreme power of God which rendered him impenetrable to passion, while other cultures focused on the supreme justice of God which high-lighted God's major concern as "world order" (such as in traditional African religion). The narrative story of the Bible, however, portrays a passionate God who acts out of love for his people. The God of the Hebrews is at times compassionate and at other times angry. Yahweh is a God who determines to destroy Israel but in mercy changes his mind. He regrets creating humanity, but graciously favors Noah and preserves humanity. He speaks to Hosea about his love affair with Israel. God is hurt and moved by the suffering of his people. He is neither distant nor unin-volved. God himself shares in the suffering of his people. God acts to redeem by sharing himself and taking their pain up into his own divine life.

Too often the history of theology has started with God as power, and used philosophical concepts to define this power. It has spoken of God as impassible, immutable, omnipresent, omnipotent, and omniscient. It has started here and only then proceeded to define the character of God in relation to his power. However, the narrative story of the Bible calls us to understand the power of God in the light of his character, deeds, and redemptive acts. Israel worships God because he is their covenant God. He acts out of his redemptive love for his people. His power serves the goal of redemption, and the goal of redemption arises out of God's holy love.

Divine Empathy: How Does God Suffer with Us?

God suffers with his world. He is not the Aristotelian "Unmoved Mover" who is unaffected by what his creatures do, nor is he the Platonic "Idea" which is self-contained per-fection totally disconnected from the world. God is often described in terms of power, but God's love values vulnera-bility and weakness rather than power. The essential char-acter of God is that he "loves in freedom,"[1] and this love is expressed in creation and redemption. God freely loves in creation. When he creates, he becomes vulnerable. He has created a freedom which images him — the ability to love in freedom. But with freedom he risks that the creature will not return his love. God, then, becomes vulnerable to pain. As Placher appropriately observes,

> Love means a willingness to take risks, to care for the other in a way that causes the other's fate to affect one's own, to give to the other at real cost to oneself, to chance rejection.[2]

The greatest expression of this vulnerability is the incarnation of the Son. God triumphs not just as a Lion, but as a Lamb. God risks involvement in the human race as a human being. It is a love that becomes vulnerable. The incarnation was the humiliation of God, even to the cross, for the sake of his sinful creatures. The Crucified One is the Christian definition of God. God revealed himself in a weakness motivated by love rather than in a power driven by egoism. In the weakness of the cross, Christ became the power and wisdom of God for salvation (1 Corinthians 1:17-29).

The Suffering of God in the Old Testament

The suffering of God, however, did not begin in the incarnation. God has suffered ever since his people chose their own way and fell into sin. God grieves the loss of his people. Ever since the grief of God asked, "Who told you that you were naked?" (Genesis 3:11), God's heart has been heavy. Yet God showed his mercy to Adam and Eve by renewing life among them with a child (Genesis 4:1-2). It reached a boiling point in Genesis 6 when God saw how wicked humanity had become and he "was grieved that he had made man on the earth, and his heart was filled with pain" (6:6). Yet God showed his mercy in Noah (Genesis 6:8-9). God was grieved in the wilderness when his people rebelled against him and put him to the test (Psalm 78:40-41). Yet God showed his mercy by ultimately bringing his people through the wilderness and into the promised land (Psalm 78:54-55). Humanity's sin is God's sorrow, and when we rebel or forsake his love, God's Spirit is grieved (Isaiah 63:10; Ephesians 4:30).

God suffers when his people seek their own path instead of finding joy in his loving fellowship, and God truly rejoices when his people return to that fellowship. God has a heart. He hurts when fellowship is broken and is enriched when fellowship is restored. While God is devoid of uncontrolled passions, God is nevertheless filled with the emotions of love, jealousy, compassion, mercy, patience, and anger. God is emotionally involved with his creation so that he shares their sorrows and their joys. God is not impassible. God is moved and stirred by the course of human history. While God cannot be manipulated or controlled by some outside power, God responds, relates, and reacts to the tragedies and victories of human existence. The weeping prophet Jeremiah speaks for the weeping God (Jeremiah 8:21–9:3; 9:8-10; 12:7-12; 15:5-9).

God's relation to his people is pictured under several metaphors in the Old Testament. These metaphors underscore God's loving care for his people, and how he yearns for them and suffers with them. One is the husband/wife analogy. God remembers when Israel was his young bride as they came out of Egypt. They followed the Lord through the desert as a wife follows her husband. "Israel was holy to the LORD" (Jeremiah 2:3). But in their sinful rebellion, they have forsaken God and "exchanged their Glory for worthless idols" which fills the creation with horror (Jeremiah 2:11-12). Despite their sin, however, God invites them to return: "for I am your husband. I will choose you . . . and bring you to Zion" (Jeremiah 3:14). When God renews his presence among his people, just as a "bridegroom rejoices over his bride, so will your God rejoice over you" (Isaiah 62:5).

The prophets often used this imagery to picture the relationship between God and Israel. Two texts are particularly striking. The first is Hosea 1–3. God told the prophet Hosea to love his adulterous wife Gomer "as the LORD loves the Israelites" (3:1). Hosea's remarriage was a symbol of God's renewed love for unfaithful Israel. God suffered the pain of a broken promise. He suffered, like Hosea, the betrayal of an unfaithful wife. Nevertheless, so great is the love of God that he pledged that a day would come when Israel would no longer say "my master" but would say "my husband" (2:16). On that day God will show his love for his people and declare, "You are my people!" In turn, they will respond to him, "You are my God" (Hosea. 2:23).

A second striking example of this metaphor is Ezekiel 16. God pledged himself to Israel in covenant and entered into a marriage relationship with her (16:8). He showered her with gifts, including costly garments, jewels, and exquisite food. Israel's fame spread among the nations because of the beauty the Lord had given her (16:9-14). But Israel "trusted in [her] beauty," and she became a prostitute (16:15). Even the children she bore to the Lord, she sacrificed on the altars to other gods with whom she prostituted herself (16:20-22). Because of her sins, God divorced her and in his "jealous anger" (16:38) he rained his wrath down upon her. Nevertheless, God declares his faithful love. "Yet I will remember the covenant I made with you in the days of your youth, and I will establish an everlasting covenant with you" (16:60). God will renew his love for her on the ground of his own covenant and by his own atoning work. God will act in love for his adulterous wife, and he will "make atonement" for her (16:63).

Another metaphor is the parent/child analogy, particularly as parents care for, weep over, and suffer with their children. The prophet Hosea (11:1-4) pictures God as a loving parent who redeemed his child from Egyptian bondage, taught him to walk, healed his broken spirit, and stooped to feed him. God loved Israel and treated them with wonderful kindnesses. He bound them with ties of love. God treated Israel like a mother eagle treats her young. He hovers over them and catches them when they fall. God "shielded [Israel] and cared for him; he guarded him as the apple of his eye" (Deuteronomy 32:10-11). Yet they rebelled and turned against him. As rebellious children they spurned the love of their parent. Isaiah draws upon the same imagery. The Lord says, "I reared children and brought them up, but they have rebelled against me" (Isaiah 1:2).

Nevertheless, the compassion of the Lord is great. "How can I give you up, Ephraim? How can I hand you over, Israel?" (Hosea 11:8). God will not treat them like any other nation. Rather, he declares, "My heart is changed within me; all my compassion is aroused" (11:8). God will not fully vent his wrath against his own child. Rather, God "will roar like a lion," and when he roars, "his children will come trembling from the west" (11:10). God will again settle them in their own homes (11:11). So also, in Isaiah, God is pictured as a mother who wishes to once again embrace her children, and as a determined mother, God will do so. "As a mother comforts her child," the Lord declares, "so will I comfort you" (Isaiah 66:13).

God will not forget his people. He bore them and cared for them like a mother though he disciplined them like a father. Despite their sin, God's people must not say, "The Lord has forsaken me, the Lord has forgotten me." God responds, "Can a mother forget the baby at her breast and have no compassion on the child she has borne? Though she may forget, I will not forget you" (Isaiah 49:14-15). God will act to redeem because he suffers with his children. God suffers because of his children — as rebels they have broken his heart — but God also suffers with his children in his yearning to renew the fellowship that has been broken.[3] God will not forget. Rather, God will redeem (Isaiah 54:5-8).

God suffers in the same way that a betrayed spouse or a heartbroken parent suffers. God understands the hurt of betrayal and he understands the hurt of a rebellious child. God yearns for his people as a mother yearns for her children. God empathizes with hurt spouses and abandoned parents.

God is willing to humble himself for the sake of his people. Because he loves, he is willing to receive back an adulterous wife. Because he loves, he will embrace a returning prodigal. The God who sits above the heavens will descend to earth in order to help his people, demonstrate his love, and seek a people for himself. This is the "incarnational" character of God. The one "who sits enthroned on high" also "stoops down to look on the heavens and the earth." He will raise up the poor and the needy and seat them "with princes," and he will settle "the barren woman in her home as a happy mother of children" (Psalm 113:5-9). The Sovereign God humbles himself to care for the poor and needy. "Though the LORD is on high, he looks upon the lowly" (Psalm 138:6).

The Incarnation of God

The empathetic character of God fully revealed itself in the incarnation, life, and ministry of Jesus Christ. The Son did not "exploit" his equality with the Father (Philippians 2:6, NRSV), but humbled himself. The one who existed from eternity in the form of God took on the form of a servant (Philippians 2:7). Though the Son is the one "through whom all things came" (1 Corinthians 8:6), he became a creature. Though he was Son, yet he learned obedience by the things which he suffered (Hebrews 5:8). He was "rich," but he became "poor" (2 Corinthians 8:9). The Word, the instrument of creation, became flesh and dwelt among us. The one who from the beginning was with the Father came into the world as one of us (John 1:1-3,14-18).

God in Jesus Christ humbled himself. As one who became human, he shared the fullness of our fallenness. The Son was tempted. He hungered, thirsted, experienced pain, and ultimately died. The humiliation of God in Christ was his identification with us in our fallenness. From his birth, to baptism, to death — he stood with the lowly. He stood with sinners. He was born among shepherds, baptized with those who confessed sin, and died between transgressors. Without the guilt of sin and without ever sinning himself, he shared our fallenness. He suffered the curse which Adamic sin brought upon the world. He experienced the world's fallenness through its pain, tears, and death.

The Nature of the Incarnation

Scripture does not provide a theory of incarnation. It offers us the story of the life and ministry of Jesus Christ. While the exact nature of the incarnation is ultimately mysterious, there are certain parameters given in the story that are important for understanding what the incarnation entailed. Three points are particularly significant.

First, we must affirm that the Son is divine and shares the divine nature with the Father. In other words, the Son is one of the triune community. Hebrews 1:3 identifies the Son as one who is the radiance of God's glory and the exact representation of his being. The Son shines with the glory of God and reflects the sunlight of God's being. The Son is the exact image of God. The Son is so completely identified with the Father that they share the same divine nature. They are Father and Son. The Son has a unique relationship with God and a unique name (1:5). Angels worship the Son (1:6). He is eternal (1:8-12).

The divinity of the Son must retain its own integrity. He cannot be less than what is essential to being God and still be given the title of "God." Yet he is given this title, even while in the flesh. When Thomas saw the resurrected Jesus, he cried "My Lord and My God" (John 20:28). The Gospel of John begins and ends with the affirmation that the Son is "God" (John 1:1; 20:28). Jesus is the one in whom the fullness of Godhood dwells (Colossians 2:9). A biblical understanding must retain the truth that Jesus is

God in the flesh so that all the fullness of the Godhood dwelt in him.

As the divine one, then, the Son reveals the Father through the incarnation. As the exact image of the Father, the Son shows us who the Father is and what the Father is like. Even though no one has seen God (John 1:18), yet when we see the Son we see God. When we see the Son, we see the Father (John 14:9). The Son exegetes the Father (John 1:18). As the image of the Father, he is the personal revelation of God. This bridges the gap between the finite and the infinite. If Jesus is God, then our knowledge of God has a personal human focus. In Jesus' character and acts we see the character and acts of God himself. In Jesus we see what God would be like if he were one of us. Jesus is the human face of God. In Jesus we encounter God as a human being.

Second, we must affirm that the Son became human. The Son was "made a little lower than the angels" (Hebrews 2:9). The agent of creation (Hebrews 1:2) became a creature. The goal of the incarnation was to suffer death. He shared in the "flesh and blood" of humanity in order to destroy the Devil and the fear of death (Hebrews 2:14-15), and he destroyed them through his own participation in suffering.

Jesus is the "author" of salvation through his suffering (Hebrews 2:10). He is the leader (author, pioneer, pathfinder) who brings others to glory. He participates in what he establishes (Hebrews 12:2). He is both the initiator and source. Jesus leads his people to glory through suffering. He is perfected by that suffering (Hebrews 2:10; 5:7; 8:28). The pioneer must suffer. As a result, he is now able to perfect others through fellowship with him (Hebrews 10:14; 11:39; 12:23). His perfection through suffering is the ground of empathy with humanity (Hebrews 2:17; 4:15; 12:2). The obedience of Jesus has a sacrificial meaning for his whole life and not just for his death (Hebrews 10:5-8). The Son, through his humanity and suffering as well as through his death, was appointed High Priest. He was perfected (not morally) in that he gained the capacity for empathetic intercession as well as qualifying as a sacrificial victim for the sins of the world (2:17-18). The perfective suffering of Jesus involves his complete identification and empathy with humanity.

Just like the divinity, the humanity of Jesus must retain its own integrity. He cannot be less than what is essential to being human. He must be everything that is necessary to being human. This means he fully identifies with and experiences human existence in a fallen world just as we do (Hebrews 4:15). Yet he lived as true human rather than sinful human. He was what human beings should be. He was authentically human whereas in our sinfulness we are subhuman. The divine Son, then, fully experienced human life. Matthew, Mark, and Luke give us this human picture of Jesus. He is born, he grows in wisdom and stature, he is tempted, he thirsts, he hungers, he agonizes in prayer, and he ultimately dies. Jesus did not stand on the periphery of human experience. He was fully immersed in it. He was human in every way that we are human.

Third, we must maintain the continuity between the preexistent Son and the human Jesus. The Son exists in eternal union with the Father. He exists alongside the Father and the Spirit in divine community with a distinct identity. Yet the Son, not the Father, becomes human. The one who is the divine Son is the same one who became human. This is the continuity of the divine and human in the incarnate one. Jesus is not someone distinct from the Son, but the Son in human form is Jesus. The divine one became human. "The Word became flesh" (John 1:14). Whatever that may entail — and it is beyond our comprehension — it means that there is continuity between the Son and Jesus. The one through whom the world was created is the same one who walked on this earth in human flesh. The one who shared fellowship with the Father before the creation of the world is the same one who was humbled in human suffering and died on a cross. Our redeemer, then, is "Jesus the Son of God" (Hebrews 4:14).

The incarnation is the personal presence of God among human beings. God became flesh and "made his dwelling among us" (John 1:14). The claim of the incarnation is unique. There is a difference between God making himself known indirectly through the awe-inspiring media of a mystical experience and God himself coming incognito in human flesh. Just as the king can only win a poor maiden's love if he lays aside his royal robes and woos her as an ordinary man, person to person, in her own village, so God wooed us through his personal presence in the incarnation. God is not merely present in Jesus, but Jesus is God. He himself is the presence of God. God did not simply come to us through Jesus — as if through a mere human prophet, but the triune God came to us through one who himself shares in the triune fellowship. God the Son came to us as a human being. What God did in Jesus Christ was a genuine incarnation. God himself became a human being. God did not remain distant and beyond human touch. Rather, God came near.

The Empathetic Experience of the Incarnation

The nature of divine experience is different from human experience. God sympathizes with us. He feels our pain through his own loving nature. He hurts with us. He knows what we know, but has not experienced what we have experienced except in the incarnate one. The divine experience does not involve hunger, thirst, or temptation. The divine experience does not have a human experiential content. The incarnation is the human experience of God. In the incarnation God actually experiences what his divine nature cannot: hunger, thirst, temptation, death. In the incarnation the divine one becomes a fully empathetic God rather than simply the sympathetic God.

There is a sense in which God is empathetic in the Old Testament. God hurts with his people. He knows the pain of a rebellious child. He knows the pain of losing someone in death. God shares the experience of grief with his world. However, the incarnation renders God empathetic with us in a unique way. In the cross God shared our experience of death rather than merely sympathizing with that experience at a distance. God as human being participates in death itself. In the incarnation, God and human beings have the same experience. God identifies with us. In his incarnation, he takes upon himself the suffering of the world's ills. God bears the brunt of evil by subjecting himself to its cruelty and horror. God himself enters fallenness and experiences it. By so doing, he reveals, as he could in no other way, the reality, depth, and costly nature of his forgiving love. Divine love and forgiveness are shown most clearly in the lengths to which our God is prepared to go to win the love of the loveless. God did not send a representative, but he came personally. God actually bore the suffering rather than simply sending his condolences. God not only sent a sympathy card, but he joined in the suffering empathetically.

The events in Jesus' life give theological meaning to this empathy. While his whole life and ministry involve him in the human experience, there are three historic symbols of this identification: (a) his birth where he took on human flesh, (b) his baptism where he identified with sinners, and (c) his cross where he identified with our fallen suffering, pain, and shame. In each case, God participates in human fallenness and experiences the suffering associated with each. In each case, God humbles himself to identify with sinners. In his birth, God joined the human race in the context of a fallen world. God came in the flesh so that he could experience authentic suffering along with his people. God's flesh was no sham but a genuine participation in human reality. Jesus submitted to a baptismal ritual designed for penitent believers who had confessed their sins. It was a baptism of repentance for the remission of sins (Luke 3:3; Mark 1:5). Jesus, then, identified with sinners through his own baptism, just as he also identified with them in his death (Luke 22:37; 23:32-33). He was crucified in weakness between two thieves. God became weak for our sakes (2 Corinthians 13:4) and the one who knew no sin became sin for us (2 Corinthians 5:21). He suffered the curse for us (Galatians 3:13).

Through sharing this suffering, Jesus, the Son of God, is able to empathize and understand human weakness. He can understand it because he has personally experienced it. He empathizes with our weaknesses because he has shared our fallen life. He is able to intercede for us and help us because he himself was tempted (Hebrews 2:18), and he is an empathetic high priest because he has experienced human weakness himself though without sin (Hebrews 4:15). Jesus, the Son of God, was so fully immersed in human experience that he was tempted in every way that we are, yet without sin.

God suffered with us in Jesus Christ. He lamented with us in his own suffering. He himself voiced lament as he hung on the cross (Matthew 27:46 quoting Psalm 22:1). But it is only in our own suffering that we learn that God suffers. It is only in our own risking that we learn the depth of God's risk-taking love. It is only when we behold the cross that we see the tear-filled eyes of God. God is not only the God of the sufferers but the God who suffers, and who suffers with sufferers. Wolterstorff aptly writes: "And great mystery: to redeem our brokenness and lovelessness the God who suffers with us did not strike some mighty blow of power but sent his beloved son to suffer like us, through suffering to redeem us from suffering and evil. Instead of explaining our suffering, God shares it."[4]

The Atonement: What Did God Do to Sin?

Atonement means reconciliation (at-one-ment). It is God's work whereby he provides the basis for and accomplishes the goal of reconciliation between himself and sinful humanity. Reconciliation is God's re-creative (redemptive) act whereby his original intention of communion between himself and his creatures is fulfilled. The atonement reflects both the holiness and the goodness of God. God's love initiates the sacrifice which is suited to God's holiness.

Sin is the spoiling of God's good creation. It is rebellion and selfishness. Sin breaks the peace of the world and destroys our relationship with God. Consequently, sin must be destroyed so that the curse which it brought might be removed. Sin must be atoned so that life might replace death. God works an atonement to restore, redeem, and renew a fallen world, and this work is initiated by his love for his people. God entered history through the incarnation to deal with sin as well as to share our suffering. He not only came to suffer with us, but also to suffer for us.

Atonement means that God makes a "holy place" for himself by removing sin from his people so that he dwells among them in his transforming, life-giving presence. Atonement accomplishes a reconciliation between God and his people so that they dwell together in a loving, holy fellowship.

God accomplished this mighty act of atonement through Jesus Christ. The earliest Christian confession, as Paul records it in 1 Corinthians 15:3-5, is (1) that Christ died for our sins, (2) that he was buried, (3) that he was raised on the third day, and (4) that he appeared to Cephas. The gospel, in its most basic form, is proclaimed in those four facts. Jesus really died (as his burial verifies) and he was really raised (as his appearance to Cephas verifies). But these are not mere facts — they have meaning. They accomplished something. The death and resurrection of Jesus are God's mighty acts by which he reconciled the world to himself (Romans 5:9-11; 2 Corinthians 5:18-19). God removed sin and offered his life-giving presence through the gospel. God destroyed sin through Jesus Christ.

The mystery of the atonement lies beyond the images and metaphors Scripture provides. The mysterious reality which lies behind the fact that "in Christ God was reconciling the world" (2 Corinthians 5:19, NRSV) and "God made [Christ] . . . to be sin for us" (2 Corinthians 5:21) is beyond our finite minds. We will spend eternity not only worshiping God and the Lamb, but exploring the mystery which inspires our worship. The atonement is more than an example, a martyrdom or a revelation. Christ died for sin. Christ died for us. Our finite minds will never fathom the mystery of that relationship, but it speaks volumes about who God is (a holy love that cannot deny himself), what he has done (humbled himself), and how he has loved us (substituted himself).

Atonement for Sin

Paul's summary of the gospel essentially locates the importance of Christ's death in the idea that Christ died "for our sins" (cf. Galatians 1:4). In other places, Paul summarizes this divine work as Christ's death "for us" (cf. Romans 5:8; 2 Corinthians 5:15; Galatians 2:20; 3:13). The mystery of the atoning function of Christ's death lies behind these two ideas, that is, that Christ died (1) for sin and (2) for us.

This is not simply Paul's version of the mystery, but it is the witness of the whole New Testament. Peter writes that "Christ died for sins once for all, the righteous for the unrighteous" (1 Peter 3:18; cf. 2:24). The writer of Hebrews talks about the expiatory significance of Christ's death ("to take away the sins of many people," Hebrews 9:28; cf. 2:17; 7:27; 10:12) but also its substitutionary character ("he might taste death for everyone," Hebrews 2:9). John also testifies that Jesus' death was "for our sins" (1 John 2:2; 4:10) as well as "for us" (1 John 3:16). Jesus taught that his death was both "for the forgiveness of sins" (Matthew 26:28) and "for many" (Matthew 20:28).

But what does it mean to say that "Christ died for sin" and "for us"? If this is the most basic Christian confession,

why are so many Christians ambiguous in their understanding and inept in their articulation of its fundamental
meaning? What does it mean to confess that "Christ died
for our sins"?

God Himself Removed Sin from His People through Jesus Christ.

This is the most basic idea of atonement. The death of
Jesus removed sin. It took away sin. It expiated sin. As a
result of his death, sin no longer exists as a barrier between
God and humanity. The wall that separated them was broken down at the cross. God reconciled himself to sinful
humanity by removing sin.

This was the function of the Levitical sacrifices. They
removed sin from the presence of God's people and created
a "holy place" where God could dwell among them. The
"blood of the covenant" cleansed and sanctified the people,
the tabernacle, the altar, and the scroll. The law required
"that nearly everything be cleansed with blood" (Hebrews
9:22). Through sacrifice, through the removal of sin, God
made "holy space" for himself so that he could dwell among
his people in a holy communion.

This was also the function of the death of Jesus. Since
sin has been removed through Jesus, God has created a holy
place in our hearts for the indwelling of his Holy Spirit. We
are now God's holy temple in which he dwells through his
Spirit (Ephesians 2:18-22). We are God's saints, his holy
ones. God lives within his holy people instead of merely in
a holy temple. Indeed, the Levitical sacrifices were inade-
quate for God's ultimate purpose. They were provisional
and patterned after God's own design in Jesus Christ
(Hebrews 9:1–10:18). In the eternal mind of God sin is
only removed through the expiatory work of Jesus
(Hebrews 9:15) though provisionally given to God's people
under the old covenant.

But in what sense did the death of Christ remove sin?
Paul offers several metaphors for this work. One is commercial. God canceled the debt of sin. He nailed the debt to the

cross. Paul writes that our certificate of indebtedness, our "I owe you," was canceled at the cross. It was nailed to the cross (Colossians 2:13-15). By whatever means, God forgave our debt at the cross and removed sin from our account. The ransom was paid and we were freed from indebtedness.

Another metaphor is legal in character. God no longer charges us with sin. The indictment has been revoked and we have been declared not guilty. God reconciled himself to the world by "not counting men's sins against them" (2 Corinthians 5:19). In Jesus Christ God no longer "imputes" sin and, therefore, there is no "condemnation" for those who are in him (Romans 8:1).

Yet how can the holy God remove the sin of a depraved people? How can God declare the guilty "not guilty"? How can God forgive a debt that is justly owed? God removes sin, but on what basis? We need to say more.

God Identified Himself with Sinners in Jesus Christ.

God did not keep his distance from his fallen, sinful people. Rather, he came near. He joined them in their fallenness and identified himself with sinners. The holy God entered the fallen world and shared the shame, pain, and death of this world.

God's first act of identification was the incarnation itself. God joined us in our fallenness by sharing our flesh, our sickness, our fatigue, our hunger, and our death. God became a slave for our sakes by becoming one of us. Jesus Christ "did not regard equality with God as something to be exploited," rather "he humbled himself" by "being born in human likeness" (Philippians 2:6-8; NRSV). God did not send a sympathy card, but he came to sit with us on the mourner's bench in order to groan with us in our shame and pain.

Jesus identified with sinners when he was baptized. Jesus underwent a rite designed for those who (a) repent of sin; (b) confess their sin; and (c) are immersed for the forgiveness of sins (Mark 1:4-5). The righteous one submitted to a ritual designed for sinners. The righteous one joined sinners in an act of humility and submission. Jesus identified himself with sinners.

The cross, however, is the moment of God's ultimate self-humiliation. There Jesus was "numbered with the transgressors" (Luke 22:37). There Jesus "became sin" for us (2 Corinthians 5:21, NRSV). There "he humbled himself and became obedient to death — even death on a cross!" (Philippians 2:8). There he became a "curse" for us (Galatians 3:13). There he "bore our sins in his body" (1 Peter 2:24). There the one who knew no sin became one with sin as he died "for us."

But what does it mean for Christ to identify with sinners? How does he become "sin" for us? How does this remove sin? We need to say more.

God Substituted Himself for Sinners in Jesus Christ.

The cross is not fundamentally a human sacrifice. It is God in the flesh sacrificing himself for humanity. God himself takes upon himself the substitutionary role. This is not a human substitute, but rather one of the triune community representing the Godhead in this act of self-humiliation offers himself for sinners. The triune community itself experiences the hideousness of sin through the Godforsakenness of the crucified one. The triune community offered its own life, community, and fellowship for the sake of reconciliation with the world it loved.

God acts against sin in Jesus Christ. He punishes sin. But he does so within his own life rather than externalizing that punishment by tormenting sinners. God himself experiences the torment of sin rather than inflicting that torment on us. The Lord of glory cried, "My God, My God, why have you forsaken me?" (Mark 15:34). The triune community suffered within itself rather than inflicting that suffering upon humanity. The triune community internalized the horror and punishment of sin rather than punishing humanity with eternal wrath. God saved us from the "coming wrath" by experiencing that wrath himself in his own triune life through Jesus Christ (1 Thessalonians 1:10). This is the love of God that sent his Son into the world as a propitiation for sin (1 John 4:10).

The cross is the moment of God's self-substitution. God substitutes himself in such a way that it is just for God to "justify the ungodly" and "not impute sin" to sinners. God substituted himself in that he experienced and internalized within himself the wrath that was due to us. Jesus Christ experienced the curse we deserved, paid the debt we owed, and suffered the eschatological death we earned.

But why did God substitute himself? Why did he not just "forgive" without substitution? Why did anyone have to "pay"? We need to say more.

God Satisfied Himself in Jesus Christ

We do not satisfy God. We do not live up to his holiness and emulate his character. We are unworthy servants even if we are obedient. We cannot deal with our sin or make up for our mistakes. We cannot pay the ransom for our own iniquities. Only God could pay it.

To whom or what did God pay it? Some believe that he paid it to Satan as if God owed Satan something. Some believe that he paid it to some principle to which he was obligated as if there is a principle of justice that stands above God to which he must submit. God does not satisfy a law higher than himself. God is not subservient to some higher principle. On the contrary, God's character is the highest principle in the universe. He does not owe anything to anyone (Job 41:11; Romans 11: 35).

Atonement must deal with sin. Wrath must be propitiated, but it is a divine self-propitiation. In this context satisfaction is a biblical concept. "Satisfaction is a proper word," Stott notes, "as long as we realize that it is [God] himself in his inner being who needs to be satisfied, and not something external to himself" (as a higher moral order, or a sense of honor, or some kind of personal offense that must be placated).[5] God cannot disown himself (2 Timothy 2:13) and he must satisfy the law of his own being. The reason why a propitiation is necessary is not that God is irascible, spiteful, capricious or arbitrary, but that evil always provokes. His wrath is his steady, unrelenting, uncompromising antagonism to evil. It is God's holy love. It is neither we who make the propitiation or a human Christ. Rather, God himself took the initiative in his sheer grace and mercy. The propitiatory sacrifice was not a thing, but a person, and the person offered was God himself. God himself is at the heart of the propitiation. The cross is the self-substitution of the divine community which absorbs the eschatological wrath. God inflicts wrath upon himself rather than upon his fallen creatures. The divine community internalizes this satisfaction rather than externalizing it in eschatological wrath.

God acts consistently with his own character. He does not deny himself (2 Timothy 2:13). God must act in character and with integrity. This is the ground of God's own faithfulness. He must be faithful to himself. He could not do otherwise and remain who he is. So God determined to redeem sinful humanity but he decided to do so in a way consistent with his character. Therefore, out of his mercy and because of his great love, God determined he would justify the ungodly, but in a just way. Because he loved his creation and yearned for their fellowship, he determined to satisfy himself in the light of his own holiness.

The cross is the moment of God's self-satisfaction. God purposed to set forth Jesus Christ as the means of averting his just wrath. The first chapters of Romans are replete with references to God's wrath and just condemnation (1:18,32; 2:2,3,5,8,12,25; 3:8-10,19-20,23). God's solution is to demonstrate his righteousness by a propitiation so that he could remain righteous and at the same time declare believers righteous. The clear implication of Romans 3:25-26 is that God could not have been just in declaring the ungodly righteous if Jesus had not been offered as a propitiation. God's own self-satisfaction was necessary if God was to remain both just and justifier. God's work in Christ is a divine self-propitiation whereby the triune community absorbs the eschatological wrath due us. Because of this self-propitiation God may now justify the ungodly (Roman 4:5). Cranfield summarizes this point well:

> We take it that what Paul's statement that God purposed Christ as a propitiatory victim means is that God, because in His mercy He willed to forgive sinful men and, being truly merciful, willed to forgive them righteously, that is, without in any way condoning their sin, purposed to direct against His own very Self in the person of His son the full weight of that righteous wrath which they deserved.[6]

Atonement, then, takes place as *substitution*. Jesus stands in our place and in our stead. He paid a ransom. This is the self-substitution of God. This substitutionary function is the heart of the gospel message. It is "divine self-satisfaction through divine self-substitution."[7]

This understanding of the atonement has been criticized as unintelligible to the modern mind. It appears to value human sacrifice and thus sounds rather mythological and hideous. But the principle of inner moral conflict whereby one sacrifices himself in self-giving love rather than compromising his own principles is still valued. We see it in parents who are torn apart with conflicting emotions when their children go astray. They long to forgive, but not in such a way that condones or encourages the wrongdoing. True forgiveness is costly. It cost God something. God decided to deal with sin by taking it up into his own life where he destroyed its power. God offers himself as a substitute in order that his holiness might meet his love for the sake of his people. The triune community sacrificed its own unbroken bliss so that others might join their communion. I am not sure we can say much more than that about the "great exchange."

Resurrection: What Did God Do to Death?

Before the beginning of time, God had purposed that he would have a people for himself and that nothing would stand in the way of that purpose. When the world fell into death, the purpose of God was not frustrated because God from eternity had determined to overcome death. Christian confidence arises out of God's eternal purpose for us. God will not permit death to reign forever. He will defeat the enemy, and God defeated that enemy through the death and resurrection of Jesus. God saved us by his own grace according to his own purpose. As Paul writes, "this grace was given us in Christ Jesus before the beginning of time, but it has now been revealed through the appearing of our Savior, Christ Jesus, who has destroyed death and has brought life and immortality to light through the gospel" (2 Timothy 1:9b-10). The resurrection is the conquest of Satan, sin, and death actualized, confirmed, and announced.

The Cursed One Vindicated

Jesus experienced the shame and condemnation of sinners through his death on the cross. Jesus hung on a "tree" (Acts 5:30; 10:39; 13:29; cf. 1 Pet. 2:24). "Tree" has a significant cultural meaning. It functions to root "death" in the concepts of "shame and condemnation." The death on the cross was no mere martyrdom or a participation in the general experience of death. Rather, the cross identified the sufferer with condemnation and shame. It was a humiliating as well as painful means of death. It was the condemnation of a criminal.

But "tree" also has a theological meaning. The condemnation is more than a criminal one. It is a theological one. It is no mere legal condemnation, but a divine condemnation. This theological understanding is rooted in Deuteronomy 21:23 where the law proclaims that "anyone who is hung on a tree is under God's curse." Paul quotes this text in Galatians 3:13 and applies it to Jesus. The tree represents a curse: the one who hangs on a tree is divinely cursed. God's curse is his curse upon sin, sinfulness, and fallenness. It is a divine condemnation. It is the curse of God's law. Indeed, Jesus became a "curse for us" in order to redeem us from the "curse of the law" (Galatians 3:13).

There can be little doubt that Jewish opponents of the gospel often appealed to this "curse" in rejecting the cross as God's messianic redemption. The cross, of course, was a stumbling block for the Jews. It scandalized them (1 Corinthians 1:23) because it represented the curse of God. God's Messiah and God's redemptive power could not be found on a "tree." The Messiah was a conquering hero, not a crucified peasant. Consequently, those who knew the Deuteronomic text would naturally say "Jesus is accursed" rather than "Jesus is Messiah." While the cross in our post-Christian culture is an object of love, gratitude, and appreciation, to first century culture it was an object of horror, curse, and humiliation. The preaching of the cross, therefore, was scandalous.

God, however, transformed the scandal. The preaching in Acts contrasts what Jewish leaders did in condemning Jesus to death and what God did in raising him from the dead. Peter accuses his audience of putting Jesus to death, but "God raised him from the dead" (Acts 2:23-24). They "disowned the Holy and Righteous One . . . [and] killed the author of life, but God raised him from the dead" (Acts 3:14-15). Peter tells the Jewish Sanhedrin, "you crucified [Jesus] but . . . God raised [him] from the dead" (Acts 4:10). And in another meeting with the Sanhedrin, Peter proclaimed: "The God of our fathers raised Jesus from the dead — whom you had killed by hanging him on a tree" (Acts 5:30). Recounting the story to Cornelius, Peter remembers that "they killed him by hanging him on a tree, but God raised him from the dead on the third day" (Acts 10:39-40; cf. Acts 13:26-31).

If Jesus' life had ended on that tree, he would have
been an accursed, condemned criminal. But the resurrection of Jesus is the vindication of the accursed one. When
God raised Jesus from the dead, he reversed the curse and
vindicated the just one. Paul balances the cross and resurrection in terms of sin and vindication when he states: "He
was delivered over to death for our sins and was raised to
life for our justification" (Romans 4:25). His own death was
death for sin — he suffered the curse of the law by becoming sin for us, but his resurrection was his justification —
God vindicated his righteous one through raising him from
the dead. The accursed one was vindicated. God reversed
the judgment of death. Now Christ stands cosmically triumphant, victorious, and vindicated.

The "mystery of godliness" (1 Timothy 3:16) is that
Jesus appeared in the flesh (incarnation and death), but was
"vindicated by the Spirit" (resurrection). Death did not
win. Satan was defeated. God's anointed one was not left in
Hades, but God raised him from the dead and proclaimed
him Lord (Acts 2:24-28). The resurrection of Jesus proclaims God's victory over Satan, sin, and death. His victory
is our victory. His resurrection is our resurrection.

Christ Was Raised for Our Life

While we often describe the death of Christ as "for us,"
we rarely say this about his resurrection. We more readily
speak of rising "with Christ" — and this is the more dominant language of the New Testament (2 Corinthians 4:14;
Romans 6:5-8; Colossians 2:12; 3:1). However, it is also
appropriate to say that Christ was raised "for us." Jesus was
raised for "our justification" (Romans 4:25) so that we
might be saved by "his life" (Romans 5:10). In much the
same way that Christ died for us, he was also raised for us.
Indeed, Paul explicitly says this in 2 Corinthians 5:15
(NRSV): "And he died for all, so that those who live might
live no longer for themselves, but for him who died and was

raised for them." Just as with the death of Christ "for us," so we must ask what it means to say that Christ was raised for us and for our life.

Our Resurrection with Jesus Is the Presence of God's Transforming Spirit.

Since Christ died to sin and we are dead to sin in him, we are now alive to God. Paul writes: "count yourselves dead to sin but alive to God in Christ Jesus" (Romans 6:11). The life we now live is not our own — it is the resurrected life of Jesus. We have been crucified with Jesus, and we have been raised with him. So the life we now live is his (Galatians 2:20). We live in the power of the life-giving Spirit who has given us "new life" in Christ.

The presence of the Spirit is God's gift by which he transforms us into the image of his Son. The work of the Spirit is sanctification (1 Peter 1:2; 2 Thessalonians 2:13). God's Holy Spirit empowers our sanctification (Ephesians 3:16-17). By the presence of his Spirit, God transforms us "into his likeness with ever-increasing glory" (2 Corinthians 3:18). God calls us to live holy lives and he gives us his Holy Spirit as a transforming power.

This power is the vigor of a resurrected life that is lived out in the present as we anticipate the fullness of that power in the resurrection of the body. Paul presses this point in Romans 8:10-11: "But if Christ is in you, your body is dead because of sin, yet your spirit is alive because of righteousness. And if the Spirit of him who raised Jesus from the dead is living in you, he who raised Christ from the dead will also give life to your mortal bodies through his Spirit, who lives in you." Thus, the present experience of the transforming power of the Spirit by the fruit he bears in us is but a foretaste of our full redemption by the power of the Spirit in the resurrection.

Consequently, the sanctified life we now live is by the power of the life-giving Spirit who gave life to the dead body of Jesus Christ. We are called to be holy, then, because God has given us the power to be holy.

OurRresurrection with Jesus Transforms Our Experience of Death.

Since God has defeated death, we no longer fear its hostile grip. The resurrection has destroyed death so that the keys of Hades are in the hands of Jesus (Revelation 1:18). His resurrection is a revelation of our future resurrection because he is but the "firstfruits" of the harvest to come. The resurrection of Jesus actually belongs to the end of time, but God raised him in the midst of history as a revelation of the end. God raised Jesus in order to show us what the end of history is. He gave us the "firstfruits" in order to assure us of the coming harvest in which we will participate. Even though the future has not yet arrived, we know what the end is because of the resurrection of Jesus. The gospel has brought the light of resurrected immortality into the darkness of this fallen world (2 Timothy 1:10).

Consequently, our experience of death is transformed from hopelessness, fear, and despair into hope, expectation, and anticipation. We no longer fear death though we hate it. We hate it because it is God's enemy, but we do not fear it because God in Christ has conquered it. As the author of Hebrews writes, Jesus "shared in [our] humanity so that by his death he might destroy him who holds the power of death — that is, the devil — and free those who all their lives were held in slavery by their fear of death" (Hebrews 2:14-15).

Our Resurrection with Jesus in Our "Spiritual" Bodies Enables Full Communion with God in the *Eschaton.*

Since God has raised Christ with a "spiritual body," we yearn for our spiritual bodies when we will experience the fullness of God's Spirit in the new heaven and new earth. Indeed, the indwelling Spirit is our promise that we will be raised, and the power of the Spirit that now works in us to transform us into his glory will transform our vile bodies into the glorious body of Jesus Christ (Romans 8:11; Philippians 3:21). Our present mortal, weak, and fallen bodies will be transformed into immortal, powerful, and glorious bodies. We will have "spiritual bodies," that is, bodies energized and empowered by the full transforming presence of the Spirit of God (1 Corinthians 15:42-44).

The present work of the Spirit which offers us daily renewal (2 Corinthians 4:16) will bear its full fruit in the resurrection when the Spirit will sanctify our whole person (body and soul). The Spirit who now sanctifies us will animate our bodies throughout eternity. The Holy Spirit will complete his work of sanctification through the resurrection so we may abide in the presence of God forever by his power and by his holiness. God will fully dwell among his people when they are fully sanctified by his Spirit in the new heaven and new earth. That work is still in process and not yet complete. The indwelling of the Spirit is God's promise that he will complete that work as we continue to trust in him (Ephesians 1:13-14; 2 Corinthians 1:22; 5:5).

The resurrection is not a mere resuscitation. It is a transformation. Metamorphosis describes the transfiguration of Christ, as well as the transformation of the inner person into the image of Christ. This metamorphosis has already begun. We are constantly renewed in the inner person by the Spirit of God who seeks to conform us to the glorious image of Christ (2 Corinthians 3:17-18; 4:16; Ephesians 3:16-17; Colossians 3:10). The resurrection is the metamorphosis of the outer body (and the perfection of the inner person). It is the redemption of the body (Romans 8:23). It is the final stage of "Christification" (Philippians 3:9-21) where we are fully conformed to the image of Christ in both body and soul (Romans 8:29-30).

Just as the death of Christ is the culmination and representation of all about the world that is fallen, so the resurrection is God's pledge to restore the world to its original goodness. God acted decisively to reverse the effects of Good Friday. The resurrection is God's pledge of eschatological reversal in a new heaven and a new earth. The resurrection is a new day of creation/redemption and signals the defeat of God's enemies, especially the last enemy which is death.

The Second Adam and the Revelation of the *Eschaton*

First Corinthians 15:22 states the second Adam theme succinctly: "For as in Adam all die, so in Christ all will be made alive." Paul unpacks this theme in Romans 5:12-21.

ADAM	CHRIST
The Condemnation	The Gift
Just Judgment	Gracious Gift
Sin of Adam	Righteousness of Christ
Disobedience of Adam	Obedience of Christ
Made Many Sinners	Made Many Righteous
Death Reigns	Life Reigns

Jesus acted as the second Adam in order to reverse the effects of the fall that Adam had introduced. Jesus is the New Humanity where life reigns instead of death; righteousness instead of sin; obedience instead of disobedience. Jesus came to redeem what was fallen and through his obedience bring life to all. The work of God in Jesus Christ reverses the fallen condition of the world and restores life. Just as one person brought the world under the curse of death, so through one person God renews the world through life.

Paul's point in Romans 5:12-21 is that whatever Adam has done to the world, Christ has undone it. Whatever fallenness Adam introduced into the world through his sin, Christ has reversed through his faithful obedience. Whatever consequences Adam's sin brought upon the cosmos are reversed in Christ. Whether that consequence involves the death of children, the corruption of creation or the reign of death, those consequences have been totally destroyed. While I do not believe infants are born guilty of sin as a result of Adamic sin, Romans 5 teaches that if Adam's sin entailed guilt for his future generations, it is reversed in Christ. Consequently, no matter what one's theological persuasion, the work of Christ means that all Adamic guilt and consequences are null and void in Christ. Therefore, no one is eschatologically condemned because of Adam's sin. Rather, everyone will be judged for their own personal guiltiness. Thus, no one should wonder about the destiny of children who die in infancy. God has redeemed them in Christ. God has restored in Christ whatever Adam corrupted through his sin.

The resurrection of Christ is the "firstfruits of those who have fallen asleep" (1 Corinthians 15:20). The concept of "firstfruits" involves the promise of harvest. Jesus is the first part of the harvest that is yet to come. Christ has already been raised as a promise of the coming harvest. "But each in his own turn: Christ, the firstfruits; then, when he comes, those who belong to him." Christ's resurrection is, as Pannenberg calls it, a "proleptic" revelation of the end.[8] "Proleptic" is derived from a Greek term meaning "to receive before." It assigns an event or person to a period earlier than the actual one. In other words, the resurrection of Jesus is an eschatological event. It belongs to the *eschaton*. Indeed, the incarnation, ministry, and cross of Jesus are eschatological events. In the incarnation, God dwells among his people just like he will in the *eschaton*. In the ministry of Jesus, God heals his people and defeats demons just as he will in the *eschaton*. In the cross of Jesus, God experiences the eschatological wrath so that we are saved from it.

Yet, though the Christ Event is an eschatological event, it also occurred in history. The Christ Event is the center of history, not in chronology, but in eschatology. It is the moment in history when God revealed the *eschaton*. He declared the goal and end of history itself. Thus, in order to secure the anchor of hope and ground our confidence in God's victory, God proleptically revealed the end of history in Jesus. God raised Jesus from the dead in order to show us what the end of history will be like. He gave us the firstfruits in order to assure us of the coming harvest in which we will participate. Consequently, the resurrection of Jesus is our resurrection. Just as we have been raised with him in baptismal waters to walk in a new life, so we will be raised with him in the new heaven and new earth.

God has revealed the end and goal of history in the resurrection of Jesus. That end is the defeat of death in resurrection. As Paul writes, Christ "must reign until he has put all his enemies under his feet. The last enemy to be destroyed is death" (1 Corinthians 15:25-26). The last enemy, death, is fully conquered in the *eschaton* when the full harvest is reaped. Though we know that death has been conquered because God has raised Jesus from the dead, the fullness of that eschatological reality has not yet arrived. The last enemy has not yet been defeated. But we do have, through the resurrection of Jesus, a proleptic vision of that harvest. While the eschatological future has not yet arrived, we know what the end will be like because of the resurrection of Jesus.

Conclusion

These three soteriological events are God's mighty act to redeem the fallen cosmos. The incarnation is God's empathy for his creation. The death of Jesus is God's redemption of fallenness. The resurrection of Jesus is the firstfruits of redemption. The gospel is the incarnation of God for our sake, his death for our sins, and his resurrection on the third day for our justification. Jesus sanctified fallen human existence, and destroyed sin and death through his incarnation, death, and resurrection. He defeated the curse and gave humanity life again.

There is a cosmic spiritual struggle involved in the redemption of humanity. This cosmic battle involves the reordering of creation itself. Given the fallenness of the cosmos, God engaged the battle climactically in the incarnation, ministry, death, and resurrection of Jesus, the Son of God. The Christ Event (from his incarnation through his exaltation) reorders the universe. It overcomes fallenness and triumphs over evil. Atonement is the work of God for us through the death and resurrection of Jesus. It is not our work. God does what we cannot do. He defeats evil in the cosmos and triumphs over fallenness on our behalf.

In Jesus Christ, God suffered with us and for us. He did not distance himself from our suffering, but joined us in it by becoming one of us. He was not satisfied to leave us in that suffering, but acted to destroy Satan, sin, and death in the death and resurrection of Jesus. Christology — the incarnation, ministry, death, and resurrection of Jesus — is God's answer to suffering. It is God's response to fallenness. There God reveals his own character and demonstrates his authentic love for us.

The incarnation is the foundation of this act. Atonement for sin is a divine act. Resurrection is the defeat of death. As a work of God, redemption is carried out by God himself. By becoming one with humanity, God redeemed us from Satan by freeing us from death and the fear of death. In his incarnational ministry, Jesus defeated Satan in temptation and destroyed his works. He exorcised demons, healed the sick, and raised the dead. God came in Jesus to destroy the works of Satan (1 John 3:8) and to proclaim the in-breaking of God's kingdom. The kingdom of God came in the person of Jesus. The kingdom of God was revealed through his ministry. The *eschaton* made its appearance in a provisional way when Jesus exorcised demons, healed the sick, and raised the dead. His ministry proclaimed the presence of the kingdom of God and provided a glimpse of eschatological glory (Matthew 10:5-8; 11:4-6; 12:28). The ministry of Jesus testifies to the reality of the eschatological kingdom and the ultimate defeat of Satan. God redeemed us because he loved us.

Yet sometimes the love of God does not seem so obvious. For example, Israel was sometimes skeptical. "How have you loved us?" they asked (Malachi 1:2). From their perspective, the love of God was not so evident. Probably living during the time of Nehemiah, Israel was oppressed by its regional neighbors, under heavy taxation from the Persian King, suffering through crop failures and famine, selling their children into slavery, and mortgaging their lands to survive (Nehemiah 5:1-5). Israel could not see God's love in the midst of this suffering.

I recalled this Malachi text after a conversation with my then six-year-old daughter Rachel. As she went to bed each evening either my wife or I would pray with her. We would always include others who needed our prayers, especially those whom she knew were sick. During a particular stretch of time, every evening she would pray for Miss Pat and for Joshua.

Miss Pat, her Sunday school teacher at the time, had been diagnosed with breast cancer. Joshua, her brother, had been diagnosed with Sanfilippo Syndrome. Through surgery and chemo, Miss Pat's cancer went into remission. Joshua's condition is genetic and terminal.

One evening, after we had thanked God for healing Miss Pat and prayed for Joshua, Rachel's tear-filled eyes looked into mine. "God healed Miss Pat, didn't he?" "Yes," I replied. "God loves Miss Pat, doesn't he?" "Yes, he does," I answered. Her next question shocked me though I suppose it should not have. "Doesn't God love Joshua, too?" Her reasoning was clear. Her logic was faultless. God healed Miss Pat because he loved her, and if he loves Joshua, why doesn't he heal him? Her question was Israel's question, "How have you, O Lord, loved Joshua?"

Her innocent, honest question raises the most difficult conundrum we face. How do we make sense of the love of God in the midst of suffering? How do we thank God for healing one, and praise God despite the fact he does not heal another? How do we continue to believe in God's love when he does not heal our children or our siblings?

When Israel asked that same question, Malachi pointed them back to Israel's beginnings. Israel existed as a nation out of the free, sovereign choice of God. Israel did not create itself, but God created Israel. Israel was not a nation because they were so numerous or because they were so righteous, but Israel was a nation because God loved them (Deuteronomy 7:7-9; 9:4-6). The history of Israel, from the promise to Abraham through the Exodus and Conquest to the restoration of Israel after the Babylonian exile, is God's testimony of his love. Malachi's message is that God had demonstrated his love through his faithfulness to Israel. Israel should not doubt that testimony.

Our answers must follow a similar pattern. We must remember God's testimony to his love. God demonstrated his love for us, even while we were his enemies, when Christ died for us (Romans 5:8). The supreme expression of God's love — beyond any temporary healing of cancer, beyond any temporary prosperity — is that God so loved the world that he gave his only Son to die for us (John 3:16). The supreme expression of God's love is that he was willing to share our pain and shame — the Father now knows the grief of death and the Son now knows the experience of death — and, at the same time, to redeem us from our pain. This love of God is ultimately redemptive and it will renew us in a place where all pain is relieved and every tear is wiped away (Revelation 21:4).

When we look down and around us, our troubles will overwhelm us. There is always a reason to doubt the love of God when we seek evidence of that love in our health, wealth or prosperity as if God's primary concern is that we have those things. But God is more interested in our faith than he is our pleasure. Health and prosperity are only temporary, for one day health will give way to sickness and prosperity will give way to death. When we look down, the waves will convince us to doubt God's love, but when we lift our eyes to gaze upon the cross, we will remember how God has loved us. The incarnation, cross, and empty tomb stand as the unshakable testimony of God's love. "For," with Paul, "I am convinced that neither death nor life, neither angels nor demons, neither the present nor the future, nor any powers, neither height nor depth, nor anything else in all creation, will be able to separate us from the love of God that is in Christ Jesus our Lord" (Romans 8:38-39).

"Yes, Rachel, God loves Joshua, too. Jesus died for Joshua, too, and even though God may not heal Joshua now, he will one day. Just like Jesus, Joshua will die one day, but just like Jesus, one day God will raise him from the dead and we will all live together with God forever. One day God will heal everybody who trusts him. So if God heals them now, we thank him, but if he decides not to heal now, we still praise him because we know one day he will."

Rachel, now eleven, continues to pray for Joshua. O Lord, give me the faith of a child.

---

[1]Karl Barth, *Church Dogmatics*, 2(1), ed. by G.W. Bromiley and T.F. Torrance (Edinburgh: T. & T. Clark, 1957), pp. 301-307.

[2]William Placher, *Narratives of a Vulnerable God: Christ, Theology and Scripture* (Louisville: Westminster John Knox Press, 1994), p. 16.

[3]Fretheim, *The Suffering of God*, pp. 107-148.

[4]Nicholas Wolterstorff, *Lament for a Son* (Grand Rapids: Eerdmans, 1987), p. 81.

[5]John R.W. Stott, *The Cross of Christ* (Downers Grove, IL: InterVarsity, 1986), p. 123.

[6]C.E.B. Cranfield, *A Critical and Exegetical Commentary on the Epistle to the Romans*, International Critical Commentary (Edinburgh: T. & T. Clark, 1975), 1:217

[7]Stott, *Cross*, p. 159; cf. pp. 133-169.

[8]Wolfhart Pannenberg, *Jesus — God and Man*, trans. by Lewis L. Wilkins and Duane A. Priebe (Philadelphia: Westminster Press, 1968), p. 108.

Chapter Ten

What Are We Waiting For?
The Glorious Goal of God's Story

> *Then I saw a new heaven and a new earth, for the first heaven and the first earth had passed away, and there was no longer any sea. I saw the Holy City, the new Jerusalem, coming down out of heaven from God, prepared as a bride beautifully dressed for her husband. And I heard a loud voice from the throne saying, "Now the dwelling of God is with men, and he will live with them. They will be his people, and God himself will be with them and be their God. He will wipe every tear from their eyes. There will be no more death or mourning or crying or pain, for the old order of things has passed away.*
>
> *Revelation 21:1-4*

"Your kingdom come, your will be done on earth as it is in heaven" (Matthew 6:10). These familiar words express the eschatological yearning and expectation of God's people. They are a cry for the consummation, the heavenly kingdom, where there will be no more pain, tears, and death. It has been the prayer of God's people since the Fall. From the beginning promise that one day the seed of the woman would crush the head of the serpent (Genesis 3:15) to the closing act of Revelation where John prays "Come, Lord Jesus" (Revelation 22:20), the people of God have expected the fullness of God's reign in the world. They pray that God would fully implement his reign over the world, destroy his enemies, and live among his people.

The prayer for the consummation is the cry of God's oppressed people for deliverance from the bondage of death. One day God will answer this cry and reveal his heavenly kingdom (2 Timothy 4:1). While that kingdom has not yet come, God has revealed his intention through various mighty acts within redemptive history. When Israel cried out to God under the burden of their slavery, God heard them, came near, and delivered them through Moses (Exodus 2:23-25; Numbers 20:16; Deuteronomy 26:7; 1 Samuel 12:8). When Israel cried out to God during their oppression under the King of Aram, God heard them, came near, and delivered them through Othniel (Judges 3:8-9). When Israel cried out to God during their oppression under the Midianites, God heard them, came near, and delivered them through Gideon (Judges 6:7-12). When Israel cried out to God during their oppression under the Philistines, God heard them, came near, and delivered them through Samuel (1 Samuel 7:5-11). When individuals within Israel's history cried out to the Lord in their distress, God heard them, came near, and redeemed them from their troubles (Psalm 18:6; 34:6; 40:1; 107:13,19; 145:19). This pattern of oppression-cry-deliverance is the cycle of fall and redemption. The people of God fall, they are oppressed by trouble, then they turn to God who answers them through his redemptive work. Nehemiah recalls this gracious pattern: "And when they cried out to you again, you heard from heaven, and in your compassion you delivered them time after time" (Nehemiah 9:28).

This theme is carried into the New Testament as well. It appears in Luke where the birth of Jesus is understood as God's remembrance of Israel (Luke 1:54-55,72-75). Jesus is announced as the one who will reign forever and his kingdom will never end (Luke 1:32-33). The prophet of the Most High, John the Baptist, will "give light to those who sit in darkness and in the shadow of death" (Luke 1:79, NRSV). God has remembered his people in order to rescue Israel from the hands of its enemies (Luke 1:74). Mark announces a new Exodus through the prophet John. God will make a way through the wilderness (Mark 1:2-3). This is the good news of the kingdom of God (Mark 1:14-15). Matthew announces that Jesus comes to bring light to darkness and to deliver God's people from the shadows of death (Matthew 4:15-17). Quoting Isaiah 9:1-2, Matthew interprets the ministry of Jesus as God's mighty act of redemption for the oppressed. Through the ministry of Jesus, God breaks the back of the oppressor as he did in the day of Midian (Isaiah 9:4). Jesus will sit on the throne of David and there will be no end to his kingdom (Isaiah 9:6-7).

In the ministry of Jesus Christ, then, God reveals his kingdom and he acts to destroy the oppressor. He heals the lame, blind, and sick; exorcises demons; and destroys death (Matthew 11:4-6; Luke 4:18-19). It is good news for the oppressed. Jesus hears the cries of the oppressed, the hurting, and sick, and he answers their cry with compassionate redemption. When two blind men cried out for mercy, Jesus heard them and healed them (Matthew 9:27-31). When the father of the demoniac cried out for help, Jesus heard him and exorcised the demon (Mark 9:24). As Jesus proclaimed the "good news of the kingdom," he also cured "every disease and sickness" (Matthew 9:35). In his ministry of compassion, healing, and proclamation, Jesus "carried our infirmities and bore our diseases" (Matthew 8:14-17, NRSV). The ministry of Jesus is God's answer to the cry of fallen humanity who seek release from the power of Satan, sin, and death.

This is epitomized in the cry of the one who not only suffered with us but also suffered for us. In the Garden, his tears express his anguish, and his voice cries out to his Father for deliverance (Luke 22:39-46). His Father heard his cry and delivered him. He asked for a way out, and when he submitted to the Father's will, he cried on the cross, "My God, My God, why have you forsaken me?" (Matthew 27:46 quoting Psalm 22:1). God heard his cry. The writer of Hebrews notes, "During the days of Jesus' life on earth, he offered up prayers and petitions with loud cries and tears to the one who could save him from death, and he was heard because of his reverent submission" (5:7). The pattern of God's history with his people is repeated: the faithful cry out, God hears, and God delivers. Psalm 22 reflects this same pattern. The cry of verse 1, and the anguish of the first few verses ("I am a worm," 22:6), are answered by God. Just as God had answered the cries of his people in the past when they trusted him (22:4-5), so God answered the cry of this faithful one (Psalm 22:22-24):

> I will declare your name to my brothers;
>> in the congregation I will praise you.
> You who fear the LORD, praise him!
>> All you descendants of Jacob, honor him!
>> Revere him, all you descendants of Israel!
> For he has not despised or disdained
>> the suffering of the afflicted one;
> he has not hidden his face from him
>> but has listened to his cry for help.

God heard the cry of Jesus, and he answered him. God delivered him through resurrection. God did not leave his holy one in Hades, but he raised him from the dead. In this remembrance, in this act of resurrection, God reveals that "dominion belongs to" him (Psalm 22:28). God has acted to destroy Satan, sin, and death. God has declared victory in the resurrection of Jesus.

Now the people of God wait for the fullness of that victory. Just as the souls under the altar "called out in a loud voice" with their lament of "how long?" (Revelation 6:10), so we wait with our groanings, tears, and cries for the consummation. We wait for the final revelation of God's kingdom. We wait for the time when, like Israel, God will take note of our groaning, hear our cry, and send his Son one more time to reveal his heavenly kingdom. Our confidence is that just as God has acted in the past for Israel, and just as he acted in the resurrection of Jesus, so he will act on our behalf when his Son returns.

The Old Testament Expectation

The Old Testament anticipated a divine deliverance from death in the form of a restored kingdom of Israel. The idea of "restoration" is central to the expectations of exilic Israel (e.g., Jeremiah 16:15; 23:8; 24:6; 50:19). However, this is not the only vision which shapes Israelite expectations. The vision of the original Garden, where the wolf and the lamb lie down together, is also central, especially in pre-exilic Israel (Isaiah 11:1-9). The kingdom of God as it appears in Israel expects a fuller revelation in the future. It expects a time when the serpent will be crushed, when a new heaven and new earth will be established, and when God's peace and reign is fully manifested in the earth.

Consequently, the Old Testament has something to say about God's final eschatological restoration. Peter makes this clear in his temple sermon (Acts 3:17-21):

> Now, brothers, I know that you acted in ignorance, as did your leaders. But this is how God fulfilled what he had foretold through all the prophets, saying that his Christ would suffer. Repent, then, and turn to God, so that your sins may be wiped out, that times of refreshing may come from the Lord, and that he may send the Christ, who has been appointed for you — even Jesus. He must remain in heaven until the time comes for God to restore everything, as he promised long ago through his holy prophets.

The prophets not only foretold the sufferings of Christ but also the restoration of all things. The Old Testament prophets, then, had an eschatological vision of the end time. Without understanding everything about that vision (cf. 1 Peter 1:10-12), they anticipated the renewal which God's anointed would accomplish (cf. 2 Peter 1:16-21 where the Second Coming is something to which the prophets give witness). The prophets promised the restoration of all things, and the New Testament expects that Christ will fulfill that promise when he returns again.

These Old Testament themes anticipate New Testament eschatology. The New Testament takes up the apocalyptic language of the Old Testament in order to testify to its fulfillment in Christ and their ultimate implementation in the consummation. There will be a time of "regeneration" when the Son of Man comes again and sits on his glorious throne (Matthew 19:28). The eschatological expectations of the Old Testament are fulfilled in Christ who is the eschatological king that will bring about the consummation. He will restore all things. Two texts from Isaiah illustrate this Old Testament expectation.

Isaiah 24

Isaiah 24 appears at the end of a series of oracles against the nations. In successive order, Isaiah prophesies against Babylon (13:1–14:23), Assyria (14:24-27), Philistia (14:28-32), Moab (15:1–16:13), Damascus (17:1-14), Cush (18:1-7), Egypt (19:1–20:6), Babylon (21:1-10), Edom (21:11-12), Arabia (21:13-17), Jerusalem (22:1-25), and Tyre (23:1-17). In each of these judgments, the nations are condemned for their pride and idolatry. Each contains a picture of the day of destruction when God would judge each nation for their sins. God will "cut off" Babylon (14:22), "crush" Assyria (14:25), "destroy" Philistia (14:30), fill Moab's waters with "blood" (15:9), turn Damascus to a "heap of ruins" (17:1), leave Cush for the birds of prey (18:6), cause Egypt to "stagger" (19:14), bring night down upon Edom (21:12), bring the sword to Arabia (21:15), topple the leaders of Jerusalem (22:19), and humble Tyre (23:9). Indeed, as Isaiah announces, "See, the LORD is going to lay waste the earth and devastate it" (24:1).

God will judge the whole earth and no one will escape. Whether you are a master or a servant, a seller or a buyer, a priest or a lay person, the earth will be "completely laid waste and totally plundered" (24:2-3). God acts against the earth's sinfulness because it has been "defiled by its people" (24:4-5). Consequently, "a curse consumes the earth; its people must bear their guilt" (24:6). God sits in judgment and no one escapes his justice. Everyone, whether the nations or Jerusalem, will suffer the curse they have brought upon themselves. In that day, God will reveal himself as the "LORD Almighty" who reigns on Mount Zion in Jerusalem (24:23).

However, the holy God is also a redeemer God. The God who reigns from Mt. Zion will renew and redeem the earth he has judged. In the wake of this judgment and in the hope of renewal, Isaiah praises God for his mighty deeds which he had planned long ago and will accomplish in the future (25:1). God is faithful, and he will be a "refuge for the poor, a refuge for the needy in his distress, a shelter from the storm and a shade from the heat" (25:4). God will act to redeem the poor and needy as he silences the ruthless. When God reigns on Mount Zion, God will destroy the prideful and exalt the humble (25:11-12). What will God do? Isaiah tells us (25:6-9):

> On this mountain the LORD Almighty will prepare
> a feast of rich food for all peoples,
> a banquet of aged wine —
> the best of meats and the finest of wines.
> On this mountain he will destroy
> the shroud that enfolds all peoples,
> the sheet that covers all nations;
> he will swallow up death forever.
> The Sovereign LORD will wipe away the tears from all faces;
> he will remove the disgrace of his people from all the earth.
> The LORD has spoken.
> In that day they will say,
> "Surely this is our God;
> we trusted in him, and he saved us.

> This is the LORD, we trusted in him;
>   let us rejoice and be glad in his salvation."

God will sponsor a banquet on Mount Zion in Jerusalem and he will take away death. God will replace the mourning and tears of death with the rejoicing of life and salvation. God will save his people who trust in him by destroying death and offering festive celebration in his holy presence. God promises to live among his people where death is destroyed and there are no more tears.

The New Testament applies this language to the consummation. Paul quotes this text as he celebrates the victory of life over death in the resurrection (1 Corinthians 15:54). Revelation 7:17 and 21:4 place God's removal of tears from the eyes of his people in the *eschaton*. The Old Testament expected a time when the earth would be consumed and judged, but also a time when death itself would be destroyed. Isaiah 24 expects the consummation — the destruction of death. It expects a heavenly banquet in God's presence. This is the essence of the *eschaton*. It is God's goal in redemption: to destroy death and renew communion with his people.

Isaiah 65–66

Isaiah 65–66 addresses God's people in Babylonian exile. This oracle offers the hope of restoration. Isaiah 40–48 announced a new time of redemption among God's people. They will return to their land once again. They have suffered for their sins, and now God acts in compassion toward them once again (Isaiah 40:1-2). The climax of this hopeful message is the last two chapters of Isaiah which offer a vision of the new Jerusalem.

Isaiah 65–66 may be divided into three major sections.[1] Isaiah 65:1-16 portrays God's judgment of his city, but also offers hope to a remnant. God judges the sins of his people and he has given "full payment" to their sins (65:7). God destroys those who did not answer when he called and chose evil over good (65:11-12). God's enemies are put to death (65:15). Nevertheless, God does not totally destroy his people (65:8). Rather, God will provide Sharon as a pasture for flocks and the Valley of Achor as a resting place for herds. He will restore blessing to the cursed land. God will bless those who seek him (65:9-10). The servants of God will neither hunger nor thirst, but they "will sing out of the joy of their hearts" (65:14).

Isaiah 65:17–66:5 offers a picture of a new Jerusalem set in a new heaven and a new earth. God will create a new heaven and a new earth and he will create a new Jerusalem to be a "delight." God himself will reign from this Jerusalem, the people will rejoice, and "the sound of weeping and of crying will be heard in it no more" (65:17-19). The contrast between the "former things" (65:17) and the new things denotes the radical change that will take place in the world.

The Former Things	The New Things
Crying and Mourning	Rejoicing
Infant Death	Infant Life
Premature Death	Full Life
Stolen Homes	Live in Own Homes
Stolen Food	Own Food
Fruitless Labor	Fruitful Labor
Loss of Children	Descendants
No Answer to Call	Answer Before Call
Violence and Destruction	Peace and Harmony

The new creation is God's reign over the world fully established. Heaven is God's throne and the earth is his footstool (Isaiah 66:1). God is the creator, and he is the re-creator. God will redeem his earth and his people. But whom will God redeem? The answer: "he who is humble and contrite in spirit, and trembles at my word" (Isaiah 66:2b).

The third section (Isaiah 66:6-24) offers comfort. God will punish the guilty and his enemies with his fury (66:14-

16), but he will comfort Zion with peace and wealth (66:12-13). Just as a woman suffers labor pains before the joy of birth, so the fallen creation suffers the pains of the curse before it gives birth to the joy of the new creation (66:7-11). In that new moment God promises (66:12-13):

> I will extend peace to her like a river,
>> and the wealth of the nations like a flooding stream;
> you will nurse and be carried on her arm
>> and dandled on her knees.
> As a mother comforts her child,
>> so will I comfort you;
>> and you will be comforted over Jerusalem.

God will renew his affection like at the beginning when God chose her as his new child. In the beginning God loved Israel and hovered over her like an eagle over her young (Deuteronomy 32:11). God will renew this relationship in a new Jerusalem in a new heaven and a new earth. God will recall the beginning and make the end like the beginning. God will restore Eden. But the rebellious will not experience this newness because their dead bodies will be strewn across the battlefield where "their worm will not die, nor will their fire be quenched" (66:24). God's people, however, will have a name that endures as long as the new heavens and the new earth endure (66:22-23).

The New Testament applies this "new heaven, new earth, and new Jerusalem" motif to the consummation. It is the picture quoted at the beginning of this chapter. When the Son returns, God will renew the earth and recreate the heavens as God's people live in a new Jerusalem (Revelation 21:1-4). The new heaven and the new earth will be the home of the righteous (2 Peter 3:13). The New Testament also applies the language of the undying worm and unquenchable fire to the *eschaton* as well. It is Gehenna (Hell; Mark 9:48). God will defeat his enemies and cast them into Gehenna, and at the same time create a new heaven and new earth for his people. The New Testament applies this to the day when Jesus Christ comes again.

The New Heaven and the New Earth

The first advent of Jesus was the incarnation. He came in humility, weakness, and poverty. However, the second advent will display his greatness, power, and majesty. The second coming of Jesus will involve the full revelation of God's glory and kingdom. He will save his people from the eschatological wrath of God and execute justice upon the earth. God will accomplish his goal of a new heaven and a new earth when Jesus comes again.

God has always wanted to dwell among his people where he can be their God and they can be his people (cf. Genesis 17:7; Leviticus 26:11-12; Jeremiah 24:7; 32:38; Ezekiel 36:28; Zechariah 8:8; 2 Corinthians 6:16; Revelation 21:3). The eschatological promise of God is that we will be with him "forever." This is the central hope of God's people, that is, that God will be present among them. To dwell in the house of the Lord forever is the singular hope of God's people, and it is a hope that will find fulfillment when Jesus returns. Then we will see the face of God and dwell with him forever (Revelation 22:1-5).

However, the "new earth" will be a very different one than the one we now inhabit. Sin, corruption, decay, tears, and death will no longer fill it. The old earth with its old age problems will have passed away and a new earth will have arrived "for the old order of things has passed away" (Revelation 21:4). We will live with the Lord in a new heaven and a new earth where everything old and fallen will be renewed and restored (Revelation 21:1-4). This new heaven and new earth will be the home of the righteous. The old heaven and the old earth will be destroyed, purified by fire, and renewed for inhabitation by God's saints (2 Peter 3:10-13). Just as God judged and destroyed the old world through the Noahic flood and then renewed the world through the descendants of Noah, so God will judge and destroy the old world by fire and then renew it as the place where his saints will live with him forever. This has been

God's intent from the beginning. He created an earth to be inhabited and filled by human beings who reflect his glory (Isaiah 45:18). He created Eden for that purpose, but sin destroyed that world, and a curse was laid upon it (Genesis 3:14ff). Now the creation itself groans to be released from the futility and bondage of that curse (Romans 8:20-21). The creation yearns for redemption.

God will redeem creation itself, just as he will redeem our souls and our bodies (cf. Romans 8:23). God's redemption is cosmic in character (Colossians 1:20 — things in heaven and things on the earth). He will turn everything back to its original purpose, both things in heaven and things on the earth. Just as he will redeem fallen bodies through resurrection, so he will redeem the fallen creation through re-creation just as he now transforms us through his Holy Spirit. This is the point of Romans 8:19-23:

> The creation waits in eager expectation for the sons of God to be revealed. For the creation was subjected to frustration, not by its own choice, but by the will of the one who subjected it, in hope that the creation itself will be liberated from its bondage to decay and brought into the glorious freedom of the children of God. We know that the whole creation has been groaning as in the pains of childbirth right up to the present time. Not only so, but we ourselves, who have the first-fruits of the Spirit, groan inwardly as we wait eagerly for our adoption as sons, the redemption of our bodies.

The creation, including our bodies, was subjected to the futility and bondage of a fallen world. God subjected the world to frustration in the hope of liberating the creation from its bondage. Because of the fall, our bodies die, we grieve, and we suffer. This world, full of its sin and disease, is not the world God created. God will judge this world, and in the flaming fire of vengeance he will destroy those rebels who continue in their sinful refusal to acknowledge and obey him (2 Thessalonians 1:7-9). But God's redemptive intent is to renew the world just as he intends to redeem our bodies. God will create a new heaven and a new earth (Revelation 21:1-4; 2 Peter 3:13; cf. Isaiah 65:17; 66:22). God will make his dwelling place among human-kind in a new heaven and new earth, in a new city, in a new Eden, and in that garden there will be no more curse. There will be no more pain, no more tears, and no more death (Revelation 21:1-4; 22:1-5). Through the work of Christ, God reverses the fall and renews the earth. He redeems us from our sins and resurrects our dead bodies. Once again, God will live among his people just as he did in the Garden of Eden. The original intention of God's creative work will be fulfilled through his redemption of the fallen creation.

Sometimes our view of heaven is too other-worldly. We think that heaven is some ethereal, almost surreal, place somewhere in the sky. We think heaven is out there, over there, or somewhere other than here. Certainly, here and now is not heaven — it is far from it. This place is full of sin, death, mourning, tears, and pain. But this is not what God created. He created Eden where the voice of God was heard in the midst of the garden; where harmony, peace, and joy were experienced throughout creation; where God communed with his newly created human community. One day, God will destroy this fallen earth and redeem it through renewing it so that it might be inhabited by his saints. On that new earth we will live with God forever. It is described as a great city — the size of the Mediterranean sea (Revelation 21:9-27). It is described as a wedding celebration between Christ and his Church. It is described as a new heaven and a new earth. Sin destroyed this world, but God will renew it. Heaven is not out there or over there. Heaven is where God will dwell with his saints forever, and he will dwell with them on a new heaven and a new earth.

Hokema rejects the total annihilation of the old heaven and earth in favor of a renewal for four basic reasons.[2] First, the newness of the heavens and the earth (2 Peter 3:13; Revelation 21:1) is described by *kainos* (new in quality or

nature) rather than *neos* (new in time or origin). Consequently, the point is that something old is given a new quality rather than totally annihilated. Second, Romans 8
teaches that the physical earth will be redeemed along with
our own bodies. Third, the analogy between our resurrected
bodies and the new earth points in the direction of materi-
ality. While there will be discontinuity between the old and
new earths, there will also be, just like with the resurrection
body, continuity between the old and new earths. Fourth,
"if God would have to annihilate the present cosmos, Satan
would have won a great victory." Has Satan so corrupted
this world that it must be destroyed and a new one erected?
Did God lose the battle for this earth? God's victory is deci-
sive and complete. He will redeem the earth he created.

The hope of a new earth is not another earth but this
earth redeemed and renewed. This earth will be purged by
fire and its old elements will melt away so that it might be
renewed by God's grace.[3] Our hope is that this earth will be
refurbished and given its original condition once again. This
is more concrete than the spiritualized and ethereal hopes of
many Christians. Perhaps it makes more sense of certain biblical phrases like, "the meek will inherit the earth" (Matthew
5:5; cf. Psalm 37:11), or that Gentiles, as part of the promise
of Abraham, would inherit the cosmos (Romans 4:13). The
meaning of the new heaven and the new earth is that God
will redeem the cosmos — everything in heaven and earth
will be reconciled to him again. Everything will be made
new, the Garden of Eden will be restored, and there will no
longer be any curse (Revelation 22:1-5):

> Then the angel showed me the river of the water of life,
> as clear as crystal, flowing from the throne of God and
> of the Lamb down the middle of the great street of the
> city. On each side of the river stood the tree of life,
> bearing twelve crops of fruit, yielding its fruit every
> month. And the leaves of the tree are for the healing of
> the nations. No longer will there be any curse. The
> throne of God and of the Lamb will be in the city, and

his servants will serve him. They will see his face, and his name will be on their foreheads. There will be no more night. They will not need the light of a lamp or the light of the sun, for the Lord God will give them light. And they will reign for ever and ever.

The restored tranquillity of the Garden, absent the curse, and the renewed access to the tree of life is the essence of the new Jerusalem where God himself dwells. God will bring everything full circle — what he created fell, but what fell, he will redeem. God will offer us the Garden once again, but this time it is a Garden where we will be with the Lord forever.

Whether Scripture has in mind this literal earth or some other physical realm is inconsequential if we understand that heaven is defined by the fullness of God's presence. It is not really worth debating the exact character of the new heavens and the new earth. We really do not know much about what the new heaven and new earth will be like. We only have some juicy hints. Whether we return to a renewed earth, or whether we live in the sky, or whether there is no real space/time location to heaven as we know space and time, these considerations are secondary to the primary point. The primary point is that our eschatological home is where God fully dwells among his people — where he will be our God and we will be his people. We might debate some of the fine points of the new heaven and the new earth but that debate does not undermine the fundamental point of eschatology which is that God will dwell with his people and we shall forever be with the Lord. Eschatology is not about when or where, but whom — with whom will we dwell? God will dwell among us.

Whatever God may do and however he may do it are secondary to the promise that when Christ comes again, we will live with God forever in a new heaven and a new earth. This is our hope. This is our goal. Eschatological speculation which distracts us and detracts from that goal is unbiblical. Instead of debating exactly how or when God will achieve the goal he has in mind for us, we ought to be a people who live ethical lives so as to bring glory to God's name. As Peter indicates, one reason we talk about eschatology — about what God will do when Jesus comes again — is to answer the question, "what kind of people ought [we] to be?" as we are "looking forward to a new heaven and a new earth, the home of righteousness" (2 Peter 3:11,13). Eschatology is important because of how it affects the way we live now. It gives us hope as we look forward to the day when we will live with God forever with a newly transformed body on a new earth. It also motivates holy living as we seek to be the kind of people God wants to live with him. Christ is coming, he will raise the dead, and he will commune with us forever. Those are the basics, and they give us hope and inspire our desire to please God.

Patiently Waiting through the Spirit

We live in a fallen world where the redemption of God is already at work but has not yet reached its full potential. God has already acted in Jesus Christ to accomplish our redemption, but that redemption has not yet been fully revealed. Consequently, the people of God wait for the fulfillment of God's work. As Paul writes, "by faith we eagerly await through the Spirit the righteousness for which we hope" (Galatians 5:5).

Our existence in the present age is characterized by three horizons (Romans 8:18-26). First, there is the present fallenness which pervades our world. We lament and groan. Our bodies suffer and decay. We live in bondage to death. Our second horizon is the "alreadiness" of God's presence through his Spirit, through prayer and intercession. We wait for God's final victory as we seek his face in prayer through the Spirit. God has already given us his presence by the indwelling of his Spirit. We already have the firstfruits of the *eschaton* in the person of the Spirit. However, we have not yet experienced the full revelation of our sonship. Our third horizon is the "not-yetness" of our hope. We do not yet experience the glory and freedom of resurrected life in the *eschaton*. As a result, we live within three horizons: (1) the present age is fallen, but (2) God has already given us his presence though (3) he has not yet fully revealed himself. The chart below represents this threefold understanding of the present age.

Fallenness	Already	Not Yet
Groaning	Holy Spirit	Adoption
Suffering	Hope	Revelation
Bondage	Waiting	Freedom
Decay	Prayer	Resurrection
Futility	Intercession	Glory

"Not Yet" – The Persistence of Fallenness

God has subjected the world to futility and frustration (Romans 8:18-21). Paul uses the term *mataiotes* to describe this futility. This is the only time Paul uses this term except for describing the futility of the pagan mind (Ephesians 4:17). In the context of Romans 8, this is particularly significant because the Septuagint uses it to translate the Hebrew term for "vanity, futility, meaningless" in Ecclesiastes. Of the Septuagint's fifty-four uses of this term, thirty-nine are in Ecclesiastes (1:2[5],14; 2:1,11,15,17,19,21,23,26; 3:19; 4:4,7,8,16; 5:5,9; 6:2,4,9,11,12; 7:6,15; 8:10,14; 9:2,9; 11:8,10; 12:8). Paul identifies the fallen cosmos with the meaninglessness and pessimism which characterizes the world in the eyes of the Teacher.

God placed a "burden" on his fallen cosmos (Ecclesiastes 1:13). The term for "burden" only occurs in the Hebrew text in Ecclesiastes (1:13; 2:23,26; 3:10; 4:8; 5:2,14; 8:16). He created the world full of joy, harmony, and peace. Sin, however, destroyed that original harmony, and God subjected the world to futility. God put the cosmos under a curse and rendered life futile except as God gives his gifts to life. Despite the "burdenness" of life, despite the horizon of death, God gives "wisdom, knowledge and happiness" to those who please him, but to the "sinner he gives the task of gathering and storing up" for another (Ecclesiastes 2:26). He may give wealth or poverty to either, but he only enables those who please him to be happy in their work and to recognize God's gifts (Ecclesiastes 5:18–6:2). While the futility of life is revealed in the prospect of death, God yet gives his good gifts to his creation and enables believers to enjoy them even while they live in a fallen world.

The present time, then, includes suffering. It is inescapable and believers should not think that they can evade the effects of a fallen world. Suffering is part of fallenness and the cosmos will remain fallen until the consummation. The kind of suffering that Paul envisions here is not simply persecution. According to the context, this suffering also involves any kind of hardship or trouble. It includes nakedness and hunger (famine) as well as persecution or threats with a sword (Romans 8:35). It includes all the power of the fallen cosmos itself (Romans 8:38-39).

The Christian perspective on suffering is that this is a suffering "with Christ" (Romans 8:17). The suffering is not simply generic, but it is to be viewed in a particular way. All suffering is suffering with Christ, and all suffering with Christ will be exchanged for glory with Christ. To suffer with Christ is to share his experience of fallenness. It is to identify not only with the pain and humiliation of his fallenness, but it is also to share in the redemptive agenda of his suffering.

Paul uses this image several times in his writings. For example, Paul wants to know Christ so that he might attain to the resurrection from the dead, but his knowledge of Christ involves both the suffering and power of Christ. Suffering and power refer to the experiential dimension of the Christian life (Philippians 3:10-11). Paul views his suffering as the expression of his identification with Christ, and he views his experience of power as that which raised

Jesus from the dead. Indeed, Paul believes that his own sufferings are so identified with Jesus that his suffering fills up what is lacking in the suffering of Christ (Colossians 1:24). Paul rejoices in his suffering because it is the continuation of the suffering of Christ through his church. Christ himself suffers as his church suffers. As the church continues the ministry of Christ, it experiences the suffering of Christ and Christ empathizes with the suffering of his church.

Consequently, the Christian perspective on suffering is fundamentally christological. We see our suffering as an identification with Jesus Christ so that we might also see his glorification as our own. Suffering comes because the world is fallen, but our suffering is characterized by the redemptive purposes of God in Christ. Our suffering is christological. We participate in suffering as people who share the ministry of Christ. Through that suffering we experience the power of Christ's resurrection. This experience of power through suffering emboldens our hope.

Believers, therefore, yearn for the revelation of their glorious freedom as the children of God. Paul calls this the "groaning" of believers. It is a groan that arises out of the expectation of something new, something redemptive. We groan for the consummation because we are perplexed, struck down, and persecuted by the fallen world. But we are not crushed, desperate or destroyed because we believe in the hope of the resurrection (2 Corinthians 4:7-14). Yet our hope generates a yearning. Paul expresses this groaning for the *eschaton* in 2 Corinthians 4:16–5:5:

> Therefore we do not lose heart. Though outwardly we are wasting away, yet inwardly we are being renewed day by day. For our light and momentary troubles are achieving for us an eternal glory that far outweighs them all. So we fix our eyes not on what is seen, but on what is unseen. For what is seen is temporary, but what is unseen is eternal.
>
> Now we know that if the earthly tent we live in is destroyed, we have a building from God, an eternal

house in heaven, not built by human hands. Mean-
while we groan, longing to be clothed with our heavenly dwelling, because when we are clothed, we will not
be found naked. For while we are in this tent, we groan
and are burdened, because we do not wish to be
unclothed but to be clothed with our heavenly
dwelling, so that what is mortal may be swallowed up
by life. Now it is God who has made us for this very
purpose and has given us the Spirit as a deposit, guar-
anteeing what is to come.

Paul pictures our present fallenness in terms of a decay-
ing body which is like living in an impermanent tent. It is
frail and fragile. It will die. Consequently, we groan under
this burden. We lament, complain, suffer, and hurt. We are
burdened by fallenness. Even though we hope for the resurrection, we still hurt in the present. Because we hope for the
resurrection, we cry out for God's eschatological victory. We
cry, "how long?" We cry because we know there is a heavenly building (a resurrected body) waiting for us. God offers
his people renewal in the midst of their fallenness and he
promises an eschatological reality that provides hope.

But God has not left us without a witness in the present. God has given his witness in the incarnation, death,
and resurrection of Jesus Christ, but he has also given us his
witness by the presence of his Holy Spirit. God has poured
out his love into our hearts and has given us a deposit of his
eschatological communion. He has given us the Holy Spirit
as a down payment of the fullness of his triune presence.
Consequently, though the outer person decays day by day,
the inner person is renewed by the life-giving Spirit of God.
The Spirit strengthens the inner person and generates hope
within us (Ephesians 3:16-17; Romans 15:13).

Already – The Presence of the Spirit

The groaning of believers for the consummation is balanced with the present experience of hope through the
firstfruits of the Spirit (Romans 8:22-27). The "not yet" is

balanced by an "already." It is the "alreadiness" of our present Christian experience which yields eschatological hope and enables peace and joy in the midst of fallenness.

The victory has already been won even though the battle is not yet over. Christ reigns even now, but he has not yet put every enemy under his feet. The last enemy is death. Death has been defeated in the resurrection of Jesus, but death still rules the fallen world. In principle death has been defeated, but the skirmish continues. The skirmish is not meaningless even though the victory has already been won (Revelation 12). On the contrary, while Christ has defeated Satan and the kingdom of this world has become the kingdom of God, Satan still pursues the church in the wilderness and seeks to destroy the saints of God. The struggle is real and it continues. Consequently, this calls for "the endurance and faith of the saints" (Revelation 13:10, NRSV). Nevertheless, the victory song of Moses and the Lamb is sung around the throne of God. A mighty host stands on Mount Zion with the Lamb as the firstfruits of those whom God has redeemed from humanity (Revelation 14:1-5).

The indwelling of the Spirit is the "alreadiness" of God's victory in the fallen world. It is God's down payment on eschatological glory. God dwelt among his people in Israel through the tabernacle and the temple (Leviticus 26:11-12). God dwelt among humanity through the incarnation (John 1:14-18). God will dwell eschatologically with his people in the New Jerusalem (Revelation 21:1-4). Now, however, in fulfillment of God's dwelling among Israel and in anticipation of his dwelling in the New Jerusalem, God dwells among his people through his Holy Spirit. We are the temple of God (2 Corinthians 6:16). The presence of the Spirit means that we are heirs of God's kingdom (Romans 8:16-17). Paul calls this the "down payment" or "earnest" (*arrabon*) of God's eschatological intention.

> ## THE SPIRIT AS *ARRABON* (NRSV)
>
> *2 Corinthians 1:22*: By putting his seal on us and giving us his Spirit in our hearts as a *first installment*.
>
> *2 Corinthians 5:5*: He who has prepared us for this very thing is God, who has given us the Spirit as a *guarantee*.
>
> *Ephesians 1:14*: This is the *pledge* of our inheritance toward redemption as God's own people, to the praise of his glory.

Christians have received the Spirit of adoption by whom we cry, *"Abba*, Father." God has sent his Spirit into our hearts as a witness to our relationship to him (Galatians 4:6). This is the relational dimension of the Christian faith as the Spirit bears witness to God that we are his children and we, by the Spirit, address the God of the universe as *"Abba."* It is the Holy Spirit who speaks our prayer through us. It is only by the Spirit that we are able to address God as "Father."

The presence of God's Spirit bears fruit in believers (Galatians 5:22-23). The Spirit transforms believers into the image of Christ (2 Corinthians 3:16-18) and assures their hearts of God's love (Romans 5:5). Joy, peace, and comfort are gifts of the Spirit to the hearts of believers who endure (Romans 5:5; 15:13; 1 Thessalonians 1:6).

For Paul it appears that this experience of the Holy Spirit is especially seen in prayer. For example, he invites readers to "pray in the Spirit at all times" (Ephesians 6:18, NRSV), and we receive through prayer and the power of the Spirit "abundantly far more than all we can ask or imagine" (Ephesians 3:20, NRSV). Paul asks the Romans to struggle for him in their prayers to God "by our Lord Jesus Christ and by the love of the Spirit" (Romans 15:30, NRSV). Paul prays that the Colossians will be filled with the knowledge of the divine will "in all spiritual wisdom and understanding" (Colossians 1:9, NRSV). Epaphras prays that the Colossians may be enriched with every will of God (Colossians 4:12). Paul speaks of prayer and Spirit in the same breath, and that relationship is particularly evident in Romans 8 when Paul describes the intercession of the Spirit. According to Paul, it is the Spirit himself who speaks in prayer through us.[4] In this way also the Spirit bears witness with our spirits that we are the children of God.

The Spirit of God actively works on behalf of God's people through their prayers. The Spirit, Paul writes, "helps us in our weakness" (Romans 8:26). In the immediate context, Paul is thinking about prayer. But it is important to note that the topic of the Spirit is not far from Paul's mind when he thinks about suffering, groaning, and hope. As he turns from the present suffering to a sense of the "already," it is the Spirit who is uppermost in his mind. The presence of the Spirit is an "already." The wait through which we endure, we endure by the Spirit of God as we groan for the "not yet." Fallenness remains — it is what makes us weak and needing the help of God's Spirit. Even in our praying — our most desperate attempt to seek God's face — we are weak and need help. The Spirit is present to assist and provide sufficient aid so that our weakness is conquered by God's power through prayer.

The Spirit's function in this context is to intercede for us through our prayers. This is one form of the Spirit's help. There is an assumed intimacy here. The Spirit knows our hearts and because he knows us so well, he is able to offer intercession for us. The Spirit is the relational dynamic that connects us with God. God knows the mind of the Spirit just as the Spirit knows our inexpressible groanings as he himself groans for us. This is the language of intimacy, fellowship, and shared experience.

What does it mean for the Spirit to intercede for us with his own groanings? The Spirit groans with us through the intimacy of our relationship with God. The Spirit suffers with us, just as God suffered with Israel in the Old Testament and just as Jesus suffered with us incarnationally. Now the Spirit too suffers with us and shares this experience with God in ways that words cannot describe. The triune community — Father, Son, and Spirit — shares our suffering and helps us.

God is not removed from his people as if the ascension of Jesus has left God without a presence on earth. On the contrary, God has poured out his Spirit generously upon his people (Titus 3:5-6) and he dwells among them through his Spirit (1 Corinthians 3:16; 6:20; 12:13; Ephesians 2:22). God has a dynamic relationship with his people through the Spirit who intimately shares the experience of the believer and offers God's presence, comfort, and peace to the believer. In other words, and in more traditional terms, the believer has a personal relationship with God through the indwelling Spirit. The Spirit provides communion and fellowship between God and his people (2 Corinthians 13:14). We approach God through the Spirit (Ephesians 2:18), we pray through the Spirit (Ephesians 6:18; cf. Jude 20), and we worship by the Spirit (Philippians 3:3). Our relationship with God is grounded in the work of Christ and personally mediated by God's Holy Spirit. This is our dynamic experience of God through prayer and personal transformation. We approach the Father by Christ through the Spirit (Ephesians 2:18). The presence of the Spirit, then, is our personal fellowship with God.

Waiting – The Endurance of Believers

Believers are caught between the "not yet" of fallenness and the "already" of the *eschaton*. This tension means that believers live in two worlds. They live in the futility of suffering, death, mourning, and pain, but they also live in the Spirit who gives hope, peace, and comfort. They are oppressed by the world's fallenness, but they are liberated and renewed by the indwelling Spirit of God. This tension creates the situation where believers must wait for something they already partially possess. Believers wait for the *eschaton* with a hope that overcomes the futility of fallenness. This is an important theme for Paul.

WAITING IN PAUL (NRSV)

1 Corinthians 1:7: So that you are not lacking in any spiritual gift as you wait for the revealing of our Lord Jesus Christ.

Galatians 5:5: For through the Spirit, by faith, we eagerly wait for the hope of righteousness.

Philippians 3:20: But our citizenship is in heaven, and it is from there that we are expecting a Savior, the Lord Jesus Christ.

Titus 2:13: While we wait for the blessed hope and the manifestation of the glory of our great God and Savior, Jesus Christ.

Waiting in Hope

Our hope is the experience of glorious redemption. We wait for freedom from the bondage of corruption and mortality. We wait for the redemption of our bodies. God's glorious intent is to conform us to the image of his Son, both in body and soul.

Our hope is grounded in the work of God in Jesus Christ. Just as God subjected the world to fallenness, so God redeems the world through Jesus Christ. God gave his Son for the work of redemption. God is for us even though fallenness sometimes distorts our perception of God's redemptive intent. The evidence of God's redemptive love is that he gave us his Son, and if he gives us his Son, then "how will he not also, along with him, graciously give us all things?" (Romans 8:32). God is not against us. On the contrary, through Jesus Christ, God justified us.

Our hope is established through the intercession of Jesus Christ. Believers do not fear condemnation even when fallenness may distort our perception of how God feels about us. Nothing condemns us because God in Christ has justified us, and Jesus Christ sits at the right hand of God to intercede for us. God has already made his judgment in our favor through the intercession of Jesus Christ.

Our hope is produced by the presence of God's Spirit in our hearts (Romans 15:13). The firstfruits of the Spirit bear witness to our relationship with God. We are his children and through the Spirit we cry, "Abba, Father." God produces joy and peace in our lives by the power of the Spirit whom he has poured into our hearts. The love of God fills our hearts, and our hearts are comforted in the midst of fallenness.

Waiting with Confidence

We are confident because God has loved us in Jesus Christ. Fallenness creates doubt about God's love. Suffering causes us to question God's intent, motive, rationale, and power. But the demonstration of God's love in Jesus Christ dispels our doubts even if it does not answer all our questions.

We are confident because God works in all things for our good. The promise of Romans 8:28 is significant not only because of its meaning but also because of its context. Trapped in fallenness, yet given hope by the Spirit, Christians are caught in uncertainty about the present. The present is filled with suffering though the future is filled with hope. The constant promise of God which answers this uncertainty is that God is at work in all things for good.

God is active. He is active in everything. He has a good intention in everything he does. God is not distant or uninvolved. There is nothing outside of his activity. In everything he seeks to accomplish good, and, given that it is God, he will achieve good in every situation.

The "good" here does not refer to a human definition of happiness. It does not mean that nothing bad will happen, but that in everything that happens God intends something good or God's will is actively accomplishing something good. The "good" here refers to God's ultimate intent. The good that God works is the highest good — it is the good of fellowship with him. It is the good of conformity to the image of his Son (Romans 8:29-30). This is the purpose of God in the world.

Waiting through the Suffering

There are many obstacles in the way of God's people. Some of these are given in two lists in Romans 8:35,38-39, but Paul intends these lists as all-encompassing. He is not simply talking about persecution or human hostility toward the gospel. Rather, he is talking about every form of suffering which appears in this futile world. These tribulations form the fundamental obstacles of endurance and create despair within the people of God.

We must be willing to suffer for God's sake (Romans 8:36). Paul quotes Psalm 44:22 to make this point. Psalm 44 is a communal lament that raises the issue of whether God has forgotten his people (44:20) and rejected them (44:9). God has crushed his people (44:19) and made them a reproach (44:13). The psalmist raises the "Why?" questions. "Why do you sleep?" (44:23). "Why do you hide your face and forget our misery and oppression?" (44:24). He petitions God to wake up and act on behalf of his people. "Rise up and help us; redeem us because of your unfailing love" (44:26).

Paul quotes from the end of the psalm where the psalmist expresses the attitude of God's suffering people. God's people face death for God's sake, and indeed they are slaughtered as sheep. God's people do not escape fallenness, but God's people remain faithful and endure suffering. Their petition, however, is for redemption, and their confidence is, as the last line of the psalm expresses, God's unfailing love (44:26). The unfailing love of God to which the psalmist clung is also the same thing to which Paul appeals. God's unfailing love has been demonstrated in Jesus Christ.

Endurance produces hope because the love of God is in our hearts (Romans 5:5). Paul believes we ought to "boast" or "rejoice" in our sufferings because those sufferings produce perseverance, character, and hope (Romans 5:2-4). When believers persevere through suffering, God refines and builds a character out of which hope arises by the power of the Holy Spirit. The perseverance of faith through a tribulation is the means by which God makes us worthy of his kingdom. Paul wrote to the Thessalonians (2 Thessalonians 1:4-5):

> Therefore, among God's churches we boast about your perseverance and faith in all the persecutions and trials you are enduring. All this is evidence that God's judgment is right, and as a result you will be counted worthy of the kingdom of God, for which you are suffering.

This is the only time Paul uses the verb "to make worthy" (NRSV) or "to count as worthy." It is used in an eschatological sense. This is another way of expressing the more typical understanding of "first suffering, then glory." The suffering refines and perfects the character of God's people. It prepares them for glory. Endurance, then, has a goal in mind. We endure in view of the prize that is set before us. We endure suffering, as Jesus did, for the sake of the joy set before us (Hebrews 12:2).

But the suffering is not meaningless. It is purposeful. God uses it in order to "make us worthy" of his kingdom. Just as the suffering of Jesus was meaningful in the accomplishment of redemption, so our suffering is meaningful as it perfects us for the glory God will give in the *eschaton*.

Even more, our suffering is also redemptive. We seek to introduce the kingdom of God into the world through our lives and actions. This means that we act sacrificially for the sake of the world. We approach suffering within a redemptive framework. As Beker comments, "both suffering and hope must be embodied and concretized by the 'hopeful' suffering of the church at the hands of the powers of injustice," and "there can be no authentic hope in the church unless it is willing to suffer for its hope in its daily life."[5] If the "ground" of hope is the cross and resurrection of Christ by which Christians celebrate the inbreaking of God's kingdom, and if the "horizon" of hope is the promise of God's eschatological kingdom where all injustice and idolatry is destroyed, then the "object" of hope is "those strategies and possibilities that the church devises as inroads of the dawning kingdom of God in the midst of an idolatrous and suffering world."[6] The church, as God's redemptive instrument in the world, must be willing to suffer for the redemption of the world and thus share in the suffering of Christ so that they might also share in his glory.

Conclusion

The inaugurated eschatology of "already, but not yet" is important for biblical theology. In one sense it has always been present. Though the creation is cursed, God yet provides good gifts to his people. He is even gracious to the wicked through his good gifts. Though Israel suffered because of their sin, yet they had the promise of blessing in their land. When blessed, they anticipated the *eschaton* itself. Paul's theological structure is his eschatology. God has already defeated Satan, sin, and death, but he has not yet fully revealed this redemption.

At present the people of God do not expect to live without suffering because we understand that only in the *eschaton* is fallenness reversed. The cosmos has been subjected to futility, but God has subjected it in hope. God has a goal for his creation. He intends to redeem it. While God has already given evidence in Jesus Christ that he will redeem, that redemption is not yet fully realized. Consequently, the people of God wait for eschatological redemption.

Nevertheless, God has given his Spirit to his people as evidence that the redemption has already begun and that the *eschaton* has already been inaugurated. God's Spirit dwells among his people as a down payment of the consummation when God will dwell fully with his people as their God and they as his people. God's Spirit intercedes, witnesses to, and produces hope in God's people as they wait through their suffering. Because God has poured out his love into the hearts of his people, God's people endure with hope.

The people of God, then, are people who live in the Spirit. They breathe the Spirit of God and the Spirit of God gives them breath and life. This is an eschatological life that ushers us into the hope of God's redemption and the expectation that God's life is our life. The Spirit is God's presence among his people in a fallen world.

Because we groan "here" under the oppression of fallenness, we yearn for "there" where that fallenness is destroyed. We yearn for a day without tears, without pain, without mourning and without death. We yearn for the fullness of God's presence which will satisfy our deep longings for communion with him. We yearn for God's light which will dispel all darkness. Consequently, we pray, "Maranatha," or, "Come, O Lord!" (1 Corinthians 16:22).

---

[1]John D.W. Watts, *Isaiah 34–66*, Word Biblical Commentary (Waco: Word Books, 1987), pp. 337ff.

[2]Anthony A. Hoekema, *The Bible and the Future* (Grand Rapids: Eerdmans, 1979), pp. 280-281.

[3]Second Peter 3:12 may teach that the old earth will be totally dissolved, but the language of "melt" or "burned up" may simply be an apocalyptic (thus, metaphorical) description. For example, Isaiah 34:4 refers to the melting of the stars of heaven in the judgment of a nation and Micah 1:4 talks about mountains melting before God.

[4]Oscar Cullmann, *Prayer in the New Testament*, Overtures to Biblical Theology (Philadelphia: Fortress Press, 1995), pp. 72-80.

[5]J. Christiaan Beker, *Suffering and Hope: The Biblical Vision and the Human Predicament* (Grand Rapids: Eerdmans, 1994), p. 89.

[6]Ibid., pp. 88-89.

Chapter Eleven

What Do Sufferers Need to Remember?

Faithful Endurance in Our Own Stories

When Job's three friends, Eliphaz the Temanite, Bildad the Shuhite and Zophar the Naamathite, heard about all the troubles that had come upon him, they set out from their homes and met together by agreement to go and sympathize with him and comfort him. When they saw him from a distance, they could hardly recognize him; they began to weep aloud, and they tore their robes and sprinkled dust on their heads. Then they sat on the ground with him for seven days and seven nights. No one said a word to him, because they saw how great his suffering was.

Job 2:11-13

When Job's friends heard about his plight, they decided to visit Job. Their intention was benevolent. They came to "sympathize with him and comfort him" (2:11). The same Hebrew words (though translated differently) are used again in the epilogue where his friends and relatives "comforted and consoled him over all the trouble the LORD had brought upon him" (42:11).

Their genuine sympathy for Job is expressed in a traditional Near Eastern manner (2:11). They not only raised a great lament with loud cries, they also tore their clothes and threw dust on their heads. Job's reaction to his trouble was similar (1:20). They sat with Job on the trash heap for seven days in silence (2:13). Their friendship could not have been demonstrated more appropriately. Often it is better to be silent in the face of another's suffering than to attempt to soothe their pain with words. Now Job was no longer alone. His friends were with him. "Finally," Job might have thought to himself, "I have someone who will share my pain with me and provide a comforting presence." But Job, and the reader, soon discover that the friends are "miserable comforters" (16:2).

Community is important in suffering. The help of friends is immeasurable. But suffering can also destroy community. In the midst of suffering, humans tend to seek their own interest. We want to preserve our own theology in a way that evidences the basic selfishness of the fallen human spirit. Job rose above this basic inclination to selfishness when he maintained his integrity. But his friends did not. They counseled a false self-incrimination. They sought to preserve their theology by questioning Job's integrity. They cut Job loose from their community because God, in their view, had judged him. Job was without a community. We moderns are no different. Recently, a minister discovered he was HIV positive through a past blood transfusion. He disclosed this to his congregation and the congregation fired him. What was once a loving community turned on him when they believed that God had judged him for some secret sin. The theology of Job's friends is alive and well.

The dialogue in Job is as much about the destruction of community as it is about bad theology. The reader, who evaluates the dialogue from the standpoint of the narrative prologue, sees the tragedy of both. The friends model Satan's approach to suffering. Indeed, they are Satan's third attempt to destroy Job's faith. His friends are as much an attack on Job's integrity as were the Sabeans and his wife. His wife counsels Job to maintain his integrity and curse God's injustice. The friends counsel Job to deny his integrity and submit to their version of God's justice. Either way,

Satan wins the wager. Job's wife serves God only when he blesses. The friends serve God so that he will bless. In the end, both serve God for profit. But Job rejects both alternatives. Instead, he worships, laments, and trusts.

What Do You Say to a Sufferer?

In the face of tragedy, the community of God "talks with each other" about the fear of the Lord (Malachi 3:13-18). The Lord listens, remembers, and he will one day redeem his people as his own possession. One day redemption will overcome tragedy, and grief will give way to joy. But as the community waits for that day, how does it "talk with each other?" What does the community of faith say, for example, to those who have experienced the tragic death of a child?

First . . . Don't Say Anything

Sometimes silence is better than speaking, listening better than advice, and sympathy better than instruction. Job's three friends sat with him on the trash heap for seven days in silence (2:11-13). Job broke that silence with a heartbreaking lament where he cursed the day of his birth (3:1). Eliphaz, displeased with Job's lament, counseled him to confess his sin because trouble comes to the wicked (5:3-7). Indeed, the wicked suffer the kind of trouble that Job has experienced, and God has judged Job (4:5-8). Job's house had been cursed due to his sin (5:3), and Job must now submit to God's discipline (5:17). Job must humble himself, confess his sin, and seek God's mercy so that God might redeem him (5:11). Though God has wounded Job, God may yet heal him if Job repents (5:18). Only when Job humbles himself will God restore his wealth, children, and security (5:24-26). Eliphaz is confident about his advice. "So hear it," he says to Job, "and apply it to yourself" (5:27).

Job is discouraged by Eliphaz's words. Eliphaz had not eased Job's burden, but increased it. Job is struggling to persevere in faith, but Eliphaz accuses him of faithlessness. Job cries out to God for relief through death. Job wants his life to end without denying "the words of the Holy One" (6:9-10). Job is still faithful, but his pain tempts him to deny God. Eliphaz offers no sympathy. On the contrary, he assails Job's integrity and tells him to repent of his hidden sins. Job hoped for comfort from his friends — even "a despairing man should have the devotion of his friends" (6:14). Instead, his friends are like dried up streams (6:15-17) for which caravans hope, but are disappointed when they reach them (6:18-20). His friends are "no help" (6:21), and instead of easing his burdens they increase them.

Job is willing to listen (6:24-26). Job will be silent if his friends will say something useful. Eliphaz's descriptions of the plight of the wicked were insinuations that Job himself was one of them. Job is willing to listen to any accusations or charges that the friends know. But he wants proof. Job complains that his friends had not really listened to him. His words were honest (Hebrew, sweet). They were the words of a person in great distress and despair. But Eliphaz had treated them as if they were nothing but hot air ("wind"). Eliphaz listened to Job's lament in order to critique rather than suffer with him.

Eliphaz's callous response evokes Job's assessment of his heart (6:27). Eliphaz is the kind of person who would gamble over fatherless children or barter away a friendship. Eliphaz is the sort of person who turns every situation to his own advantage. Rather than help a friend, Eliphaz becomes defensive of his own traditions and beliefs. Eliphaz's rebuke is more concerned about his traditions and values than it is about Job's troubles and spiritual health.

Job gets to the point (6:28-30). The kindness he expects from Eliphaz and his other friends is trust. Job simply wants his friends to believe him. Job is not a liar. He wants to be treated justly and compassionately. What is really at stake in this dialogue is not the traditions of the friends, but the integrity of Job. God affirmed Job's integrity both before and after trouble enveloped him (1:1; 2:3). Job does not belong among the wicked. He is a righteous sufferer. He does not deceive nor does he speak evil. As the narrator commented after Job's second trial, "In all this, Job did not sin in what he said" (2:10; cf. 42:7).

How, then, do we approach sufferers? First, we should approach them in silence. We are often too quick to speak to sufferers. We are uncomfortable with silence, so we feel we must say something. "Do you see a man who speaks in haste? There is more hope for a fool than for him" (Proverbs 29:20). A lengthy silence is better than a hasty sentence.

But silence is awkward. Silence burdens us so that we feel like we are not helping. But comfort comes more in the form of presence than words. I do not remember everything everyone said at Sheila's funeral. However, I do remember who was there. Primary comfort for the griever does not come through the words of comforters, but through their presence. The comforter's presence at the funeral home is much more significant than anything that might be said. The fact that they sent a card is more significant than anything they wrote in the card. The first rule of comfort is: be there and be silent.

Second, we should approach them as listeners. We should give them permission to speak. We should sit with them in their lament, offer our sympathy and share their tears. Eliphaz was shocked by Job's words. He did not hear Job's anguish. He did not give Job permission to speak his heart and cry out to his God. We must be willing to sit with sufferers and give them permission to speak to God in deep lament with all the doubts, fears, and questions those laments contain. Too often we divert the conversation to mundane topics because we are uncomfortable listening to the griefs and pains of another. God listens to our laments, and we should listen to each other's.

It is not the comforter's task to lead a discussion but to be a silent listener. But as listeners we must be willing to listen, even when our pain is increased by what we hear. When the griever laments, do not rebuke or chastise. Listen silently, and listen in such a way that it gives the griever permission to speak. When the griever is ready to speak, we should be ready to listen. We must give the griever permission to be angry and to speak to God or about God with bitterness and impatience, just as righteous Job did. We need to give the griever permission to remember and cry. As uncomfortable as it makes us, it is an important aspect of healing for those who are hurting. We are God's instruments of comfort, and just as God listens, so should we.

Third, we should approach them in sympathy with expressions of love. The context of tragedy is no place for theological diatribes. It is not a place for interpreting what has happened. It is not a time for bombastic, simplistic, and pithy platitudes. "A fool finds no pleasure in understanding but delights in airing his own opinions" (Proverbs 18:2). We should suffer with our friends rather than attempting to restructure their theology or probe their life circumstances so we can offer them a correct understanding of their situation. We should weep with them rather than explain what has happened.

Job's friends made the mistake of correcting Job rather than sharing his suffering. They thought they could explain his suffering, but all Job wanted was someone to share it with him. Instead of helping him, his friends became "miserable comforters" (Job 16:2).

Nicholas Wolterstorff, lamenting the death of his son in a mountain-climbing accident, reflects on this point:

> What do you say to someone who is suffering? Some people are gifted with words of wisdom. For such, one is profoundly grateful. There were many such for us. But not all are gifted in that way. Some blurted out strange, inept things. That's OK too. Your words don't have to be wise. The heart that speaks is heard

more than the words spoken. And if you can't think of anything to say, just say, "I can't think of anything to say. But I want you to know that we are with you in your grief."

Or even, just embrace. Not even the best of words can take away the pain. What words can do is testify that there is more than pain in our journey on earth to a new day. Of those things that are more, the greatest is love. Express your love. How appallingly grim must be the death of a child in the absence of love.

But please: Don't say it's not really so bad. Because it is. Death is awful, demonic. If you think your task as comforter is to tell me that really, all things considered, it's not so bad, you do not sit with me in my grief but place yourself off in the distance away from me. Over there, you are of no help. What I need to hear from you is that you recognize how painful it is. I need to hear from you that you are with me in my desperation. To comfort me, you have to come close. Come sit beside me on my mourning bench.[1]

Don't Say . . .

When in the presence of grieving parents, the loss of words is stunning. We do not know what to say, how to say it, or whether to say anything. Indeed, it is often better to say nothing. But there are some things we should never say during the trauma of grief.

"This was the will of God." In the context of grief, this statement is no comfort. Rather, it becomes an accusation against God. It generates anger, doubt, and bitterness. It may be a statement the sufferer can make, but it is not something a comforter should say. It may be that sufferers can have such confidence in God's work in the world that they are able themselves to say this in a way that offers comfort, but when it is offered by a would-be comforter it is counterproductive. It invokes an image that associates God with the horror of a child's death. Should we believe that God could want something so horrible? What do you mean

it "was the will of God"? Did God want my child to die? These are questions which the sufferer may ask. But they are questions which the comforter should not raise or answer because in the midst of suffering there is no reasonable answer. Wolterstorff struggled through similar thoughts:

> Seeing God as the agent of death is one way of fitting together into a rational pattern God, ourselves, and death. There are other ways. One of these has been explored in a book by Rabbi Kushner: God too is pained by death, more even than you and I are; but there's nothing much he can do about it.
>
> I cannot fit it all together by saying, "He did it," but neither can I do so by saying, "There was nothing he could do about it." I cannot fit it together at all. I can only, with Job, endure. I do not know why God did not prevent Eric's death. To live without the answer is precarious. It's hard to keep one's footing.
>
> . . . I cannot fit these pieces together. I am at a loss. I have read the theodicies produced to justify the ways of God to man. I find them unconvincing. To the most agonized question I have ever asked I do not know the answer. I do not know why God would watch him fall. I do not know why God would watch me wounded. I cannot even guess.[2]

The sufferer will probably never fit the pieces together. This is part of the struggle of suffering itself. It is what opens up our hearts to discover whether we serve God for profit or whether we serve him out of love. But it is the struggle that each sufferer must endure, and the sufferer is not helped to be told by a would-be comforter that the death of a child was the will of God. Perhaps there will be opportunity to discuss those dimensions of suffering when faith has had time to settle the heart, but in the initial stages of grief these words offer turmoil, not peace.

"God plucked a rose out of his garden." This is a wonderful metaphor because it pictures God as a concerned gardener. It offers us a serene picture of death — God picking roses out of his garden for his use and display. God has taken

them home to enjoy his presence. But in the midst of grief this is a horrible picture of God. The griever does not see this sentimentalism, but rebels against the notion that God stole a rose. God has many roses, why did he pick mine? God may have plucked this rose, but it was my rose! The griever sees this image more along the lines of a thief than a loving gardener. The griever is not ready to hear this in the midst of grief, and the comforter offers no comfort with such a statement. Rather, it antagonizes the pain of grief and incites further bitterness toward God.

"Some good will come out of this." What good would justify the death of a child? Would not anyone gladly exchange that good for the life of their child? In the midst of suffering, there is no good that is worth the pain of the moment, especially when it is your child that is dead. To raise the hope or the potential that something good can arise out of a child's death is to ask the sufferer to compare the imagined good with the life of their child. In the midst of grief, there is no contest. There is no good that God could achieve that is worth the life of a child. The darkness of suffering does not permit the acknowledgment of a greater good, and even if there is a greater good, the one sitting in darkness cannot see it. That good arises out of suffering may not be questioned — look at the good God accomplished through the death of his own Son — but whether any particular good is worth any particular suffering is always doubted, especially in the initial moments of that suffering. Again, listen to Wolterstorff's pain:

> Have you changed, someone asked. He did not mean whether the world looks different to me now. He meant whether my character has changed. Have I changed?
>
> . . . I have changed, yes. For the better, I do not doubt. But without a moment's hesitation I would exchange those changes for Eric back.[3]

What is the greater good? Is it simply to change my character for the better? Is that worth the death of my son?

In the heart of a sufferer, there is nothing so absolutely good as the life of the child, and so there is no good that could be achieved through the child's death that is worth that price. What good would I exchange for the life of my son? What would I not give back to God for the life of my son? What "good" is worth that price? Perhaps later on, perhaps when the good is perceived as communion with God, the sufferer may see the greater good, but during grief these words reveal to the sufferer that the comforter does not understand the depths or darkness of suffering.

"It was for the best." How can the death of my son be "for the best"? While this is usually said about those who have suffered intensely or died in their elderly years, it is still an extremely interpretative statement. It may be true, but the comforter is not an interpreter. The comforter should not offer an explanation. Rather, the comforter is there to share the pain and the grief, to rebel against death and complain about its presence in the world. Only God can judge the relative "better" or "best" of a death; only he can judge the relative "good" of a death. Interpretation is best left up to him, and secondarily to the sufferer, but never for the comforter.

"You need to take a hard look at your life. God is telling you something." These words force sufferers to look into their own hearts for the rationale of their suffering. They may even imply that God is punishing the sufferer, or at least that some character flaw in the sufferer is the reason God permitted a child's death. The parent, then, feels responsible and interprets the statement as an accusation. Is there something so wrong with me that God would take my child? Am I to blame for my child's illness? Did God strike my son just to change me, just to make me better? Wolterstorff also struggled with this thought:

> In the valley of suffering, despair and bitterness are brewed. But there also character is made. The valley of suffering is the vale of soul-making.
>
> But now things slip and slide around. How do I tell

my blessings? For what do I give thanks and for what
do I lament? Am I sometimes to sorrow over my
delight and sometimes to delight over my sorrow? And
how do I sustain my "No" to my son's early death
while accepting with gratitude the opportunity offered
of becoming what otherwise I could never be?

How do I receive my suffering as blessing while
repulsing the obscene thought that God jiggled the
mountain to make *me* better?[4]

Is the death of a child really worth the soul-making
value it might produce? In grief, parents do not exalt the
value of their own character development above the life of
their child. It is an incredulous thought that God should
strike a child for the sake of the parent. Perhaps, however,
given time, when character development is seen as a means
to communion with God, then the sufferer will see what
God has taught and value suffering itself.

There is a sense in which each of these statements is
true. It is legitimate to believe that God willed this death in
the sense that he could have prevented it if he had chosen
to do so. It is also legitimate to believe that God will bring
good out of tragedy. It is also legitimate to use every
tragedy as an occasion for introspection and to seek the
meaning of that tragedy through prayer and reflection. God
uses every event in our life to teach us something and to
further his eschatological intent for us. But while there is
some truth in each of these statements, the grieving parent
cannot hear it in the initial moments, even months, perhaps
years, of their grief. These truths have an ugly ring in the
ears of grieving parents. Consequently, they should not be
offered by would-be comforters, even if they are well-inten-
tioned. They sound like superficial platitudes in the midst
of suffering.

These kinds of statements are unhelpful because they
seek to interpret the meaning of a child's death. If it is
God's will, what did he intend to do through this child's
death? What did God want to accomplish? What good

could possibly come from the death of children? Is God punishing me? Is God testing me? What does God want me to learn, and is that lesson worth the death of my child? These are all interpretative questions. They seek the meaning of a child's death. But this quest for meaning cannot be sustained in the midst of grief. Grieving parents need to lament, question, accuse, even doubt. It is not the time for interpretation and introspection. Later, as the initial shock dissipates, the sufferer will reflect on its meaning and purpose. Sufferers will do their own interpreting, and they may ask for help. Only then does the comforter have permission to interpret with them. But ultimately interpretation belongs only to sufferers. And, certainly, the funeral home or the initial months, is not a time for an outsider to offer an interpretation of the tragedy (much like Job's friends did). Interpretation is best left to sufferers, and then it only comes with hindsight.

Remind Them . . . Five Theological Anchors[5]

The role of the comforter is not to interpret, but to remind. The comforter is present as the instrument of God's presence among those who weep. The comforter is not there to explain, theologize about the meaning of suffering or to render a judgment about why a child died. Job's friends made that mistake. The comforter is there, well, just to be there. The comforter sits beside the sufferer and shares the suffering. The comforter is there to sit on the mourning bench with the mourner, to share the lament, the protest, and the questions. Comforters know how to share suffering, to weep with those who weep and to sit silently with the weeping sufferer.

However, when the sufferer speaks and seeks personal engagement with another, the comforter first listens and then speaks. But what do comforters say? Comforters can reinforce the loving relationship that exists between the two; they can express love, as Wolterstorff wrote. Comforters can speak words of sympathy and pain. They might say, "I am so sorry to hear about your loss." Or, "I can't imagine how painful this must be for you; I am so sorry." Or, "I am praying for you and I want you to know that I love you." Or, "I just wanted you to know that I am thinking of you."

But comforters can also remind the sufferer of things that are a bit blurry in the midst of grief. They can remind the sufferer about what is easily forgotten because suffering is so painful. I believe those reminders must be focused on who God is, how God feels about tragedy and what God will one day do about it. I believe we need to remind sufferers that God is sitting on the mourning bench with them.

I am sometimes asked, "What helps you endure your trials? What gets you through the tough times?" The full answer to those questions involves the theological story which I have tried to tell in this book. But I think the story boils down to five simple but profound theological anchors. These five principles summarize the story and anchor faith. When the waves of doubt and despair assail, I often reflect on these five points. They provide a foundation and, through the Spirit of God, they empower whatever endurance I might have.

Consequently, these are the words I speak to myself and the words that I would, under appropriate circumstances, speak to others. They are the anchors I want to cultivate in the life of a church. These principles do not offer an interpretation of God's work in my life, but they remind me of who God is and what he has done. They are reminders of God's story. Sufferers need to first remember, and then they may interpret (though only cautiously and tentatively). Comforters must remind, but resist interpretation. While comforters need to leave the interpretation to the sufferers, these principles provide a framework for interpretation. They are the lens through which we read our own stories. They are the context in which we should interpret

God's work in our lives. But interpretation is a task for the sufferer, not the comforter.

Consequently, these five principles not only summarize the story of God, but they are also the essence of what I think sufferers need to remember, what comforters need to offer, and what teachers need to provide their communities in preparation for suffering.

The Unrelenting Love of God

Creation was God's first act of unrelenting love. God created out of his overflowing love to include others in his loving communion. He created so he could share what he already possessed. The Father, Son, and Spirit in their eternal nature communed with each other, and they intended to share it with others through creating a people in their image. God initiated creation for the sake of others so that they too might experience the wonder of blissful communion. The love of God is so great that he is willing to risk the bliss of his own communion so that others might participate in it.

When humanity rebelled and fell into its sinful habits, God's unrelenting love took the initiative to redeem. The biblical idea of election is focused in the thought that God took the initiative in redemption. Election means that God acted first. He decided that he would redeem the world through Christ even before its foundation. God elected us in Christ (Ephesians 1:3-5). God made the first move. Our sin did not discourage his love, but his redemptive acts flow from that love.

Even though we wounded God's love, it could not be quenched. Even when Israel refused to know him, God would not give up on his people. Even when Israel was an unfaithful wife and had sold herself into prostitution, God pursued her as a husband who yearns for reconciliation with his loved one (Hosea 1–3). Even when Israel committed adultery with Baal, God's heart cried, "How can I give you up, Ephraim? How can I hand you over, Israel? . . . My heart is changed within me; all my compassion is aroused" (Hosea 11:8). God's love pursued Israel from the time he led them out of Egypt till the time he ransomed them from their exile. God's love meant that he would not give up on his people.

The climactic demonstration of this love is God's work in Jesus Christ. "While we were still sinners," Paul wrote, "Christ died for us" (Romans 5:8). This is how we know that God is love, John wrote, because he "sent his Son as an atoning sacrifice for our sins" (1 John 4:10). The unrelenting love of God is expressed in the lengths to which God went to accomplish his goal of fellowship with us. God joined the human race, shared its weaknesses and its burdens, experienced its shame, and died on a cross. God sacrificed himself in Jesus Christ for the sake of others, and his love knew no limits. There was no cost that God would not pay for fellowship with his people, and he demonstrated this at the cross. God sacrificed all for the sake of his people. "He who did not spare his own Son, but gave him up for us all," Paul wrote, "how will he not also, along with him, graciously give us all things?" (Romans 8:32).

God intends to have a people for himself with whom he can share his love. This is why he created, and it is why he redeems. This is why he unrelentingly pursues humanity, and this is why he became one of us and went to the cross. God has demonstrated his love.

When we look at the fallen world with all its pain and death, we can easily doubt that love. Where is God when evil surrounds us? Where is the love of God when my child dies? When we look within our fallen selves, we can easily doubt that God could ever love people like us with all our faults. How can God love me when my own parents abuse me? How can God love me when even my own husband divorced me? How can God love me when I am so full of sin? The fallen world is filled with reasons for doubting God's love. But that is why God gave us his story.

The plot of the biblical story is the unceasing pursuit of God's love for a people who will return his love and share his communion. God is not looking for excuses to punish, nor is he looking for opportunities to show off his wrath. God yearns for his people, pursues them with compassion and humbles himself in costly self-sacrifice for the sake of his people. God is not seeking an excuse to punish, but an opportunity to share. God is not seeking a pretext for his wrath, but an occasion for fellowship.

When the doubts creep in and the fears debilitate, I remember the cross of Jesus Christ. I can stand beside the coffin of my wife and doubt God's love, but I cannot kneel at the foot of the cross and doubt it. God has offered me an indubitable testimony of his love. Despite all the contrary witnesses that fill a fallen world, God entered history and demonstrated his love for us in the incarnation, ministry, death, and resurrection of Jesus Christ.

The Inviting Presence of God

When fallenness invades our life, when pain, disease or death strike our loved ones, our hearts cry out in protest. We sense that something is terribly wrong with the world. We sense that this is not the way things are supposed to be. Indeed, it is not the way God created the world. God created peace, life, harmony, and joy in the Garden, but sin has decimated that world. It has broken the original harmony. Death has entered God's good creation. Our protests, then, are yearnings for the original harmony. They are a natural response to the fallenness we now experience. We protest against death and we refuse to accept its appropriateness in God's creation.

The laments of Scripture are filled with those kinds of protests. The people of God cry out to their God under the burden of fallenness. The Psalms provide example after example of faithful lament. The people of God confront their God in anger, bitterness, doubt, confusion, and bewilderment. They ask God, "Why?" and "How long?" They ask God, "Where are you?" and "Why have you hidden yourself from your people?" They ask God, "When will you bring justice to the earth?" They complain, question, and weep. The story of God is filled with the protests of his people because his people have nowhere else to turn.

Yet those laments are in Scripture precisely because God invites us to lament. He invites us into his presence to speak our hearts to him. God seeks communion — real communion. He does not want ritual repetitions or high-sounding platitudes. He wants to hear the hearts of his people. He wants his people to share their hearts with him. God wants to engage them in genuine communion. But there is no authentic communion when God's people are not honest with their God. Can we deceive God by "putting on a good face" in prayer while our heart is breaking? God does not seek such superficiality. Rather, he yearns to hear the cries of his people so he can respond to their hurts and share their burden.

God invites us to speak our protests and to voice our laments. God is not offended by such protestations. He is patient. He understands lament because he himself has experienced it. God lamented the sinfulness and destruction of Israel through the weeping prophet Jeremiah (Jeremiah 8:21–9:2). Jesus lamented the stubbornness of Israel as he wept over Jerusalem (Matthew 23:37). Indeed, Jesus voiced his lament on the cross in the words of the psalmist, "My God, My God, why have you forsaken me?" (Psalm 22:1; Matthew 26:46). God himself in Jesus Christ has lamented. God understands the pain and alienation that gives rise to lament, and he understands how faith must complain because the world does not look like faith expects.

God is a loving father who listens to his children. He does not listen to scold, but to heal. He does not respond in anger to these protests. Rather, he responds in love. These protests do not repulse God. On the contrary, they evoke

God's loving presence. Like a parent who comforts a hurting child, so God wraps his arms around the protesting believer. God absorbs the pain of these protests and his love overwhelms them. God's presence invades our laments to comfort and reassure us of his love. This is why the laments in Psalms end in praise. The people of God sense God's presence, his comfort, and his faithfulness. God listens and he responds. God offers his "sanctuary" presence to lamenters.

When fallenness cripples my life, I go to God in protest. My faith laments the brokenness of the world and cries out for God's deliverance. It yearns for the inbreaking of God's full reign in the world. As I watch my son slowly deteriorate and I foresee his eventual death, I protest and I pray for the fullness of God's kingdom now. I yearn for the day when death will no longer have dominion over my son. My laments protest death. They protest fallenness. And God hears my prayer and shares his comforting presence with me as I wait for the fullness of God's victory.

The Caring Empathy of God

We have all sympathized with others who have experienced the world's fallenness. We have all sat in funeral homes with friends or written the occasional sympathy card. We sympathize with people when we hurt because they hurt and we weep because they weep. God himself feels this sympathy. Our God is the weeping God who grieves over sin, pain, and death. God is no stoic statue who is impervious to our hurts. God does not sit enthroned in an undisturbed joyful bliss. On the contrary, God weeps over our fallenness. He grieves over his corrupted creation. He grieves over the loss of fellowship with his people.

But God is more than sympathetic. He is also empathetic. God does not stand off at a distance and merely pity his fallen creation. He does more. He comes near and enters into our experience, and actually shares the fallenness of the world with us. God not only weeps over my hurt, but he shares the experience of my hurt with me. God not only weeps over the eventual death of my son, he himself has experienced the death of his own Son. God not only weeps over the rebellion of a runaway child, but God himself knows the pain that rebellious children create in the hearts of their parents. God himself has experienced the pain and hurt of the fallen world. He understands. He not only sympathizes, he also empathizes.

The climactic empathetic event is the incarnation of God in Jesus Christ. In Jesus, God experienced fallenness. He experienced pain, fatigue, thirst, hunger, grief, and death. In Jesus, God wept at the tomb of a friend (John 11:35). In Jesus, God experienced the humiliating shame of the cross. In Jesus, the rich God became poor (2 Corinthians 8:9). In Jesus, God shared our weaknesses with us, experienced our temptations and trials, and endured our shame. God came near in Jesus to sit on the mourner's bench with us. He understands the pain. He has experienced it in the flesh. God experienced my humanity and my pain in Jesus Christ.

God, then, is no mere distant relative who only hears about our hurts and sends a sympathy card. God does not stand off in a corner to watch us grieve or to pity us at a distance. On the contrary, God joined us in our humanity to share our grief, to experience our fallenness, and to empathize with our pain. In Jesus, God himself shares our laments over fallenness. God truly understands because he truly became one of us in Jesus Christ. Consequently, Jesus is able "to help those who are being tempted" because "he himself suffered when he was tempted" (Hebrews 2:18).

Our hurts, pains, cries, and cares, then, are his. He knows them. He has felt them. He has prayed them. God sits with us in the funeral home because he himself has experienced the fallenness of death. He can grieve with us while sitting beside us as God himself expresses his own grief over the fallenness of the world. God empathizes with his fallen creation and understands its hurt.

When fallenness surrounds me and I again feel its pain, I remember that God himself has also experienced that same fallenness. He knows. He understands. He has been there, and so he is now here for me. He sits with me, weeps with me, and yearns for the *eschaton* just as I do.

The Unlimited Sovereignty of God

Fallenness often makes us wonder whether God really is in control of his world. Perhaps God does care, but he cannot do anything about it. Perhaps God loves us, but he cannot help. The biblical story, however, does not picture God this way. Even when it appears that Satan and his cohorts have the upper hand, as when the Roman empire persecuted God's saints, God still sits on his throne (Revelation 4). God is still in control. Indeed, God controls the extent and length of the persecution (Revelation 6:9-10). Satan cannot dethrone God. Fallenness does not undermine God's sovereignty. God still sits on his throne. God remains in control even when my circumstances are difficult.

Because God loves, because God listens, and because God empathizes, we trust that God has the best interests of his people in mind. God has a purpose for the trials and troubles his people experience. God cares and God is sovereign. Nothing on God's part, then, is malicious and nothing is arbitrary. God is praised for his "love and faithfulness" and also for his sovereignty, "Our God is in heaven; he does whatever pleases him" (Psalm 115:1,3). God intends to bless his people out of his love and to secure those blessings by his sovereignty. God has a goal for his people and everything that happens in the world serves that goal.

But that goal is not necessarily our earthly happiness, but our heavenly fellowship with him. God is more interested in our faith than our pleasure. God's goal is to establish and enjoy an eternal communion with us. God is more interested in our holy communion with him than whether we are healthy or wealthy. Whether or not God permits or causes any particular event in the world, it is enough to say that God is sovereign over all events, and that nothing happens without his permission. If nothing happens without his permission, then everything that happens serves his goal or else he would not have permitted it. God has a reason for his permission and his actions. That reason is his original intent in creation. He wants a people who share his triune fellowship. God, then, permits or causes whatever happens for the sake of this original intent.

This is climactically demonstrated in Jesus Christ. God willed the death of Jesus in order to redeem a people. God was sovereign over all the events of Jesus' ministry, life, and death. It was by "God's set purpose and foreknowledge" that Jesus was handed over to death (Acts 2:23). At any moment the plan could have changed because God was sovereign over the plan. Jesus could have called for "twelve legions of angels," but instead he submitted to the will of the Father (Matthew 26:53). In his sovereignty, God executed a plan for the redemption of a fallen world through Jesus Christ. Yet this plan involved the suffering and death of the just one, God's own Son. Nevertheless, because God's goal is communion with his people, God willed the death of his Son out of his great love for us. God sacrificed his own joy so that others might join his fellowship.

God seeks a people who seek him. God yearns for a people who love him. God desires a reciprocal relationship of mutual love. God permits or acts in the world in order to maximize the potential of that relationship. He tests, disciplines, redeems, and even punishes to secure the ends of his original intention. God permits and acts to accomplish his original goal. God uses the circumstances of a fallen world to serve his ultimate purpose.

God, therefore, is at work in everything for the good of his people (Romans 8:28). The "good" that God has in mind is not defined by human aspirations of happiness, success, and pleasure. Rather, the "good" that God intends is a conformity to the image of his Son both here and in the *eschaton*.

God intends a holy communion between himself and his people. If discipline, testing, suffering or prosperity is necessary toward that end, then that is what God will permit or do.

As a result, I am confident that whatever circumstance befalls me, God has a purpose. God is at work to promote and seek the fulfillment of his original intent for me. God uses every fallen situation for my eschatological good. God perfects me through suffering, just as he perfected his own Son through suffering (Hebrews 5:7-10). My confidence, then, is that my experience is not the random result of lucky or unlucky coincidences, but it is the work of God in my life to shape me into the image of his Son. God will use everything in my life toward the goal of building my character, shaping my faith, and ushering me into communion with him. And the biblical story tells me that God is so sovereign and so loving that nothing happens in my life that does not serve that end.

That kind of sovereignty does not frighten me. On the contrary, it comforts me. If God were a malicious tyrant, I would be terrified. But God has demonstrated his love, care, and empathy. I have reason to trust him. God's sovereignty, then, emboldens my faith, grounds my contentment, and enables me to submit to God's purposes in the fallen circumstances of my life. God's sovereignty plus his care means that I trust that whatever happens in my life serves the eschatological good that God intends for me. I may not understand, but I do trust.

The Ultimate Victory of God

Death is the epitome of fallenness. It covers the whole human race. Everyone, including children, is subject to death's dominion. This is the reverse of what God intended. God did not create so that his people would die. The opposite is true. God created for life, communion, and fellowship. Death is an alien invader. Sin created death, and as far as sin reigns, death reigns.

However, God will not let death win. Death will not claim the final victory. Rather, God's intent for his creation will find fruition in an eschatological reality, in a new heaven and a new earth. There God will plant the tree of life by the water of life and there will be no more curse (Revelation 22:1-5). There we will see the face of God and experience the fullness of his presence. There God will fulfill his original intent in creation and dwell among his people. In that place there will be no more pain, death or mourning because God will wipe away every tear (Revelation 21:1-4). Everything fallen will be renewed; everything old will become new. God will dwell among his people eternally.

But in the present circumstance, where death has dominion, it is difficult to believe that God will ultimately bring about that eschatological reality. When we stand by the coffin of our loved one, it is difficult to envision or even trust in that new heaven and new earth. Death so dominates us that faith is difficult. Death looks like a closed door that no one can open. Death conquers hope.

For this reason God entered history in Jesus Christ to demonstrate his future victory over death. God demonstrated his power over death in the resurrection of Jesus (1 Corinthians 15:12-18). Indeed, the resurrection of Jesus is an eschatological act itself. It is an event that comes from the future. Jesus is the firstfruit of an eschatological harvest. Jesus is the first resurrection of a resurrection harvest (1 Corinthians 15:21-28). God has given us a taste of the future in the resurrection of Jesus. God has shown us what the future is like. He has shown us what the end of history is. Resurrected life is the end of history. Resurrection conquers death. The only real question about the end of history is whether God will find a people who wait for him in faith (Luke 18:8). God has testified about his future work — he will raise the dead. But what is our testimony to God — will we wait in faith?

Death does not conquer hope in the eyes of faith. In the resurrection of Jesus God has given us eyes to see the destruction of death. We still grieve, but we do not grieve without hope (1 Thessalonians 4:13-18). We still experience loss, but we know that we will regain what was lost. We still lament, but we trust in God's sovereignty over death.

I do not, of course, relish the moment of my son's death. My lament continues, and I expect my grief will intensify as that moment grows closer. In fact, I yearn for the quick return of the Lord. I want him to come now. I do not want to watch my son wither away and die. I want that resurrection life for him now, and I want it for all sufferers. I want to hear Joshua say, "I love you," again. I want to see him run and play. I want, well, what I want is death destroyed. I want the eschatological reality now! So, I pray, "Your kingdom come!" So, I pray, "Maranatha." So I pray, and so I trust, and so I wait.

While this reminder is important and it offers the substance of hope for the believer, it does not dispel the grief of a parent. We still grieve because we have truly lost something. We may grieve with hope, but we still grieve. What we want is no longer here. Our dreams have been destroyed. We will not see our children's children (cf. Psalm 128:6). As Wolterstorff notes, the resurrection grounds an eschatological hope, but it does not necessarily lessen the pain of the moment.

> Elements of the gospel which I had always thought would console did not. They did something else, something important, but not that. It did not console me to be reminded of the hope of the resurrection. If I had forgotten that hope, then it would indeed have brought light into my life to be reminded of it. But I did not think of death as a bottomless pit. I did not grieve as one who has no hope. Yet Eric is gone, *here* and *now* he is gone; *now* I cannot talk with him, *now* I cannot see him, *now* I cannot hug him, *now* I cannot hear of his plans for the future. *That* is my sorrow. A friend said, "Remember, he's in good hands." I was deeply moved. But that reality does not put Eric back in my hands

now. That's my grief. For that grief, what consolation can there be other than having him back?[6]

The resurrection means we grieve in a different manner than those who grieve without hope, but it does not dissipate the grief because what was lost in the present is still lost. The loss is not regained until the *eschaton*. But the hope of restoration comforts believers.[7]

God has given us hope in Jesus Christ, and through faith we patiently wait for his eternal kingdom (Romans 8:18-23).

Conclusion

These principles are theocentric — focused on what God has done. But they are also christocentric — demonstrated in Jesus Christ. This is God's story. It is what God has done. It is how God has loved, how he has cared, and what he has willed to do. It is God's story in Jesus Christ. The story of Jesus is the climax of the biblical story. It is the story of God's love, care, empathy, sovereignty, and victory for us. The story of Jesus is the story of God.

God loves us, and he has demonstrated this at the cross. God listens to us, and he responds with his comforting presence. God understands us, and he himself experienced fallenness through suffering in Jesus Christ. God orchestrates the world for us, and he sovereignly rules it so that it serves his ultimate goal. God will destroy death and fallenness, and he has demonstrated this in the resurrection of Jesus Christ.

These reminders are revealed in Jesus Christ. This is the message of the gospel. It is good news. God has given us an indubitable testimony of himself in Jesus Christ. Whatever doubts, fears, confusions, and questions may surround us, the incarnation, ministry, cross, and resurrection of Jesus testify to God's redemption. In Jesus Christ God has shown us who he is and what he will do. That testimony assails all doubts and comforts all questions.

God loves. God listens. God understands. God rules. God wins. This is the ground and substance of faith. It enables us to endure suffering and it empowers faith. It is the substance of God's story among his people, and God's story gives faith its confidence.

---

[1]Wolterstorff, *Lament*, p. 34.

[2]Ibid., p. 66-67.

[3]Ibid., pp. 72-73.

[4]Ibid., p. 97.

[5]I would also recommend Jeffry R. Zurheide, *When Faith Is Tested: Pastoral Responses to Suffering and Death* (Minneapolis: Fortress Press, 1997).

[6]Wolterstorff, *Lament*, p. 31.

[7]See Gary R. Habermas, *Forever Loved: A Personal Account of Grief and Resurrection* (Joplin, MO: College Press, 1997), pp. 119-121.

Bibliography

Alden, Robert R. *Job.* New American Commentary. Nashville: Broadman Press, 1993.

Allen, Diogenes. *Christian Belief in a Postmodern World.* Louisville, KY: Westminster/John Knox Press, 1989.

Alter, Robert. *The Art of Biblical Poetry.* New York: Basic Books, 1985.

Anderson, B.W. *Creation Versus Chaos: The Reinterpretation of Mythical Symbolism in the Bible.* 1967. Reprint, Philadelphia: Fortress, 1987.

Anderson, Francis I. *Job: An Introduction and Commentary.* Tydale Old Testament Commentaries. Downers Grove, IL: InterVarsity, 1976.

Barth, Karl. *Church Dogmatics,* 2(1). Ed. by G.W. Bromiley and T.F. Torrance. Edinburgh: T. & T. Clark, 1957.

Beker, J. Christiaan. *Suffering and Hope: The Biblical Vision and the Human Predicament.* Grand Rapids: Eerdmans, 1994.

Bellinger, W.H., Jr. *Psalms: Reading and Studying the Book of Praises.* Peabody, MA: Hendrickson Publishers, 1990.

Berkouwer, G.C. *Sin.* Studies in Dogmatics. Trans. by Philip C. Holtrop. Grand Rapids: Eerdmans, 1971.

Bloesch, Donald. *God the Almighty: Power, Wisdom, Holiness, Love.* Christian Foundations, 3. Downers Grove, IL: InterVarsity, 1995.

Brueggemann, Walter. *Finally Comes the Poiet: Daring Speech for Proclamation.* Minneapolis: Fortress Press, 1989.

_____ . *The Message of the Psalms: A Theological Commentary.* Minneapolis: Augsburg, 1984.

Carson, D.A. *How Long, O Lord? Reflections on Suffering and Evil.* Grand Rapids: Baker, 1990.

Clines, David J.A. *Job 1–20.* Word Biblical Commentary. Dallas: Word Books, 1989.

Coleman, Richard J. *Issues of Theological Conflict: Evangelicals and Liberals.* Grand Rapics: Eerdmans, 1972.

Cook, Judith A. and Dale W. Wimberley. "If I Should Die Before I Wake: Religious Commitment and Adjustment to the Death of a Child." *Journal for the Scientific Study of Religion* 22 (September 1983): 222-228.

Cottrell, Jack. *Gender Roles and the Bible: Creation, the Fall, & Redemption.* Joplin, MO: College Press, 1994.

_____ . *What the Bible Says about God the Creator.* Joplin, MO: College Press, 1983.

_____ . *What the Bible Says about God the Redeemer.* Joplin, MO: College Press, 1987.

_____ . *What the Bible Says about God the Ruler.* Joplin, MO: College Press, 1984.

Craig, William Lane. *Reasonable Faith: Christian Truth and Apologetics.* Wheaton: Crossway Books, 1994.

Cranfield, C.E.B. *A Critical and Exegetical Commentary on the Epistle to the Romans.* ICC, 2 vols. Edinburgh: T. & T. Clark, 1975.

Crenshaw, James L. "Wisdom." In *Old Testament Form Criticism.* Ed. by John H. Hayes. San Antonio: Trinity University Press, 1974.

Cullman, Oscar. *Prayer in the New Testament.* Overtures to Biblical Theology. Philadelphia: Fortress Press, 1995.

Davis, John Jefferson. "Theological Reflections on Chaos Theory." *Perspectives on Science and Christian Faith* 49 (June 1997): 75-84.

Day, Peggy L. *An Adversary in Heaven: Satan in the Hebrew Bible.* Atlanta: Scholars Press, 1988.

Deroche, M.P. "The *ruah elohim* in Gen 1:2c: Creation or Chaos." In *Ascribe to the Lord: Biblical & Other Studies in Memory of Peter C. Craigie.* JSOTSup, 67. Sheffield: JSOT Press, 1988: 318.

Dick, Michael Brennan. "Job 31, the Oath of Innocence, and the Sage." *Zeitschrift für Altestamentliche Wissenschaft* 95 (1983): 31-53.

_____ . "The Legal Metaphor in Job 31." *Catholic Biblical Quarterly* 41 (1979): 37-50.

Dobbelaere. "Secularization: A Multi-dimentional Concept." *Current Sociology* 29 (Summer 1981): 1-213.

Dockery, David S., ed. *The Challenge of Postmodernism: An Evangelical Engagement.* Wheaton, IL: Victor Books, 1995.

Dostoevsky, Fyodor. *The Brothers Karamazov.* Trans. by Alexandra Kropotkin. Garden City, NY: Literary Guild of America, Inc., 1949.

Duffy, Joan I. "Legislature Keeps 'Acts of God' in Bill." *Commercial Appeal* (March 21, 1997).

Duke, David N. "Giving Voice to Suffering in Worship: A Study in the Theodicies of Hymnody." *Encounter* 52 (1991): 263-272.

Farrer, Austin. *Love Almighty and Ills Unlimited.* Garden City, NY: Doubleday, 1961.

Feinberg, Paul. *Deceived by God?* Wheaton, IL: Victor Books, 1997.

Fløsvik, Ingvar. *When God Becomes My Enemy: The Theology of the Complaint Psalms.* Saint Louis: Concordia Academic Press, 1997.

Foh, Susan T. "What Is the Woman's Desire?" *Westminster Theological Journal* 37 (1974/75): 376-383.

Fretheim, Terence E. *The Suffering of God: An Old Testament Perspective.* Philadelphia: Fortress Press, 1984.

Geivett, Douglas R. *Evil and the Evidence for God: The Challenge of John Hick's Theodicy.* Philapdelphia: Temple University Press, 1993.

Gibson, J.C.L. "On Evil in the Book of Job." In *Ascribe to the Lord: Biblical & Other Studies in Memory of Peter C. Craigie.* JSOTSup 67. Sheffield: JSOT Press, 1988.

Gleick, J. *Chaos: Making a New Science.* New York: Penguin, 1987.

Green, William B., Jr. "The Ethics of the Old Testament." In *Classical Evangelical Essays in Old Testament Interpretation.* Ed. by Walter C. Kaiser, Jr. Grand Rapids: Baker, 1972.

Grenz, Stanley. *Theology for the Community of God.* Nashville: Broadman & Holman, 1994.

Gutiérrez, Gustavo. *On Job: God-Talk and the Suffering of the Innocent.* Trans. by Matthew J. O'Connell. Maryknoll, NY: Orbis Books, 1987.

Habel, Norman. *The Book of Job: A Commentary.* Old Testament Library. Philadelphia: Westminster Press, 1985.

Habermas, Gary R. *Forever Loved: A Personal Account of Grief and Resurrection.* Joplin, MO: College Press, 1997.

Hamilton, Victor P. *The Book of Genesis, Chapter 1–17.* The New International Commentary on the Old Testament. Grand Rapids: Eerdmans, 1990.

Harris, J.G. "The Laments of Habakkuk's Prophecy." *Evangelical Quarterly* 45.1 (1973).

Hartley, John E. *The Book of Job.* The New International Commentary of the Old Testament. Grand Rapids: Eerdmans, 1988.

Hasker, William. *God, Time and Knowledge.* Ithaca, NY: Cornell University Press, 1989.

Hauerwas, Stanley. *God, Medicine, and Suffering.* Grand Rapids: Eerdmans, 1990.

Helm, Paul. *The Providence of God.* Contours of Christian Theology. Downers Grove, IL: InterVarsity, 1994.

Hick, John. *Evil and the God of Love.* Rev. ed. New York: Harper & Row, 1978.

Hiebert, Theodore. *God of My Victory: The Ancient Hymn in Habakkuk 3.* Harvard Semitic Monographs, 38. Atlanta: Scholars Press, 1986.

Hoekema, Anthony A. *The Bible and the Future.* Grand Rapids: Eerdmans, 1979.

Houghton, J.T. "New Ideas of Chaos in Physics." *Science and Christian Belief* 1 (1989): 75-84.

Hudson, W. Donald. *A Philosophical Approach to Religion.* New York: Macmillan, 1974.

Janzen, Gerald. *Job.* Interpretation. Atlanta: John Knox Press, 1985.

Kierkegaard, Søren. *Philosophical Fragments.* Trans. by David Swenson. Princeton: Princeton University Press, 1962.

Köhler, Ludwig. *Hebrew Man.* Trans. by P.R. Ackroyd. Nashville: Abingdon Press, 1957.

Komp, Diane M. *A Window to Heaven: When Children See Life and Death.* Grand Rapids: Zondervan, 1992.

Krumrei, Philip Dale. "The Relevance of Secularization for Interpreting and Nurturing Sprituality and Dutch Churches of Christ; An Analysis of the Relation of Pre-modern, Modern and Post-modern Paradigms of Faith and the Practice of Prayer." D.Min. diss., Harding University Graduate School of Religion, 1992.

Kushner, Harold S. *When Bad Things Happen to Good People.* New York: Avon Books, 1981.

LaCugna, Catherine Mowry. *God for Us: The Trinity & Christian Life.* San Francisco: HarperSanFrancisco, 1991.

Lasor, W.S. "Prophecy, Inspiration, and *Sensus Plenior.*" *Tyndale Bulletin* 29 (1979): 49-60.

Lewis, C.S. *A Grief Observed,* with afterword by Chad Walsh. New York: Bantam Books, 1976.

Lilley, J.P.U. "The Judgement of God: The Problem of the Canaanites." *Themelios* 22 (January 1997): 3-12.

Mays, James Luther. *Psalms.* Interpretation. Louisville, KY: John Knox Press, 1994.

Meyer, Lester. "A Lack of Laments in the Church's Use of the Psalter." *Lutheran Quarterly* 7 (1993): 67-78.

Middleton, J. Richard and Brian Walsh. *Truth Is Stranger Than It used to Be: Biblical Faith in a Postmodern Age.* Downers Grove, IL: InterVarsity, 1995.

Nelson, James S. "Divine Action: Is It Credible?" *Zygon* 30 (1995): 267-280.

Niditch, S. *Chaos to Cosmos: Studies in the Biblical Pattern of Creation.* Chico: Scholar's Press, 1985.

O'Conner, D.J. "Job's Final Word — 'I Am Consoled . . .' (42:6b)." *Irish Theological Quarterly* 50 (1983/84): 181-197.

Pannenberg, Wolfhart. *Jesus — God and Man.* Trans. by Lewis L. Wilkins and Duane A. Priebe. Philadelphia: Westminster Press, 1968.

_____ . *What Is Man?* Trans. by Duane A. Priebe. Philadelphia: Fortress, 1970.

Patrick, Dale. "Job's Address of God." *Zeitschrift für die Alttestamentliche Wissenschaft* 91 (1979).

_____ . "The Translation of Job XLII 6."*Vetus Testamentum* 26 (1976): 369-371.

Peters, Ted. *God as Trinity: Relationality and Temporality in Divine Life.* Louisville, KY: Westminster/John Knox Press, 1993.

_____ . *Sin: Radical Evil in Soul and Society* . Grand Rapids: Eerdmans, 1994.

Phillips, Timothy and Dennis L. Okholm, ed. *Christian Apologetics in the Postmodern World.* Downers Grove, IL: InterVarsity, 1995.

Piper, John. *Desiring God: Meditations of a Christian Hedonist.* Portland, OR: Multnomah, 1986.

Piper, John and Wayne Grudem, eds. *Recovering Biblical Manhood and Womanhood: A Response to Evangelical Feminism.* Wheaton, IL: Crossway Books, 1991.

Placher, William. *Narratives of a Vulnerable God: Christ, Theology and Scripture.* Louisville: Westminster John Knox Press, 1994.

Plantinga, Alvin. *God, Freedom and Evil.* New York: Harper & Row, 1974.

Pruyser, Paul W. *Between Belief and Unbelief.* New York: Harper & Row, 1974.

Resner, André, Jr. "Lament: Faith's Response to Loss." *Restoration Quarterly* 32 (1990): 129-142.

Roberts, J.J. "Job's Summons to Yahweh: The Exploration of a Legal Metaphor." *Restoration Quarterly* 16 (1973): 159-165.

Robertson, O. Palmer. *The Books of Nahum, Habakkuk and Zephaniah.* The New International Commentary on the Old Testament. Grand Rapids: Eerdmans, 1990.

Ruelle, David. *Chance and Chaos.* New York: Penguin, 1993.

Schilling, S. Paul. *God and Human Anguish.* Nashville: Abingdon, 1977.

Scholnick, Sylvia Hubermann. "The Meaning of *Mispat* (Justice) in the Book of Job." *JBL* 101 (1982): 521-529.

_____ . "Poetry in the Courtroom: Job 38–41." In *Directions in Hebrew Poetry.* Ed. by Elaine Follis. Sheffield: JSOT, 1987.

Simkins, Ronald A. *Creator & Creation: Nature in the Worldview of Ancient Israel.* Peabody, MA: Hendrickson, 1994.

Smick, Elmer B. "Another Look at the Mythological Elements in the Book of Job." *Westminster Theological Journal* 40 (1978): 213-228.

Stott, John R.W. *The Cross of Christ.* Downers Grove, IL: InterVarsity, 1986.

Tate, Marvin. "Satan in the Old Testament." *Review and Expositor* 89 (1992): 461-474.

Thompson, Michael, E.W. "Prayer, Oracle and Theophany: The Book of Habakkuk." *Tyndale Bulletin* 44.1 (1993): 33-53.

Tupper, E. Frank. *A Scandalous Providence: The Jesus Story of the Compassion of God.* Macon GA: Mercer University Press, 1995.

Vancil, Jack. "From Creation to Chaos: An Exegesis of Jeremiah 4:23-26." In *Biblical Interpretation: Principles and Practices.* Ed. by F. Furman Kearley, et al. Grand Rapids: Baker, 1986.

Vogel, Arthur A. *God, Prayer & Healing: Living with God in a World Like Ours.* Grand Rapids: Eerdmans, 1995.

Vos, Geerhardus. *Biblical Theology: Old and New Testaments.* Grand Rapids: Eerdmans, 1948.

Warren, Thomas B. "God and Evil: Does Judeo-Christian Theism Involve a Logical Contradiction?" Ph.D. diss., Vanderbilt University, 1970. Published as *Have Atheists Proved There Is No God?* Jonesboro, AR: National Christian Press, 1972; and also as *Sin, Suffering and God.* Jonesboro, AR: National Christian Press, 1980.

Watts, John D.W. *Isaiah 34–66.* Word Biblical Commentary. Waco, TX: Word Books, 1987.

Wenham, Gordon J. *Genesis 1–15*. Word Biblical Commentary, 1. Waco, TX: Word Books, 1987.

Wenham, John W. *The Enigma of Evil: Can We Belieue in the Goodness of God?* Grand Rapids: Zondervan, 1985.

Westermann, Claus. *Genesis 1-11: A Commentary*. Trans. by John J. Scullion. London: SPCK, 1984.

_____ . *Praise and Lament in the Psalms*. 2nd ed. Trans. by K.R. Crim and R.N. Soulen. Atlanta: John Knox Press, 1981.

_____ . "The Role of Lament in the Theology of the Old Testament." *Interpretation* 28 (1974): 20-38.

_____ . *The Structure of the Book of Job: A Form-Critical Analysis*. Trans. by Charles A. Muenchow. Philadelphia: Fortress, 1981.

Wiesel, Elie. *Night*. Trans. by Stella Rodway. New York: Avon Books, 1960.

_____ . *The Trial of God*. Trans. by Marion Wiesel. New York: Random House, 1964.

Wolfers, David. *Deep Things Out of Darkness*. Grand Rapids: Eerdmans, 1995.

Wolterstorff, Nicholas. *John Locke and the Ethics of Belief*. Cambridge: Cambridge University Press, 1996.

_____ . *Lament for a Son*. Grand Rapids: Eerdmans, 1987.

Yancey, Philip. *Disappointment with God: Three Questions No One Asks Aloud*. Grand Rapids: Zondervan, 1988.

_____ . "When the Facts Don't Add Up." *Christianity Today* 30 (June 13, 1986): 19-22.

Zuck, Roy B. *Job*. Everyman's Bible Commentary. Chicago: Moody Press, 1978.

Zurheide, Jeffry R. *When Faith Is Tested: Pastoral Responses to Suffering and Death*. Minneapolis: Fortress Press, 1997.

About the Author

Since 1991 John Mark Hicks has been Professor of Christian Doctrine at Harding University Graduate School of Religion in Memphis, Tennessee. Prior to his current position he most recently taught in Alabama Christian School of Religion, Montgomery, Alabama and Magnolia Bible College, Kosciusko, Mississippi. Hicks received his B.A. from Freed-Hardeman College (1977), M.A.R. from Westminster Theological Seminary (1979), M.A. from Western Kentucky University (1980), and Ph.D. from Westminster (1985).

John Mark has served as minister with the Northeast Philadelphia (Pennsylvania) Church of Christ, education minister with Prattville (Alabama) Church of Christ, adult education minister with Ross Road Church of Christ in Memphis, and teaching minister for a new church plant in Cordova (Tennessee). Hicks has spoken on a number of occasions in the United States and has taught in missions and graduate settings in Korea, Germany, Italy, Croatia, Japan, and Uganda.

In addition to five lectureship books, he has contributed chapters to four edited works: *Theology Matters: Answers for the Church Today* (In Honor of Harold Hazelip), ed. by Gary Holloway, Randall Harris and Mark C. Black, published by College Press (1998); *Building a Healthy Minister's Family, ed.* by Don Kinder, published by Gospel Advocate (1996); *Grace, Faith, Works: How Do They Relate?* ed. by C. Philip Slate, published by Publishing Designs (1992); and *Baptism and the Remission of Sins: An Historical Perspective*, ed. by David Fletcher, published by College Press (1990). John Mark has published numerous articles in academic and church publications, among which are: *Restoration Quarterly, The Journal of the American Society of Church Growth, Lexington Theological Quarterly, Evangelical Journal, Discipliana, Image, Christian Chronicle, Gospel Advocate, Leaven, Mission, Church Growth Magazine, Magnolia Messenger, Stone-Campbell Journal, 21ˢᵗ Century Christian*, and *World Evangelist*.

John Mark and Barbara live in Memphis with their children, Ashley, Joshua, and Rachel.